Contemporary Design

DESIGN MUSEUM

Dedicated to Michael McDermott 1938-2008
Mathematician and teacher

THIS IS A CARLTON BOOK

Text and design copyright © 1997, 1999 and 2008 Carlton Books Limited

This third edition published in 2008 by Carlton Books Limited
20 Mortimer Street, London W1T 3JW

First published in 1997 under the title *20th Century Design*.

A CIP catalogue record for this book is available from the British Library

ISBN 978 1 84732 177 0

Publishing Manager: Penny Craig
Junior Editor: Cressida Malins
Designer: Katie Baxendale
Production: Sophie Martin and Luca Bazzoli

Printed and bound in Dubai

Contemporary Design

DATE 1900–today

AUTHOR Catherine McDermott

DESIGN MUSEUM

CARLTON
BOOKS

Foreword

Using the word museum in the Design Museum's name twenty years ago when it was originally established was a careful decision, calculated to inject a certain sense of gravitas into a subject that has sometimes lacked confidence in its own significance. Design has certainly moved up the visibility scale since then. Design is a way of seeing, and understanding the world, through its material and immaterial objects. It's also a broad subject that, in Ernesto Rogers' words, covers the spectrum from planning a city, to detailing the tools to mass produce spoons.

As a museum, we cannot only be concerned with the present. We need to work to a different time scale; to remind the present generation of what their work, acknowleged or not, depends on.

Design is a reflection of our economic systems, and of the technology that we have to work with. It's a kind of language, and it's a reflection of emotional and cultural values. What makes seeing design in this way really engaging is the sense that there is something to understand about objects beyond the obvious issues of function and purpose, that there is a point in exploring what objects mean, as well as what they do, and what they look like.

What design means, the "why", as it were, is important. The "how" is an equally powerful way of understanding the physical, material world, not least because technologies and techniques keep changing, so that a focus on this aspect of design offers the chance to continually shift our attention to the issues that are going to be raised, as well as an understanding of past contexts.

But it is not only what it tells us about the way the world works that gives design its resonance. Let's not forget that it is also a pleasure in itself. The aesthetic, sculptural quality of a glass, or a chair, the intellectual elegance of a typeface, these are all creative expressions in themselves.

Deyan Sudjic
Director, Design Museum

PART 1

Fashion

EDWARDIAN ERA

Fashion at the beginning of the twentieth century reflected the old order, with formal clothes for men and tight-corsetted silhouettes for women still the prevailing taste. There were, however, signs of change in the taste for artistic dress that was made popular by the reforming spirit of the Arts and Crafts Movement and the even more dramatic impact of World War One. Women called on to do traditional men's work were required to wear functional clothing as a patriotic duty and that experience was to change attitudes to clothing forever. At the same time the ideas of Modernism ushered in a demand for simpler, streamlined ideas which suited the new spirit of the times. In Russia, for example, the artistic avant-garde designed clothes that would reflect the goals of the revolution: minimalist designs using bold geometric fabrics which were modern, practical and functional. These changes came together in the fashion mainstream in the form of the century's most influential designer, Coco Chanel. Inspired by English menswear, she combined this tradition with clothes that were simple, easy to wear, sporty and relaxed. Her clothes cut all ties with the past, broke away from a fussy outline and created a look for the modern woman that remains inspirational to this day. Hollywood also played a key role in popularizing these

JAEGER

ideas, and at the same time focused on the traditional elements of glamour and couture that never disappeared. After the constraints of the World War Two this theme reappeared with a vengeance in the "New Look" of Christian Dior. His full skirts and tight bodices were a revelation to a generation used to rationing and coupons and inspired not only affluent women but a new and powerful consumer group, the teenager. Now for the first time teenagers created an original style of dressing that broke the dominance of fashion designers, who had hitherto set the pace. That revolution was to have important repercussions in the 1960s when young people rebelled against the conservative and oppressive ideas of their parents and liberal reform movements throughout the world questioned all aspects of the status quo and demanded immediate change. The movement for civil liberties, the anti-Vietnam War demonstrations, the 1968 revolution in Paris and the Prague Spring produced a generation of people committed to challenging social norms and conventions. Young people experimented with sex, drugs and their personal appearance. These experiments had a profound effect on fashion. The mini skirt was the most popular expression of the new, more relaxed attitude to the body. However, some fashion designers like Paco Rabanne went further, producing topless and transparent outfits. During the same period the Gay Liberation and feminist movements demanded a public space for alternative attitudes to sexuality and lifestyles. By the 1970s themes of androgyny and cross dressing moved from the worlds of subcultures and pop music into the mainstream.

THE BEATLES

GIORGIO ARMANI

The economic recession of the 1970s meant that many design areas moved toward the classic, the safe and the conventional, and fashion was no exception. However dramatic change was about to come. Japanese designers, such as Issey Miyake and Yohji Yamamoto, were exploring alternatives to the tight silhouette, popularized in the mainstream by such television series as Dallas. At the same time Italian designers such as Giorgio Armani reworked the formal tailored jacket in soft unconventional fabrics. One undeniable influence came, however, from a more surprising source. The Punk revolution in Britain was not only about music and anti-establishment lifestyles, it also produced a new attitude to clothes. In 1971 Vivienne Westwood and Malcolm McLaren opened the first of a series of shops in London's Kings Road. Selling ripped and torn t-shirts, and clothes with references to bondage, they delighted in anarchy, irony and the Punk principle of "Do-It-Yourself". London led the way in new style directions and if you wanted to know what was directional and important in fashion you read two style magazines: The Face and i-D. London set the pace and in the early 1980s Vivienne Westwood took these ideas and placed them in the international arena of Paris couture with a series of seminal catwalk shows that would change the fashion map forever. Widely dismissed as unwearable and outrageous, she nonetheless introduced a series of original fashion ideas, including underwear as outerwear, fall-down socks, uniforms, pattern and the mini-crini that were imitated by designers all over the world. The rest of the fashion world took note and produced variants of these themes that produced inspirational clothes by leading designers such as Christian Lacroix and Romeo Gigli. The decade of the 1980s became the decade of serious devotion to designer clothes.

PRINTED FABRIC

Important fashion themes at the end of the twentieth century included the quest for wearability in clothes, stylish clothes that are both comfortable and relaxed. At the same time there was a desire for individual character in fashion, the idiosyncratic expression of the wearer through a designer look.
In the 1990s the arrival of new synthetic materials and information technology also changed the fashion industry. These new materials included paper with felted and bonded fabrics and new innovations to Lycra. Also important were a new generation of fibres and fabric finishes, which include a Teflon finish for wool that provides a fully breathable membrane, making it possible to produce waterproof cashmere and offer the consumer and the designer new possibilities for fashion. In the twenty-first century, fashion and technology continue innovative change with sensor fabrics and clothes that integrate communication technology for the wearer. Alongside such changes, fashion is also addressing the issue of sustainability in both fabrics and production. Such concerns have moved into the mainstream and show every sign of increasing.

NEW FABRIC

The Edwardian Era

DATE: 1901–10

Toward the end of the 1860s, the fashion for huge crinolines disappeared. The fashion for restrictive women's clothing did not, however, disappear but enjoyed a final flourish in the fashions of the Edwardian era. In the years leading up to World War One, women identified the dramatic curves of the hourglass with luxury, status and class and it therefore remained the style of the rich and aristocratic, inevitably filtering down to the middle classes. These outfits state clearly that the wearer leads a life of formal leisure supported by money and staff, bypassing any practical or functional demands of her clothing.

The level of applied decoration on these two dresses also places them within the tradition of late nineteenth-century and early twentieth-century decoration. Naturalistic flowers, ruffles, elaborate pleating, embroidery and lace contribute to a sumptuously layered effect that reflect the domestic interiors – also the preserve of women's taste – of the period.

Aesthetic Dress

DATE: 1900s

From the 1860s, a dress reform movement for women argued that the traditional restrictive corset and crinoline clothing of the period was unhealthy and cumbersome. Women started to demand clothing that could comfortably be worn for sports, cycling and other outdoor activities. Although this movement was generally viewed as extreme and eccentric, some of their ideas filtered through into mainstream fashion.

The artistic movements of the late nineteenth century encouraged women to adopt the loose flowing garments inspired by the medieval period from which they drew so much inspiration in their art and architecture. In the 1860s, Jane Morris – the wife of William – was famously photographed in dresses which, although conventional by twentieth-century standards, used flowing fabrics and ignored the fashion for tightly defined waists.

Aesthetic dress became a combination of the practical and the artistic, which aimed at establishing for the wearer an association with the new and the daring. By the turn of the century this fashion had been reproduced by many commercial outlets including Liberty's, the famous London department store, which produced a whole range of dresses in this style, such as the 1905 design pictured here, bringing the avant-garde into the mainstream.

Savile Row Tailoring

DATE: 1930s

British tailored clothes of the nineteenth century, particularly those designed for sporting activities, were widely admired for their quality and functionality. Tailoring as a profession emerged in the late seventeenth century when it was required for formal attire and horse riding. Stiff fabrics, such as tweeds and worsted, were sewn together using seams and darts to produce jackets reinforced with a firm structure of padding and interfacing. By the twentieth century this tradition had developed a reputation for producing some of the world's finest tailored suits, an industry centred in London and more particularly in Savile Row. This famous street in the city's West End is still the home of traditional tailors including Welsh and Jeffries, Maurice Sewell and Norton and Sons.

The classic Savile Row suit is designed to fit each individual client and is cut and constructed by hand. It takes up to eighty hours to create the template needed to create a master pattern for the client and to finish the suit by hand. There are three categories of tailoring: those made exclusively by hand; semi-bespoke, which is a combination of manufacture by hand and machine; and ready-to-wear, which is made by machine to fit a standard size.

The classic fabric for tailoring is wool cloth; other fabrics simply don't possess the durability and versatility needed for fine tailoring, although tweed, flannel and gaberdine also have the strength and body which enable them to hold a shape. The Savile Row suit has come to represent a quality and elegance that has less to do with fashion than tradition. The Duke of Windsor, seen here in 1938, epitomized this style of dress.

Coco Chanel

DATE: 1920s

DESIGNER: Coco Chanel
(1883 1971)

Gabrielle "Coco" Chanel is quite simply the most famous fashion designer of the twentieth century. She was the embodiment of the modern woman. Her clothes were based on the simple idea of producing comfortable and streamlined garments that broke away from the prevailing taste for the fussy and the elaborate. In this sense she is the fashion equivalent to the great designers of the Modern movement in the 1920s.

Her lifestyle is part of the same legend. She was brought up in an orphanage and used her many affairs with influential men to advance both her career and her financial position. Easy wearability was the key to her success. Her clothes were sporty, relaxed and well-suited to the new outdoor life promoted as a vital ingredient of modern living in the twentieth century. Significantly, Chanel is also credited with having turned the suntan into a vital fashion accessory.

Many of her ideas were adapted from men's clothing and the tradition of English tailoring, which she learnt at first hand from raiding the wardrobe of her English lover, the Duke of Westminster. Her classic suit represents this new approach. It looks simple with a geometric, box-like cardigan jacket worn over a short skirt, but she also introduced to this aesthetic the principle of couture: her clothing may have been simple, but cut, finish and fabric were always of the highest quality. Chanel also reduced her colour range to a palette of greys, black and cream with the occasional use of red.

Burberry

DATE: 1920s

The British Burberry is now synonymous with the waterproof mackintosh. Styled like an army overcoat, it became one of the most familiar fashion accessories of the twentieth century. Its origins go back to the 1860s when Thomas Burberry, the founder of Burberrys, started his own draper's business and developed a waterproof cloth that was hard-wearing, impenetrable to rain, yet cool and light to wear. The story has it that although Burberry called the cloth gaberdine, the name was changed to Burberry by one of its most famous customers, Edward VII, who on rainy days simply called for his "Burberry".

By the early twentieth century Burberry raincoats had become standard outdoor clothing as well as offering specialist protection for sportsmen and explorers. The explorer Scott and his team, for example, wore specially designed Burberry windproof suits on their ill-fated Antarctic trip. Other versions of the coat were designed as school uniforms. The coats appealed both to men and women: belted and with the collar upturned, the Burberry became a cliché of the sexy, debonair film hero and heroine. The private detective, the lone hero of Hollywood movies, had to wear the obligatory rainwear. Its role as a contemporary classic, however, has been somewhat superseded by waterproof rivals such as the Barbour jacket.

BURBERRY BOOK, patterns and prices, post free on mention of the "Queen."

A movement emerged during the twentieth century that espoused the view that clothes were not just about fashion but should be part of a rational healthy lifestyle. These ideas had their roots in the work of nineteenth-century dress reformers, in much the same spirit as English writer Edward Carpenter, forexample, had promoted the open-toed leather sandal for men. These clothes became an important statement of social belief and attracted a great deal of sympathy from individuals who felt fashion was a distraction from life's more important issues.

Using the same rationale, the German-born Dr Jaeger developed a new open-weave fabric for undergarments which were advertised with an emphasis on healthy living. A wider range of clothing, which went under the same name, was commercially successful in establishing a reputation for practical, well-made and durable outdoor wear. Inevitably Jaeger looked to the wider tradition of such garments; thus the tweed suit, such as the 1929 version seen here, using woven Scottish cloth, recommended itself as a hard-wearing and practical accessory for outdoor life. Jaeger continues to be a successful brand today.

Tailored Coat
R950
(Half lined)

West of England,
Scotch & Yorkshire
Tweeds
Fawn, Brown,
Mauve, & Grey

94/6

Costume
D105
(Coat lined)

Fawn, Mauve, Grey,
Brown, & Tan
Tweeds

79/6

Coat
P532
(Half lined)
Belt from side fastening
with slide
West of England,
Scotch & Yorkshire
Tweeds
Fawn, Brown,
Mauve, & Grey

63/-

Sheath Dress

DATE: 1920s–30s

The sheath dress of the 1920s and 1930s still retains the power to shock. Made from skin-tight fabric cut on the bias, the dress clings to the body outline and gives the impression of near nudity. Every contour of the female form can be seen and this sleek streamlined image is reinforced by the use of shiny reflective fabrics such as satin. The sheath dress is the fashion equivalent of the Modernist tubular steel chair. They are both about minimalism and purity of form, creating effects that have the technical precision of the machine. With her white hair – the effect of science not nature – cut in a geometric bob, Jean Harlow epitomizes the look of the new *femme fatale* of the twentieth century.

Trouser Suit

DATE: 1930s

Coco Chanel was the first designer to adopt men's tailoring when she wore the breeches and tweed shooting jackets of her lover, the Duke of Westminster. She adapted many of the lessons she learnt from wearing these clothes for her own couture range of the 1920s and was thus responsible for drawing a direct line from the English tailored man's suit to Paris couture and then Hollywood.

By the 1930s, trousers had crossed over to the female wardrobe and the trouser suit had been adopted by some of Hollywood's most famous film stars, including Marlene Dietrich, Katharine Hepburn and Greta Garbo. In their films and press photographs they created a fashionable sexual ambiguity, reworking an old device of using men's clothes to enhance femininity, in the same way that actresses often wore oversized male pyjamas in the movies.

Katharine Hepburn in particular used the trouser suit to project the modern image of the new American woman as an independent person who could operate on her own terms in the male professional world.

The new trouser suits needed some adaptation for the female form. The trousers needed the fly piece removed and tailored waistline darts introduced. In the jacket, the stiffened men's interfacing was replaced by two layers of fabrics.

Leather Jacket

DATE: 1940s

Fashion has a long tradition of appropriating items of functional clothing for more general usage. The brown leather flying jacket, shown here, was worn as regulation issue by the British Royal Air Force crew of a Hampden bomber in 1941. Such jackets are among the most popular and widespread garments of the postwar period. Designed to protect the early flyers from the cold temperatures of the cockpit, the jackets were fur-lined and zipped to the neck and came to be worn by flying crews all over the world. The durability of leather also protected the wearer from injury, making the jackets a popular choice for early motorcyclists. More than this, however, leather was masculine and sexy and could be worn functionally or informally with jeans and T-shirts. More recently the leather flying jacket has become a unisex garment worn by men and women.

One of the most important challenges to the restraints and conventions of nineteenth-century dress was not fashion-led but came about through the historical circumstances of two world wars. The women's movement and other dress reformers may have argued for changes to women's clothes but it was the onset of war that rapidly advanced their cause. Quite simply, women were now needed for jobs that had traditionally been the preserve of men –

and they needed functional work clothes to do this work, as demonstrated in this photograph of women working for the Land Army in 1943. Not only did it become acceptable for women to wear these clothes, it was seen as a patriotic duty. In the years after the war women were inevitably reluctant to return to the conventions of formal dress and the way was opened for women to introduce items such as men's jackets and trousers into their everyday lives.

DATE: 1940s

The New Look

DATE: 1947

DESIGNER: Christian Dior
(1905–57)

On February 2, 1947, Christian Dior's collection was dubbed the "New Look" by American fashion editor Carmel Snow. It was more than a new direction in style, it was one of the truly original moments in twentieth-century fashion. Dior's designs cut straight across the social feelings and the fashion of the time. In 1947, the general mood was still towards austerity and the need to sacrifice personal needs. Much of Europe lay in ruins and the slow process of rebuilding was a daunting programme. Many felt that during such a period Dior's look was inappropriate.

When Dior's extravagant dresses were shown on the catwalk, riots ensued: women wearing the clothes were attacked in the streets, while the American ambassador declared the style "unpatriotic". Nonetheless, Dior had struck deep feelings – after the trauma of the war, women wanted a moment of extravagance.

Interestingly, Dior chose not to look into the future for his radical collection but to the *belle époque* tradition of the 1880s, a style which saw the female body incarcerated in steel corsets and swathed in metres of material. It was ironic that Dior, from the rarefied world of Paris couture, produced the first postwar rebel look – a look which later found its way into the high streets via the rock and roll skirts worn by teenagers of the 1950s.

Teenage Consumer

DATE: 1950s

In 1959, the London Press Exchange – then one of Britain's largest advertising agencies – commissioned Mark Abrams to write a seminal study of key shifts in the consumer market. Called *The Teenage Consumer,* Abrams' research highlighted the new postwar phenomenon of teenage taste and style. Abrams, who had studied the social attitudes of working-class groups before and during the war, came to an important conclusion: that the new teenage market of the 1950s was dominated by the style aspirations of young, working-class people.

One of the most visible new aspects of teenage culture were the Teddy Boys. Wearing American-inspired "DA" haircuts, long drape jackets, crepe-soled shoes and tight trousers, they represented something totally new in British fashion. Such clothes in the 1950s were highly individual and even confrontational for a society that viewed young people's independence as a social problem. A Teddy Boy outfit also required serious commitment: the average cost of the outfit was around £20 – roughly £700 at today's prices. It is a look which has gone down in history as a classic heroic style for working-class teenagers.

1950s Casual Wear

DATE: 1950s

The rise of a new and affluent culture in postwar America encouraged informality and a more relaxed way of life. An obvious manifestation of this was the development of the first youth culture to seek new ways of dressing, independent of adult fashion. The first items to capture the imagination of this new market were sportswear – items like the sneaker, which developed from the athletic running shoe – and practical, easy-to-wear work clothes, such as denim jeans and the T-shirt vest, seen here worn by James Dean, whose style of dress typified the 1950s casual look.

Worn by manual workers for their cheapness, comfort and durability, these associations were also attractive to American bohemians and artists looking for a dress code that would reinforce their image as creative radicals in what still remained a deeply conservative society. It was unsurprising, then, that in the artistic communities of New York, white T-shirts, sneakers and jeans were worn by artists such as Jackson Pollock. Jeans – which had been produced by companies such as Levi's for over one hundred years – and T-shirts were both authentically American dress.

Jackie Kennedy

DATE: 1950s–60s

DESIGNER: Oleg Cassini (born 1913)

When Jackie Kennedy became America's First Lady she immediately became one of the most influential fashion leaders in the world. Both young and beautiful, she stepped onto the world's centre stage and influenced the look of a whole generation of women. Initially criticized for wearing the clothes of leading French couturiers, Jackie Kennedy looked for an American replacement and chose Oleg Cassini as the official dressmaker to the White House.

Cassini was brought up in Florence where his mother ran an exclusive dress shop. The family emigrated to America in 1938 where Cassini worked as a costume designer in Hollywood, creating many of the clothes worn by his wife, the actress Gene Tierney. Cassini's clothes for Jackie Kennedy were chic and stylish, most notably his trademark suit and pillbox hat which gave her a formal but modern image for the early 1960s.

Jackie Kennedy's enduring influence as a style icon was seen in the appearance of France's "first lady", Carla Bruni Sarkozy, on the occasion of the French President's 2008 visit to London.

Mini-Skirt

DATE: 1960s

Whether it was actually invented in London is not clear, but what is certain is that the mini-skirt came to represent the image of London's Swinging Sixties and became the most popular expression of a new relaxed attitude to the body.

Jean Shrimpton, shown here at the Melbourne Cup in 1965, caused a sensation when she appeared to present the fashion prize to the best-dressed lady attending the race meeting. In contrast to the prevalent dress codes, the "Shrimp" came hatless, gloveless and minus stockings, as well as wearing a mini.

The mini also represented some fundamental changes in fashion retailing. When America's *Time* magazine published its famous map of London in 1964 it did not illustrate the historical sites of interest but the new boutiques of Carnaby Street and Kings Road. These independent fashion outlets, including *Granny Takes A Trip, Hung On You* and *Lord John*, challenged the dominance of the larger department stores and more traditional fashion retailers. The most famous of these shops was *Bazaar,* opened by Mary Quant in 1957. More than any other designer, Quant popularized the mini-skirt in Britain and led the way in designing clothes specifically for young people. Although the mini-skirt gained wider acceptance – by the end of the decade even the Queen wore shorter skirt lengths – it always looked better on skinny, young and trendy models such as Jean Shrimpton and Twiggy.

The Beatles

As teenagers during the 1950s, the Beatles were part of the same revolution in style and culture that was, albeit slowly, affecting British life. As a port, their home town of Liverpool was always more open to outside influences than other English provincial cities. Deeply taken with American music and style, they first adopted the leather jackets and slicked back hair worn by 1950s cult heroes such as Marlon Brando and Elvis Presley.

For John Lennon, his seminal experience of the period was listening to Elvis sing *Heartbreak Hotel* in 1956 on Radio Luxembourg. There was the further influence of Liverpool Art College, which Lennon attended, where he met another early band member, the painter Stuart Sutcliffe. It was Sutcliffe's German girlfriend, Astrid Kirchherr, a Berlin art student, who introduced the Beatles to the famous "mop-top" haircut, a variant of the "Beatnik" style then popular among young students.

In 1962, manager Brian Epstein proposed a new image for the Beatles. They were to wear sharp grey wool suits, cropped collarless jackets, tight trousers and Chelsea boots. The Beatles swapped the uniform of American working-class teenagers for a new, confident and uniquely British style.

DATE: 1960s

Hippie Culture

DATE: 1960s

Towards the end of the 1960s the social revolution of the decade began to take a different direction. The consumer culture of Pop, with its emphasis on the throwaway and the instant, suddenly found itself challenged in a number of significant ways. Things changed fundamentally in Britain with the massive expansion of higher education places and the availability of grants. These new students became part of a widespread movement seeking alternative lifestyles and attitudes, in which clothing and image were fundamental. The search for spiritual priorities was closely linked to the widespread experimentation with drugs and a sympathy with the religions and culture of the East. Ethnic and Indian clothing became fashionable and, to reinforce the power of the individual, an eclectic mix incorporating quirky secondhand items became part of the new hippie culture.

The Chinese Revolution

Mao Tse Tung (1893–1976) has been described as the most influential fashion designer of the twentieth century, because it was his revolution that made the uniform of the single-breasted collared jacket, loose trousers and soft-peaked hat obligatory clothing for literally millions of Chinese men and women. These clothes became one of the most powerfully iconic outfits of the twentieth century. In the 1960s they were worn by Western political radicals, and items such as the hat became a popular fashion accessory among young liberals in the 1960s. The suit in soft, cotton fabric has since become a fashion perennial and inspired designers including Issey Miyake and Comme des Garçons.

Mao was the great non-European Marxist who stressed the role of the peasantry in the Revolution rather than the industrial worker – whom traditional Marxists believed would engineer social change. Mao ran China as a totalitarian dictatorship and the idea of a uniform for the people, with its underlying message of order and discipline and, more importantly, the suppression of the individual, reflected the regime's ideology.

Although the idea of loose soft cotton trousers and jacket had some links with traditional Chinese peasant clothing, the outfit owed much more to the clothing adopted by the early Russian revolutionaries, including the "Lenin"-style hat.

DATE: 1940s

Punk

DATE: 1970s

In 1971, Malcolm McLaren and Vivienne Westwood opened the first of a series of shops on the same site at 436 Kings Road, London. Believing that culture and style in London had reached a dead end, they went in search of a different direction. In 1975 they opened Sex, a shop that sold provocative soft-porn rubber clothes and accessories. Two years later this was followed by Seditionaries, London's first authentic Punk shop. McLaren and Westwood acted as a catalyst for a revolution in British music, fashion, design and culture – Punk.

McLaren had always encouraged like-minded young people to hang out at the shop and on Saturdays it acted as a kind of club for those also searching for an alternative identity. Punk sought a focus away from the tail end of the despised hippie movement: McLaren provided one. He had always loved the antics and slogans of the Dadaists and direct confrontation with the mainstream. The Punk band, the Sex Pistols, which included John Lyndon, show here in 1976, gave him the direction to develop a new attitude. An anti-fashion style quickly followed: ripped and torn clothes fastened with safety pins, aggressive tribal make-up, black lipstick and brightly coloured hair. Westwood elaborated on these themes in her own designs for the Sex Pistols which included bondage trousers, "Destroy" T-shirts and workmen's boots for both sexes.

This 1987 image shows the New York hip-hop–rap bands The Beastie Boys and Run DMC, whose distinct identity highlights a youth culture which requires specific dress codes. In this context trainers have become especially significant, the key accessory which marks the tribe to which you belong.

They have their origin in the development of footwear for sport. From the 1940s sport shoes such as the sneaker and then the trainer were worn as leisure wear, reflecting the new relaxed lifestyle of postwar America. This began a key shift in the way people used clothing: the cross-over of footwear and other sportswear from one activity to another and the idea that you didn't have to pursue a sport to wear the clothing. Now the styling and association of the trainer was more important than

its original intended use. Today what was originally designed as a high-tech and specialized sporting shoe has become a key item in the development of street style, street gangs, music fans and surfers, each selecting a particular brand as a tribal sign and wearing the appropriate sports clothing to complete the image. Major manufacturers such as Nike and Adidas quickly responded to this "street style" by developing new versions of trainers which are deliberately targeted at the youth market through their sponsorship of youth icons like Michael Jordan, Magic Johnson, and Prince Naseem.

The main players in this industry have now built up a billion dollar industry exploiting the nuances of styling and design that are so crucial in this market.

DATE: 1980s

Androgyny

DATE: 1980s

For decades, androgyny – the merging of traditional gender appearances – had remained a subcultural trend, marginalized to the private world of members' bars and clubs. By the late 1960s, however, it began to enter the mainstream. Transvestism and androgyny were made fashionable by Andy Warhol and his coterie of "superstars" who featured in films such as Che*lsea Girls* and *Trash*. Many rock musicians began to question concepts of masculinity through their dress and use of make-up over the coming decade. David Bowie and other figures of the Glam Rock movement helped to make bisexuality chic and influenced many fields of design including fashion and graphics. In the early 1980s these themes found expression once again with the emergence of the New Romantics focused on the clubs of London. An important figure in this context was Boy George who, with his friend Marilyn, turned a lifestyle of dressing up in women's clothes into a public career as a pop star. Boy George wore make-up, adapted items of ethnic dress, such as deadlocks, and converted the whole package into a trend in which androgyny became a fashion statement.

Madonna and Jean-Paul Gaultier

DATE: 1990

DESIGNER: Jean-Paul Gaultier
(born 1952)

During the 1980s, a number of openly gay figures became highly influential through their pop videos, fashion designs, theatre and dance presentations. The pop singer Boy George, the dancer and choreographer Michael Clark, the performance artist Leigh Bowery and the film-maker John Maybury have been particularly important in pushing a gay sensibility toward the mainstream.

But the most important figure to appropriate gay culture has undoubtedly been Madonna. Through her enormous fame, she has been able to borrow ideas from the periphery and place them at the centre of contemporary culture. Her use of imagery, drawn from sadomasochistic and fetishistic sexual practice, has entered the mainstream discourse through her videos and most notoriously through her *Sex* book.

In 1990 Madonna commissioned Jean-Paul Gaultier to design the costumes for her *Blonde Ambition* tour. Gaultier has redefined notions of gender and sexuality through his clothing. He has designed skirts for men and pinstripe suits for women. His longstanding fascination with underwear has produced outfits which are little more than bras, corsets and suspenders, a look which was worn to great effect by Madonna. Gaultier has always looked to street-style and nightlife culture for inspiration. He has transformed fetish clothing into items of high fashion, combining, for example, traditional suits with rubber opera gloves and cod-pieces.

Slogan T-Shirt

DATE: 1984

DESIGNER: Katherine Hamnett
(born 1948)

This image of Katherine Hamnett meeting Prime Minister Margaret Thatcher was taken in 1984 at a Downing Street reception to celebrate British Fashion Week. In her regal velvet robes, Thatcher, who was effecting her own political and economic revolution, makes an interesting contrast to Katherine Hamnett, who staged something of a publicity coup by wearing sneakers and one of her trademark slogan T-shirts, and by cross-questioning the Prime Minister on the effects of acid rain. Hamnett had worked on a number of slogan T-shirts inspired by the anti-nuclear women's protests at the Greenham Common airbase in England. Although Hamnett was deeply committed to ecological and peace movements, the meeting may have been less of a culture clash than it first appeared. Throughout the 1980s, Hamnett's fashion company proved hugely successful in selling a range of crumpled jumpsuits and casual suits to the new affluent professionals who were doing so well in Thatcher's Britain.

Printed Fabric

DATE: 1989

DESIGNER: Paul Smith
(born 1946)

Paul Smith brought about a significant shift in attitude to British menswear during the 1980s. To a traditionally extremely conservative market, Paul Smith introduced a range of classic men's clothes with a twist that gave his designs a freshness and edge that quickly attracted sales both in his home market and abroad, particularly in Japan. Paul Smith took the standard office uniform – the suit, the shirt and the tie – and introduced new fabrics and choices of colour that gradually won over his customers.

Smith had identified an important gap in the market – the new affluent professional men of the 1980s who wanted to look serious for business and the office but did not want to dress in the obligatory drab dark suit. With this design strategy as his mainstay he was able to develop more adventurous lines including his trademark patterned shirts of this period. Often printed in "Day-Glo" colours with 3D versions of fruit, flowers and vegetables, these shirts echoed the tradition of the 1960s and the 1980s fashion for colour, pattern and decoration. Now the young city highflyer could wear a suggestion of radical chic but remain perfectly safe in the knowledge that to wear Paul Smith was a mark of excellent taste.

John Galliano

DATE: 1997

DESIGNER: John Galliano
(born 1960)

John Galliano was part of the British fashion new wave of the 1980s. A graduate of St Martin's School of Art in London, he was an extremist who saw the potential for turning clothing into subversion. Although such experimentation continues to inform his work, Galliano has since moved on to become a designer of international stature – so much so, in fact, that in 1996 he was appointed chief designer to Dior, one of the world's most prestigious fashion houses and one of the most coveted design jobs in the world. Galliano has been chosen to revitalize the rather stuffy world of French couture with his extraordinarily original talent. Like other British contemporaries, his ideas derive from stories, from a narrative of cultural fragments that inspire him, including the late eighteenth century and the French Revolution.

Vivienne Westwood

DATE: 1996

DESIGNER: Vivienne Westwood (born 1941)

Vivienne Westwood is one of the world's fashion superstars. She has come to embody those elements of British creativity – the cultural export of ideas, style, anarchy, history, irony and multi-layers of culture – that have inspired new international directions. However, this was not always the case. When, in 1990, John Fairchild, editor of the tough trade paper, *Women's Wear Daily,* named her as one of the six most important fashion designers in the world, it marked a change in her reputation – Westwood's contribution to fashion design was at last taken seriously.

There is an exploratory edge to Westwood's work, a risk element that has influenced clothes from the most expensive of couture to the high street. Her genius includes a new approach to the cut of clothes and the impact of her influential ideas such as underwear as outerwear, tights under jackets, the "mini-crini" skirt and the boned corset using eighteenth-century baroque prints.

Westwood's approach is rooted in history and this preoccupation reflects the strengths and obsessions of the most creative forms of British design. Her research is in the great museums of London, such as the Victoria and Albert and the Wallace Collection.

For Westwood, fashion is a way of reappraising history: she embodies the idea that the British creative tradition is literary rather than visual. Indeed Westwood's starting points are words not pictures. Her clothes are quintessentially British and more than any single individual, she has helped place London as the world's centre for leading-edge fashion.

Synthetic Materials

DATE: 1990s

The invention of synthetic materials has offered the consumer new levels of comfort and functionality. This ongoing process of technological innovation since the beginning of the twentieth century has become an important fashion theme. Two companies producing new synthetic fabrics are Dupont and Courtaulds. Their development of high-tech fibres has helped to shift fashion emphasis from innovative cut to innovative cloth. Dupont, famous for discovering nylon in 1938, introduced Lycra as the stretch fabric of the 1980s and the company continues to develop improved versions. Courtaulds launched Tencel, produced from cellulose of harvested, managed trees. It is a soft, supple fabric with a lustre finish, offers the qualities of silk or cotton, can breathe like natural fabrics, but is more durable and easy to wash.

Other new fabrics include Berghaus's outdoor fabric, Polartec, made from recycled plastic bottles; W.L. Gore's Gore-Tex, a thin membrane applied to any cloth, which prevents water penetration but, through its micro pores, allows moisture to escape; and a material with microscopic holes, launched by the swimwear manufacturer Speedo, which allows all-over tanning. In addition to new fibre sources, Scientists are working on genetic modification of natural fibres. In the garment shown here, the British designer Hussein Chalayan has used Tyvek paper, originally used for envelopes. He has compensated for the non-stretch element of paper by reinforcing it with special cutting and stretching techniques.

Alexander McQueen

DATE: 1997

DESIGNER: Alexander McQueen
(born 1969)

One of the 1990s generation of radical young British fashion designers, Alexander McQueen started as an apprentice to Gieves and Hawkes, one of Savile Row's famous tailors. He then borrowed money to complete a postgraduate fashion course at St Martin's School of Art in London, where his work caught the eye of Isabella Blow, a well-known patron of young fashion designers. She bought his collection and ensured that his work, with its themes concentrating on the body and sabotage of tradition, attracted media attention. Blow recognized in the young McQueen the raw energy of style that provided a new look for the 1990s. His designs provided stunning images for the press – most notably his bumster trousers, cut to reveal the cleavage of the buttocks. In 1997 McQueen was appointed head of design at Givenchy in Paris. It was a shock move: Hubert de Givenchy represented the highest echelons of Paris couture, but it was felt to have lost its way, to be conservative and staid. McQueen brought radical anti-fashion into the mainstream, and did nothing to ease the transition, deliberately playing on his working-class origins. Asked to comment on Givenchy talent, he famously replied "What talent?" Nonetheless, his work revived interest in Givenchy, where he works closely with a small team of British collaborators, including stylist Katy Englander, art director Simon Costin, who has produced jewellery made from animal body parts, and hat maker Philip Treacey, who transformed the hat into an art form. The influence of Costin and Treacey can be seen here.

Marc Jacobs

DESIGNER: Marc Jacobs
(born 1963)

For a certain kind of professional, independent woman the American fashion designer Marc Jacobs defined the new look of twenty-first-century fashion. His exceptional inventiveness, referencing fashion design icons such as Audrey Hepburn, reviving the dress for the office and using quirky oversized detailing, won over an international customer base.

As a student, Jacobs showed a prodigious talent, graduating from the Parsons School of Design in 1984 as Design Student of the Year. In 1986, with business partner Robert Duffy, he launched his first Marc Jacobs collection and won the Council of Fashion Designers of America (CFDA) Perry Ellis Award for New Fashion Talent. His signature style mixed luxurious materials such as silk and cashmere to recreate the grunge look seen in his earliest collections. His catwalk shows also became high profile design events at New York's Fashion Week. For these he worked with set designer Stefan Beckman to produce a series of installations that became almost as inspiring as the clothes.

Marc Jacobs has become America's most directional fashion brand: he designs for his own company Marc Jacobs, the diffusion line Marc-by-Marc Jacobs, international fashion brands in menswear, womenswear, accessories and shoe collections, and international flagship and stand-alone international stores.

Currently Marc Jacobs is Creative Director at the French fashion house Louis Vuitton, where he transformed the classic brown Louis Vuitton monogram into bright coloured bags that became collector's items.

Christopher Kane

DATE: 2008

DESIGNER: Christopher Kane
(born 1982)

British fashion has been energized by a wave of younger twenty-first-century designers starting with Giles Deacon in the late 1990s and over the last few years Gareth Pugh and Christopher Kane. All three designers are graduates from London's Central Saint Martin's Fashion course and all three are interested in a very British, cutting-edge take on sex, re-using heritage, combining materials and radical innovation. Kane's graduating show in 2005 attracted media interest because of his strong talent working creatively with new fabrics, colour and print. His collaborator is his sister Tammy who shared with him a childhood in Motherwell in Scotland and who trained as a textile designer. In 2006 their partnership helped win him a series of fashion awards, notably New Designer of the Year in 2007.

International fashion looks to London for a contemporary take on modern styling and Kane's work delivered a modern style popular in defining fashion cities across the world. Typical here is his combination of torn denim jacket combined with a cream floating chiffon skirt, delicately layered and ruched and balanced with steel-capped boots. At first sight it appears "torn" but the effect comes from highly skilled cutting and detailing. Kane's talent is to combine skill and experimentation with a light but clever touch. In doing so he is extending a tradition in British fashion talent that first emerged in the Punk era of the late 1970s and continues to establish a unique sense of British style.

The Forster House

DATE: 1891 London, England

ARCHITECT: Charles Francis Annesley Voysey (1857–1941)

During the 1890s, British architecture was the most creative modern architecture to be found anywhere in the world. Voysey was part of a group of distinguished architects and designers which falls under the general heading of the Arts and Crafts Movement. Within this group, however, Voysey was one of the most talented and influential practitioners. For his informality of planning and simplicity of form, Voysey has been hailed as one of the fathers of twentieth-century Modernism, although Voysey himself found little to admire in the new architecture of the 1920s.

The Forster House was built in Bedford Park in London and pioneered another important British contribution to town planning – the garden suburb, which combined convenient town access with the pleasures and freedom of the country. It was in sharp contrast to the red-brick houses of the earlier development from the 1870s and this strikingly original house effectively launched Voysey's career. The exterior was simple; Voysey was not interested in reworking past styles, creating instead a generic vernacular of white roughcast walls, stone dressings and iron brackets that held a deeply pitched roof. The interior space was interesting because it attempted to create a modern way of living: a large living room with no separate parlour or dining room, with the staircase set to the side of the house to free up the living space. The interior was more conventional, using oak furniture and vernacular detailing.

Glasgow School of Art

DATE: 1897–1909
Glasgow, Scotland

ARCHITECT: Charles Rennie
Mackintosh (1868–1928)

Although Mackintosh is now one of the world's most famous architects, his work was not always highly rated. He died in 1928 a neglected figure, and the postwar period saw some of his most famous buildings threatened with demolition. It was not until the 1960s that his work was reassessed, and his importance as a key transitional figure from the historicism of the nineteenth century to the abstraction of the early twentieth century, acknowledged.

Mackintosh was part of an artistic renaissance in Glasgow at the turn of the century. He worked closely with his wife Margaret Macdonald, with whom he had trained at the Glasgow School of Art. Their original style, seen in their architectural drawings, interiors and furniture for private clients, very quickly attracted interest from all over the world, but particularly enthusiastic were the Vienna Secessionists.

Mackintosh's most famous building was the Glasgow School of Art. The first phase, including the entrance shown here, was completed between 1898 and 1899. Huge windows dominate the entrance and the front can be read as an abstracted form of traditional Scottish castle architecture. It still functions as an art school, attracting many visitors drawn to Mackintosh's distinctive detailing seen here in the railings and window brackets. The second phase of building, including a library, was completed in 1909.

Casa Battló Apartments

DATE: 1905–07 Barcelona, Spain

ARCHITECT: Antoni Gaudí (1852–1926)

Gaudí is not only one of the great individualists of Spanish architectural history but his impact internationally has made him a key twentieth-century figure. He worked almost exclusively in and around his native city of Barcelona, then as now the artistic capital of a fiercely independent region, proud of its traditions and history. Gaudí merged his native Catalan style with Moorish features and natural forms, to produce some of the most novel architecture of the late nineteenth and early twentieth century.

Perhaps his most famous work is the still uncompleted Sagrada Familia church, begun in 1883. However, his most original version of Catalan Art Nouveau, known as "Modernismo", can be seen in the remodelling of an apartment building into a residence for the Battló family, with offices on the ground floor and apartments for rent. Here Gaudí's distinctive language of ornament is no longer simply applied to a building but constitutes the essential structural elements. The facade is covered with highly coloured mosaics constructed with broken glass, while the roof outline resembles the form of an exotic reptile. Gaudí's highly original use of sculptural form established him as one of the great artist-architects of the twentieth century. However, it should be said that this does not mark the start of something new, rather the culmination of the previous century's obsession with revivalism and natural forms. Nonetheless, Gaudí became an inspirational figure for many Postmodernist architects in the postwar period.

Castle Drogo

DATE: 1910–30
Devon, England

ARCHITECT: Edwin Lutyens
(1869–1944)

In the context of British architectural history, Edwin Lutyens remains a complex figure. He worked within the tradition of nineteenth-century British Arts and Crafts yet he is arguably the most influential British architect of the twentieth century. However, his vision of architecture was not part of the quest for new forms of Modernism. Lutyens was the British establishment's chosen architect, commissioned to design war memorials, government buildings for the Empire and work for major banks. None of this endeared him to the architectural avant-garde, who saw him as a reactionary figure holding back progress.

Recently a more sympathetic reappraisal of Lutyens' work has viewed his handling of form and space, his use of traditional materials and his reinterpretation of the vernacular as qualities that seem more sympathetic than they did forty years ago. In addition to his work for the establishment he was also the last great country house architect. Castle Drogo, built for a wealthy tea merchant, is an example of this work. It is a romantic vision of a castle. Constructed of granite, it is built on a rocky outcrop on the edge of Dartmoor. The interior of the building opens into a series of dramatic spaces; particularly notable is the library and the basement kitchen which is lit from above by a glazed rotunda.

Chrysler Building

DATE: 1928–30 New York City, USA

ARCHITECT: William Van Alen
(1883–1954)

The Chrysler building is probably one of the most familiar buildings in the world. Indeed for many its opulent and dramatic profile has come to symbolize the Manhattan skyline. It was one of a number of high-rise buildings planned in the 1920s that established New York as the modern city of the twentieth century.

The building has a slightly curious history. It was designed for the Chrysler motorcar company – its foyer was planned as a showroom for new models, and the exterior metal sculptural decoration evokes car grilles and emblems. In fact, the building was never used by Chrysler. Also, during the construction of the building, Van Alen was accused of financial impropriety and, whatever the truth, he never recovered his reputation.

Standing at 320 metres (1,048 feet), the Chrysler Building remains the most flamboyant example of Art Deco in New York's midtown district that saw so many corporations vying for attention, including the Woolworth building across the street and the Chenin Insurance headquarters on the opposite block.

Empire State Building

DATE: 1931
New York City, USA

ARCHITECTS: Richmond H. Shreve (1877–1946), William Lamb (1883–1952) and Arthur Loomis Harmon 1878–1958)

In one of the most enduring images of popular culture, the giant gorilla "King Kong" hangs from the mooring mast at the top of the most famous skyscraper – New York's own "eighth wonder of the world" – the Empire State Building. Standing on Manhattan's 34th street and 5th Avenue, for forty years after its completion this 381-metre (1,250-foot) marvel was the world's tallest building. Designed by architects Richmond H. Shreve, William Lamb, and Arthur Loomis Harmon, the exterior's vertical thrust and simple, yet powerful, limestone and granite form was the very definition of a modern skyscraper. Although less exotic than its rival Chrysler building, the sleek marble lobby artfully highlighted with polished metal epitomized the Art Deco style. Widely acclaimed, the Empire State Building was not an immediate success: the Depression left much of its office space unfilled. But in postwar prosperity it flourished, becoming one of America's greatest tourist attractions. Since its opening in 1931, nearly 120 million people have visited the observatories from which, on a clear day, one can see for up to fifty miles.

Schröder House

DATE: 1924
Utrecht, The Netherlands

ARCHITECTS: Gerrit Rietveld
(1888–1964) and Truss Schröder-
Schräder (1889–1985)

The Schröder house has become a
metaphor for Modernism and a key
building of Dutch De Stijl, one of the
most coherent groups within the
Modern Movement. The house was
the first open-plan home. Its internal
organization reflected the new way
of life that Modernism advocated –
unencumbered, unostentatious,
flexible, dramatically different to the
constraints of the nineteenth
century. It opened up light and
space, with a view originally
overlooking meadows. The windows
opened out to ninety degrees,
creating the impression that the
house merged with the landscape.
It is also interesting because it was
one of the few Modernist homes
partly designed by a woman: Truss
Schröder-Schräder collaborated
with Rietveld on the design of her
own home. She seems to have
been responsible for the internal
planning and saw herself and the
house as models for the new life of
the twentieth century. The Schröder
House was distinctive in that, apart
from the fixed staircase and
bathroom, the spaces could be
opened up using a system of flexible
screens which you could simply
draw across if you wanted privacy.
The downstairs area is more fixed,
with four or five rooms but a gap at
the top of a screen wall to give a
sense of space. Another key feature
was the functional fitted furniture,
fold-down ledges and cupboards.

Villa Savoye

Le Corbusier is the most influential architect of the twentieth century, yet surprisingly few of his designs were actually built. However, it is his vision of the future, revealed in his drawings and published writings, that has dominated Modern architecture. As a Modernist, Corbusier was dedicated to the creation of a new aesthetic for a new way of life and his chief source of inspiration was the machine. He wanted to create architecture that functioned with the same slick efficiency and economy of design as a car or an aeroplane. Corbusier's philosophy is reflected in his famous aphorism "the house as a machine for living in".

In the 1920s these ideas were put into practice in a series of modern villas for wealthy clients in the Paris suburbs, the exteriors of which evoked the machine, with interiors which were largely free in plan. Placed in the interiors of houses such as the Villa Savoye was specially designed furniture, discrete sculpture within the free-flowing interior space, which rendered the house a totally designed entity. This house has become one of the best-known expressions of twentieth-century International Style; sixty years later its design continues to influence architectural practice.

DATE: 1929–31
Poissy, France

ARCHITECT: Le Corbusier
(1887–1965)

Seagram Building

DATE: 1954–58
New York City, USA

DESIGNER: Ludwig Mies van der Rohe (1886–1969)

Mies van der Rohe is one of the most influential architects of the twentieth century. His buildings became the blueprint for a modern industrial society. As an architect, Mies is famous for his ability to derive maximum effect from a minimum use of form, reflecting his legendary axiom "less is more".

Largely self taught as an architect, his formative years were spent in the German office of Peter Behrens where he supervised the construction of many important projects. After World War One he placed himself at the centre of the New Modern Movement, designing astonishingly original buildings. Between 1919 and 1929 his important works included the Wolf House at Guben and the German Pavilion at the 1929 International Exhibition in Barcelona – one of the most important buildings of the twentieth century.

After a short period as Director of the Bauhaus, political pressure forced him to leave Germany and move to the USA where, in 1938, he accepted a teaching post at the Illinois Institute of Technology, Chicago. Here he began to establish his distinctive architecture principles, using exposed metal frame structures to exploit bold rectangular forms. In the immediate postwar years his career acquired superstar status. Two of his skyscrapers – Lake Shore Drive Apartments, Chicago (1950) and the Seagram Office Building in New York (1954–58) – came to express the ambitions and spirit of the most powerful nation in the world. Mies' work symbolized the power structure of American executive life, inspiring the shape of hundreds of commercial quarters throughout the world.

Bauhaus School Building

From 1919 to 1928, Walter Gropius was the director of the most famous design school of the twentieth century – the Bauhaus. It was no coincidence that when the opportunity arose to build a new school Gropius designed it himself, to show what the new architecture should and could be. The School remains one of the seminal buildings of the Modern Movement. As its director, Gropius was responsible for establishing a new approach to design education, an approach that still influences the way design is taught. While design education in the rest of Europe remained largely dominated by outdated nineteenth-century attitudes, the Bauhaus developed a syllabus on a pattern clearly recognizable in most design colleges today. It set out a common foundation year from which students moved on to specialize in the design area of their choice, for example furniture, product design or graphics.

Within the building itself, the different elements of the course were expressed in a series of distinct areas connected by single-storey blocks. Gropius aimed to make the effect functional but spiritually pleasing, and so different activities were expressed by a different treatment of the façade. For example, the workshop block, which Gropius considered to be the heart of the school's activity and identity, used a reinforced concrete frame, hence the curtain wall, which wraps around the corner to reveal what goes on inside. Designed by Gropius and his students, the interior was equally important, most notably his office and the lecture theatre, which featured folded canvas and steel chairs by Marcel Breuer.

DATE: 1926
Dessau, Germany

ARCHITECT: Walter Gropius
(1883–1969)

Maison de Verre

DATE: 1927–32
Paris, France

DESIGNER: Pierre Chareau
(1883–1950)

Maison de Verre was designed by the architect Pierre Chareau who embraced the Modernist aesthetic with enthusiasm. For many architects and designers this private house, built for a gynaecologist and his wife, is one of the most poetic and beautiful expressions of Modern-Movement architecture and it enjoys an iconic status.

What made it so distinctive was the use of glass bricks in the main external walls. Glass bricks had been used in the past, mainly for industrial buildings, but never before had they been featured so extensively in a domestic context. Up to the present day, the use of glass bricks has come to signify modernity. In 1927, they created a sort of membrane, which gave the house a tremendous feeling of transparency and light. Inside, the complex spatiality of the design – walls which are nearly transparent, interior spaces defined with the use of screens and built-in furniture – have inspired subsequent generations of architects.

Also significant for contemporary designers was the fact that this project was a conversion of an existing building and, as such, has offered a blueprint for architects working in the same way. Maison de Verre remained Chareau's most important building. In 1940 he emigrated to America and worked on a number of private commissions, including a house for the painter Robert Motherwell.

When Eileen Gray died in Paris, aged 97, she was virtually unknown. Two decades later she is now widely recognized as one of the twentieth century's most talented and individualistic designers. Although she designed buildings, she was not strictly speaking a practising architect, nor had she any formal architectural training. Her work concentrated on a select group of interiors for a small but influential group of clients, and custom-made furniture, lamps, mirrors and hand-woven carpets. In the 1920s and 1930s Gray was unique as a designer, a women practising within a predominately male world. She was fortunate: Gray came from an affluent Irish family which supported her decision to train at the Slade painting school – circumstances that, after the death of her father, allowed her to lead an independent life in Paris.

During the 1920s Gray's work attracted much attention. Those who found her work interesting included the Dutch De Stijl architect J. J. P. Oud. While in France she became friendly with many leading architects and designers, including Le Corbusier. This encouraged her to go beyond interior decoration and experiment with architecture. In 1927 she not only designed a house – the Villa E.1027 in the south of France – but every aspect of the furnishings and interior. The floor coverings, murals, furniture and light fittings were all made in her Paris workshops. It was a brilliant tour de force. Le Corbusier admired the results so much he visited the house often. It was from here in 1965, in fact, that he swam to his death. Gray only completed two houses but produced plans for many other projects, including a scheme for a vacation centre which incorporated offices, de-mountable cabins, a restaurant and sports centre.

Gray's work required wealthy clients and remained exclusive. She did not share the machine-age preoccupations of many of her contemporaries in the European Modern Movement. The fact that her work did not translate into a wider commercial context helps to explain her low postwar public profile.

DATE: 1927–29
Roquebrune, Cap Martin, France

DESIGNER: Eileen Gray
(1878–1976)

Casa del Fascio

DATE: 1932–36
Como, Italy

ARCHITECT: Giuseppe
Terragni (1904–41)

Fascist Italy, under the leadership of Benito Mussolini, promoted the new imagery and technology of Modernism to express the ambitions of the nation. The Casa del Fascio, built for Fascist mass rallies, remains Terragni's masterpiece and one of the key projects of the Italian Rationalist Movement. Mussolini, a great admirer of new inventions and industrial advances, admired the simplicity of form of Modernism but also wanted to combine this with the monumentality of the great Italian classical tradition. For Mussolini, identification with Ancient Rome was a way of reinforcing the new power of both the state and the people. The building was to be Como's headquarters of the Fascist party and includes a meeting hall, offices and a gallery. Terragni's design for the Casa is a cube by a double cube, a model classical proportion using white marble. The

site was placed on an axis leading across Como's Piazza del Imper to the east end of the city's Cathedral, thereby suggesting a link ar an equal status with another symbol of Italian power.

Terragni was part of Gruppo 7, a collective made up fro graduates of the famous architectural course at Milan's Polytechni They disliked the stripped classicism that informed much Itali Fascist architecture. The Casa del Fascio expressed their version Modernity with its famous framed glass roof which top-lights th central hall. Technology was a feature of the main glass doors, whic were electronically controlled so they could be opened simultaneous In this way the crowds inside could flood into the square demonstrati the dynamic power of Fascism. In the 1970s, Terragni's work wa rediscovered and inspired a number of New York architects.

Einstein Tower

As a young student, Mendelsohn's friends included Paul Klee and Wassily Kandinsky, and his early drawings were inspired by these Expressionist artists. This influence can be seen in the Einstein Tower, one of his most famous buildings. It was commissioned by the Einstein Foundation as an observatory and laboratory to prove Einstein's theory of relativity, and research work began in 1924. In design terms this was one of the most important examples of German Expressionist architecture. Mendelsohn used cement stucco not to express the pure geometry of Modernism, but the dynamic, sculptural form of curves and domes.

Other commissions quickly followed, buildings which placed Mendelsohn at the centre of new German architecture. He visited the USA the Soviet Union, and brought back the new ideas he had seen. Tragically, his career in Germany was cut short: as a Jew, his position became untenable. In 1933 he emigrated to England where he worked with Sergei Chermayeff. Their most famous collaboration was the De La Warr Pavilion in Bexhill-on-Sea. At the same time Mendelsohn worked on buildings in Palestine, including the Hebrew University in Jerusalem. His last years were spent in San Francisco working for the Jewish community.

DATE: 1921
Potsdam, Germany

ARCHITECT: Eric Mendelsohn (1887–1953)

Falling Water

DATE: 1935–37

Bear Run, Pennsylvania, USA

DESIGNER: Frank Lloyd Wright

(1869–1959)

Frank Lloyd Wright was one of the great American individualists in architecture. He is important not only because of the quality of his ideas and buildings, but because almost single-handedly he created the idea of the architect as superstar. His architectural style changed throughout his career from decade to decade, almost from project to project. A common thread running through his work, however, is his attempt to create an organic architecture, which has a dialogue with nature. This reflects his readings of the nineteenth-century critics Ruskin and Viollet-le-Duc, whose romantic ideas had a tremendous influence on him. Falling Water exemplifies these ideas and remains one of his most startling and original works. It was built for the Kaufmann family as a weekend retreat, on a site overlooking the Bear Run stream which the family wanted to be incorporated into the final design. The house is a mix of natural and man-made forms. Lloyd Wright had observed that a high rock ledge beside the stream could be used to cantilever the house, so it stood above the stream and at the same time became almost part of it. Each cantilever has a balcony overlooking the stream, bringing inhabitants into contact with water and nature: the whole house seems to merge with the landscape, its layers becoming the strata of the terrain.

Notre-Dame de Haut

ssociated with the purity of Modern-Movement architecture, the pressive forms of the chapel at Ronchamp come as something a surprise. Situated on the top of a hillside, the building's organic rm dominates the site. Le Corbusier claimed that the dramatic of-line's anthropomorphic form was inspired by a "*réaction* *pétique*" to a crab's shell he had originally picked up on a Long and beach in the 1940s. For others it resembled the symbolic nclosure of a nun's veil.

Ronchamp was a project on which Le Corbusier lavished a great eal of personal attention. He wanted to create a place of peace and tranquillity, a religious and spiritual sanctuary. In this way Ronchamp exemplified a move away from his prewar work, which simulated the sleek lines of the machine by the use of pure form and white concrete. This building became one of the most accessible and popular examples of Le Corbusier's architecture. In some ways the techniques he used in the design of Ronchamp indicate a return to his very early work. This can be seen in his use of natural forms for the concave and convex walls and in the materials, which included the rubble of the destroyed church, which the chapel replaced, and reinforced concrete.

DATE: 1955
Ronchamp, France

ARCHITECT: Le Corbusier
(1887–1965)

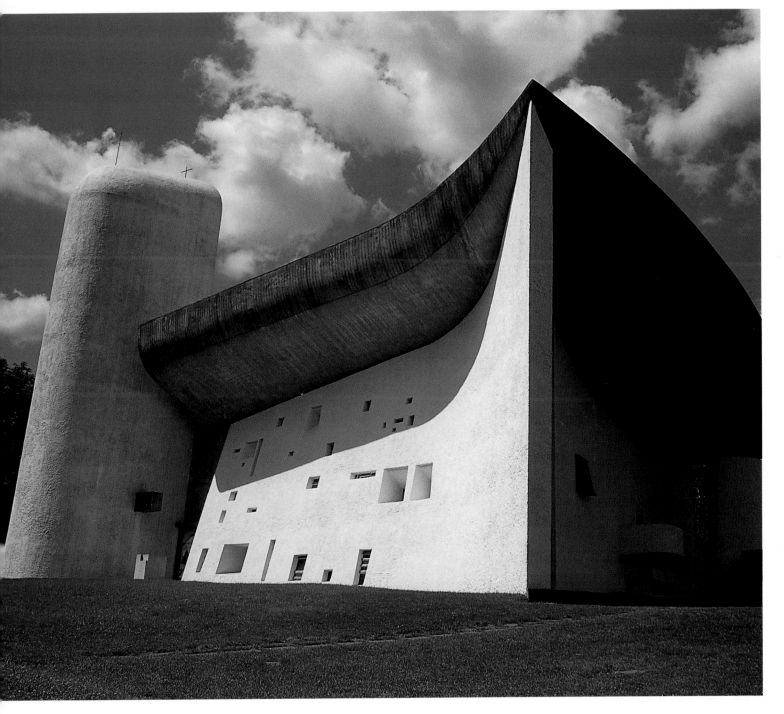

Eames House

DATE: 1949

Pacific Palisades, California, USA

ARCHITECT: Charles Eames
(1907–1978)

The name Eames is synonymous with furniture, but he preferred to describe himself as an architect: "I prefer the word 'architect' and what it implies. It implies structure, a kind of analysis as well as a kind of tradition behind it." He trained as an architect in the 1930s, producing largely conventional work, but in 1937 an important meeting changed his career and placed him at the very centre of new design experiments in America: Eames was invited by Eero Saarinen to teach at the Cranbrook Academy of Art, then a small and unknown school, but with ambitions of becoming an American Bauhaus. Here Eames worked alongside the influential sculptor–designer Harry Bertoia, and met key figures such as Florence Knoll. This shaped his attitudes to both design and architecture and marked the beginning of his fascination with new technology.

Eames never ran an architectural practice, but Eames House provided the prototype for a few private commissions. It consisted of two steel-frame prefabricated units, bought from an industrial catalogue, divided by a patio space. These frames were painted grey with infill panels, some of which are constructed from opaque materials while others are painted in bright yellows, reds and blues.

Charles and his wife Ray were true polymaths, working on children's toys, films and exhibition designs. In this respect the architecture and furniture are interchangeable – their approach and aesthetic remained a unified and single one.

TWA Terminal Building

During the 1950s, Eero Saarinen helped to establish an original American architectural style that combined the European tradition with sculptural organic forms. Saarinen was responsible for some of America's best-known buildings, including the TWA terminal at John F. Kennedy Airport, with its dramatic roofline designed between 1956 and 1962. Through a daring use of concrete, Saarinen wanted to restore to architecture a new expression of form and excitement that would contrast with the anonymity of the high-rise building.

Saarinen was originally born in Kirkkonummi, the son of Eliel, a leading Finnish architect. Although the family emigrated to America in 1923, Eero returned to Europe to study sculpture – a training that was to have an important influence on his later work. When his father became Director of Architecture at the famous Cranbrook Academy, near Detroit, Eero came into contact with America's most progressive designers, including Florence Shust – who later married Hans Knoll and established one of America's most important furniture companies – and Charles Eames. From 1937, Eames and Saarinen collaborated on a series of furniture projects using plywood, one of which took first prize at the Low-Cost Furniture Competition organized by New York's Museum of Modern Art in 1948.

From 1950, Saarinen's work with his partner Cesar Pelli developed a more inventive style. These buildings include the TWA terminal, with its distinctive parabolic arches that evoke wing forms, and Dulles Airport, Washington D.C. In London's Grosvenor Square, a late Saarinen collaboration with Yorke, Rosenberg and Mardall can be seen in the United States Embassy building.

DATE: 1956–62
John F. Kennedy Airport,
New York City, USA

ARCHITECT: Eero Saarinen
(1910–1961)

Sydney Opera House

DATE: 1956–73
Sydney, Australia

DESIGNER: Jorn Utzon
(born 1918)

The Sydney Opera House has become one of the most famous buildings in the world. It is such a potent image that it has now come to symbolize the city of Sydney and the country of Australia.

Jorn Utzon, a Danish architect, won the competition to design a new opera house for Sydney in 1957. Previously he had worked for Alvar Aalto from whom he learnt an organic approach to architecture. His other inspiration was the work of the American architect Frank Lloyd Wright. Utzon's winning design was both functional and symbolic, housing two concert halls and public spaces. Its form evoked both the sea, which provides the dramatic backdrop for the building, and the graceful flight and form of sea birds. In this way the design marks a transition in twentieth-century architecture away from the geometry of early Modernism to a more expressive and sculptural approach to building.

Between 1956 and 1966, Utzon was responsible for the main structure of the building, but it was the engineer Ove Arup who enabled him to realize the ambitious form of the roof. Utzon chose to make the roof the focal point of the design because it was the feature most people would see – it was sited on a point projecting into the bay of Sydney Harbour. In this way, the concert hall covered by the famous "prow-like" roof, became a sculpture – a fifth facade to the building.

Pompidou Centre

DATE: 1971–76
Paris, France

ARCHITECTS: Richard Rogers
(born 1933) and Renzo Piano
(born 1937)

The Centre National de l'Art et de la
Culture Georges Pompidou is an arts
complex that has become one of the
most famous and best-loved buildings
in Paris. The architects left a large
piazza at the front of the city centre
site, an extension of the building
which has created a wonderful
atmosphere of life and activity. To
increase the internal space, all the
services, air-conditioning pipes and
ducting of the building were placed
on the exterior. The most dramatic
feature is the escalator with its
transparent covering dominating the
main facade, which takes people into
the building and becomes an
extension of the street. The effect of
the brightly coloured blues, reds and
greens resembles, in Rogers' own
words, "a giant Meccano set".

The Centre proved a brilliant
solution to the brief, which
demanded a library, galleries, a
museum of modern art and research
centre. The internal spaces are
completely free of supports,
permitting maximum flexibility. This
was the first "museum" not to be
designed as an imposing monument
in the nineteenth-century tradition,
but as a flexible framework for
cultural activity.

Hong Kong and Shanghai Banking Corporation

DATE: 1985
Central District, Hong Kong

ARCHITECT: Sir Norman Foster
(born 1935)

Designed in 1979, this was Norman Foster's first skyscraper and it established the practice as one of the most prestigious in the world. The bank combined many of Foster's architectural preoccupations: his attempt to redefine the faceless office blocks associated with the Modern Movement; a concern with structure; the use of new materials and technology; and his introduction of natural light into the building. It occupies one of the most spectacular sites on the island, leading to the waterfront while the granite rock formations of Victoria Peak rise in the background.

The building is suspended from pairs of spectacular steel masts arranged in three bays, connected at key points by two-storey trusses from which the floor clusters are suspended. This staggered profile created interior spaces of varying width and depth, allowing garden terraces and dramatic east and west elevations. In addition, the combination of solid structure and transparent panels reveals the rich mixture of spaces within. These include a 12-metre (40-feet) -high public concourse from which a pair of escalators rise to the main banking hall and its ten-storey atrium.

Lloyds Building

DATE: 1978–86
London, England

ARCHITECT: Richard Rogers
(born 1933)

Richard Rogers is one of Britain's foremost contemporary architects. His work represents the "High-Tech" phase of Modernism. It emphasizes the structure and working parts of the building, often placing them on the exterior, and argues that since they are the first elements that need replacing, it is more straightforward if they are easily accessible.

As a young architect, Rogers was influenced by the new avant-garde, particularly the work of the Archigram group, elements of which appeared in his collaboration with Renzo Piano on the Pompidou Centre in Paris. The Lloyds commission was the result of a competition to design the headquarters for one of the most important financial institutions in the world located in the heart of the City of London. Again, his approach was to free the internal space by placing lifts and staircases outside the building and cranes on the roof to enable repairs and cleaning. Lloyds' requirement was for a vast underwriting room – the nerve centre of their insurance operation – which offered the flexibility of space so important for their business. Although ten years later the building would already be overcrowded, Richard Rogers & Partners nonetheless succeeded in creating a building of international prestige. The result was strikingly High-Tech, using steel, polished concrete, and making maximum use of the cramped site by layering the height of the building. Although Lloyds reflects the Modernist concern with technology, most details rely on a one-off customizing approach, rendering it a kind of Arts and Crafts High Tech.

Vitra Design Museum

DATE: 1989
Weil-am-Rhein, Germany

ARCHITECT: Frank Gehry
(born 1929)

Frank Gehry belongs to the great tradition of American individualist architects which includes Frank Lloyd Wright. His idiosyncratic, fun approach has made him America's best-known "fringe" architect. Almost single-handedly, Gehry made this fringe not only mainstream but popular, with clients as diverse as the Disney Corporation and American universities. The public has found this work much more accessible than the rival East Coast aesthetic centred on the New York 5 led by Peter Eisenman.

Gehry invited the viewer or user to reassess their ideas and preconceptions about conventional objects. He used non-traditional materials, such as corrugated iron, chain-link fencing and pieces of wood, placed in surprising contexts. Gehry's own Santa Monica house of 1977 is an early example of his approach, which helped to establish the meaning of the new Postmodernism. Sculptural qualities help to define the effect of his buildings. Gehry enjoyed close connections with the Pop Art movement, including his collaboration with Claes Oldenburg on the Santa Monica binocular building. These distinctive visual qualities made Gehry's work particularly appropriate for the design of art galleries, such as the Vitra Design Museum, the remarkable Guggenheim Museum in Bilbao, and the American Centre in Paris.

KunstHal

DATE: 1992
Rotterdam, The Netherlands

ARCHITECT: Rem Koolhaas
(born 1944)

Rem Koolhaas is not only one of Holland's best-known architects but a man who enjoys an international reputation for his buildings and writings on architectural and urban theory. Always a radical with an avowed passion for science fiction, a fascination for public space and architectural wit, he has been described as the "surrealist of the city" and cites Salvador Dali as a bigger influence than Le Corbusier. Attacking Le Corbusier's ideas of city planning as restrictive, Koolhaas believes architecture should explore and represent the full range of human emotions including sensual pleasure, memory and guilt. Like many cities in the late twentieth century, Rotterdam is reinventing itself as a cultural metropolis. It is famous for its regeneration projects, including the reclamation of the dockland area, and the KunstHal, a gallery and arts venue, a quirky take on the traditional values of public building. Koolhaas's approach to what he identifies as the random, messy qualities of urban life can be seen in the KunstHal. The entrance is not obvious, located on a lower level at the "rear" of the building, and instead of the rich and expensive materials one might expect in a major public building, Koolhaas has used throwaway materials such as corrugated plastic, old planking and exposed steel girders.

Law Firm

DATE: 1984–89
Falkestraße, Vienna, Austria

ARCHITECT: Coop
Himmelblau, Vienna, Austria

Coop Himmelblau are a radical group of architects founded in Vienna by Wolf D. Prix, Helmut Swiczinsky and Rainer Michael Holzer. The group developed a theory of architecture that was confrontational, even aggressive. Their outlook was reflected in a series of projects undertaken in Vienna, one of the best-known of which was this roof conversion for a law firm in the city. This extraordinary structure, built from glass and steel, has been attached to the top of a conventional nineteenth-century building. This exterior view of the middle construction houses the conference room, in which curved glass spans the distance between the trusses of the steel construction. The main truss bears the weight of the glass and the folded roof, the underside of which is visible here.

Coop Himmelblau seek to express and reinforce the tensions they have identified in contemporary architecture. The design of their work continues the tradition of experimental 1960s ideas that were meant to challenge the viewer and to introduce an element of dissonance, as can be seen here. For example, no wall is at right angles to the next.

Alameda Bridge

Born in Valencia, Santiago Calatrava is Spain's best known architect. He studied architecture at the Escuela Tecnica Superior de Arquitectura, Valencia and in 1979 gained a PhD in Civil Engineering from the Federal Institute of Technology, Zurich.

After graduating, Caltrava entered architecture competitions as a means of gaining commissions. His first winning entry was for the Stadelhofen Railway Station in Zurich, where he established his office. In 1984 Calatrava won the competition to design the Bach de Roda Bridge in Barcelona, the first in a series of notable bridges, including the Alameda Bridge, that established his international reputation. Since then secondary offices have been established in Paris and Valencia.

The Alameda Bridge crosses the dried up bed of the Turia River to link the old town with the new. It is a 130-metre (427-foot) span of steel with a steel suspension arch which unexpectedly leans at an angle to the vertical to counterbalance the asymmetric loading of the road on one side and the pedestrian footpath on the other. The refined structural simplicity of the bridge, which looks precarious to the uneducated eye, is typical of Calatrava's work.

Calatrava is known as an artist, an engineer and an architect, and he believes that architecture is the combination of all the artistic disciplines. His training as both architect and engineer allows him to create sculptural surfaces supported by innovative structure.

Some of his most recognizable recent works are the Turning Torso Tower, Malmo, Sweden (2005), the Athens Olympic Sports Complex (2004) and the "cathedral-like" design for the World Trade Center's new transportation hub.

DATE: 1991-1995

Valencia, Spain

ARCHITECT: Santiago Calatrava (born 1951)

Getty Center

DATE: 1997
Los Angeles, California, USA

ARCHITECT: Richard Meier
(born 1934)

Richard Meier is not only one of America's most famous architects but during the last decade he has attracted frequent European commissions, many of them for art galleries and museums, including the Museum für Kunsthandwerke in Frankfurt. Meier is famous for his white architecture and his intellectual roots lie in his membership of the New York Five, a group who, in the 1960s, sought to revitalize architecture in the USA, by developing an approach to form and theory based on the work of the inter-war Modernists. Each chose a different architect as a model: Meier took Le Corbusier's purist period and evolved, extremely successfully, a white shiny architecture, based on Platonic forms. Critics have accused his style as being too conservative and commercial but his prestigious commission for the Getty Center confirmed his status as the museum architect *par exellence*. J. Paul Getty is part of the Getty family, whose tradition of arts sponsorship is legendary and includes the J. Paul Getty Museum in Los Angeles, a reconstruction of a Pompeian villa.

This new building is a hugely ambitious project to establish th centre as a research institute of international importance. employs the latest technology for conservation, storage, and th retrieval of books. More a campus than a single building, it constructed on a desert ridge just outside Los Angeles, on the Sa Diego freeway. The project includes a gallery, conservation centr administration buildings and a library. Visitors to the centre w access the site either by foot or a purpose-built tram. Get stipulated that the building should not be "white" and so Meier ha had to abandon one of his trademarks, although the design of th building retains his attachment to basic geometry. In keeping wi the defensive positioning of the site, Meier has created a massiv and monumental architecture, one that lacks his usual "pristir sheen" due to the use of heavily fossilized marble as the ma cladding material. This is informally laid across the ridge, creatir what some critics have described as an effect similar to the Grea Wall of China.

Millennium Dome

...e centrepiece of the millennium celebrations in London, the ...me was a self-conscious reference to Richard Tubbs' Dome of ...scovery, designed as the centrepiece building of the 1951 ...stival of Britain. The Dome is a remarkable feat of modern ...gineering: it is the largest structure of its kind in the world, with ...circumference of over 1 kilometre (0.6 miles). At the centre of ...e Dome the ceiling rises to 50 metres (164 ft). Its translucent ...of is supported by more that 70 kilometres (43½ miles) of high-...ength cable; although only 2 mm (0.04 in) thick the roof is, ...vertheless, resilient enough to hold the weight of a jumbo jet.

So vast is the Dome that two Wembley Stadiums would fit inside it. Construction of the Millennium Dome kept the environment in mind; the roof was designed to collect the rainwater that falls on it every year – millions of litres – to be subsequently stored, filtered and reused within the Dome.

Designed by Richard (now Lord) Rogers, the building was controversial before it had even opened, less for its design (largely considered a success) than its proposed use. Having been empty for several years, the Dome is now the O_2 concert and entertainment venue.

DATE: 1999, London, UK

DESIGNER: Richard Rogers Partnership

CCTV Building

DATE: Completion scheduled for 2008–2009 Beijing, China

ARCHITECT: Rem Koolhaas (born1944) and OMA

The CCTV Headquarters is part of an impressive building programme in Beijing, initiated by the 2008 Olympic Games, to transform and modernize China's capital city. With the international spotlight on China, it was also a moment for the country to present a more international, outward-looking and modern political image and a key element of that strategy was the appointment of leading foreign architects to design signature buildings in the city, which included the commissioning of Dutch architect, writer and critic, Rem Koolhaas. Koolhaas founded the Office for Metropolitan Architecture (OMA) in 1975 and gained his international profile through a series of innovative entries in major architectural competitions. Koolhaas's original vision has won several awards, and the practice has made a strong contribution to architectural research due to its conceptual studio, the AMO.

Koolhaas continues his research and writing as a Professor Harvard University.

OMA won the competition for the CCTV Building in 2002 a work started in 2004. Ole Scheeren, a partner of OMA based in t Beijing office, is leading the design and construction for the proje which also involved the visionary engineer Cecil Balmond of Ar Associates. The building itself is an imaginative use of a tradition Chinese character, forming a gravity-defying loop. The complex v contain three buildings and a media park. One half of the ma building, the CCTV, will be a private building with a "Visitor's Loo while its mirror image is a public building named the Televisi Cultural Centre or TVCC, which will contain a broadcasting theat cultural facilities and a five-star hotel. The project explores structu innovation and the integration of public and private use within single building.

Performing Arts Centre

Zaha Hadid is one of only a few contemporary female architects with an international profile. Iraqi-born Hadid trained at the Architectural Association in London and founded her practice in the same city in 1980. Her early work was highly conceptual and was either impossible to build or in need of considerable investment to be realized. Her radical architectural vision however was always recognized; she designs buildings using fluid and organic lines and spaces which seem to shift as one passes through them, which hold multiple perspective points. It was not until 1993 that her first project was completed; the Vitra Fire Station, in Weil am Rhein, Germany.

The eventual realization of Hadid's work was made possible by advances in engineering and architectural structures and the development of computer software able to work out the complex calculations necessary for successful construction. In 2003, following completion of the landmark Rosenthal Centre for Contemporary Art in Cincinnati, Ohio, Hadid received a number of important commissions, including the Performing Arts Centre in Abu Dhabi. Abu Dhabi, along with other countries forming the United Arab Emirates, has undergone an intense period of development and investment in public and private building. The cultural centrepiece of this regeneration is the Performing Arts Centre, part of a complex of five major institutions forming a cultural district on Saadiyat Island. Hadid's concept for the Arts Centre is inspired by the geometries of the natural world, taking a sculptural form which seems to grow from paths in the surrounding cultural district. The 62-metre (203-ft) tall building is proposed to house five theatres with a combined seating capacity of 6,300 and may also include an Academy of Performing Arts. In 2004, Hadid was the first woman in its 26-year history to win the Pritzker Prize for Architecture.

DATE: Initial designs presented 2007, Abu Dhabi, UAE

DESIGNER: Zaha Hadid (born 1950)

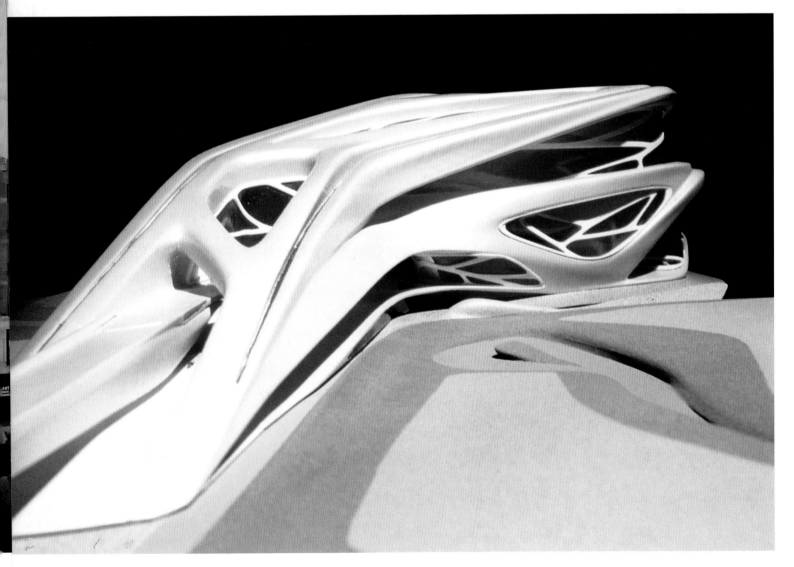

78 Southpark Avenue

DATE: 1906, reconstructed
by the Hunterian Museum,
Glasgow, Scotland

DESIGNER: Charles Rennie
Mackintosh (1868–1928)

Charles Rennie Mackintosh viewed this house as an opportunity to create "interior architecture". He designed all of the fixtures, fittings and furniture, giving the house an overall sense of harmony. In this way, the interior of the home reflected his artistic personality and the modernity and taste of its inhabitants.

In 1906, Mackintosh and his wife Margaret Macdonald remodelled a standard Glaswegian terraced house to create a modern home of simplicity and space – a dramatic contrast to the industrialized city of Glasgow. Mackintosh denoted space by changes in colour – he moves from the darker browns and greys of the hall and staircase to the pristine whiteness of the private living areas. The room is L-shaped, divided not by walls but a low arch – a continuous cornice focuses attention on the living area, helping to define a sense of vertical space. This design was a radical departure from traditional nineteenth-century room usage.

And like the use of the cornice, Mackintosh's designs for the furniture and fittings are not merely decorative, they are functional. Furniture is not used to denote status and prestige but arranged to distinguish different areas of use within the room. Furniture is often built-in – shelves, cupboards and the fireplace all contain display space. Like so many Mackintosh interiors from this period, the room is predominantly white. Colour is mainly used to enhance and mark out space.

This interior represents progressive taste for 1906 – its simplicity is extreme for the period, but it is also worth noting that as an Arts and Crafts architect, Mackintosh always placed some fine art and decorative pieces within his design, such as a stencilled decoration he designed with his wife, or Japanese prints. With its use of space and simplification of form, Southpark Avenue articulated ideas that would define the Modernism of the interwar years.

Gamble House

Greene and Greene were key exponents of the American Arts and Crafts movement, which came to maturity in the early years of the twentieth century. They were heavily influenced by the writings of William Morris and the work of British architects such as Voysey, whose buildings they could have seen in the pages of the British magazine *The Studio*. Like many other Western architects, they were inspired by Japanese culture and artifacts. More specific American influences and attitudes also shaped their work, most notably the designer Gustav Stickley. The Gamble House remains an important example of a new native Arts and Crafts style. Built for David Gamble – of Procter and Gamble – as a retirement home, it reflects a desire to produce an

American architecture for American people. In designing the interior of the Gamble House, Greene and Greene took into account four principles: climate, environment, use of local materials, and the culture of the inhabitants.

The plan focuses around a central hall, allowing free circulation of air – crucial in Pasadena's hot climate. The living zone was built on one side of the hall, with the kitchen and dining area on the other. These interlinked spaces give an underlying unity to the overall design. The house is particularly notable for its use of art glass, seen here in the doors, and the desire to include up-to-date technology, such as electric lighting covered by the famous Tiffany glass shades.

DATE: 1907–08
Pasadena, California, USA

DESIGNERS: Charles Sumner Greene (1868–1957) and Henry Mather Greene (1870–1954)

Pavilion de l'Esprit Nouveau

DATE: 1925

Paris, France

DESIGNER: Le Corbusier
(1887–1965)

The 1925 Exposition des Arts Décoratifs was planned as a major international exhibition to signal a new spirit of progress after the devastation of the First World War. Most of the exhibits tended toward the well known and conservative, with two significant exceptions – Le Corbusier's building and the Melnikovs' Russian Pavilion. These two examples offered the public a glimpse of the future – a model of the new architecture of the twentieth century.

The pavilion took its name from L'Esprit Nouveau, a magazine Le Corbusier founded in 1920 to publicize his own work and that of like-minded contemporaries. In the grounds of the 1925 Exposition site stood a prototype in which Le Corbusier wanted to show that an interior could be standardized yet still satisfy human needs. The interior space is notable for its free plan – in Le Corbusier's words: *"une surface pour circuler"* – rather than a series of individual box rooms. Two storeys high, the upper storey is a mezzanine offering a vista of open white space below. Le Corbusier does not use solid walls to divide the space; instead furniture and sliding screens create distinct areas.

The contents of the Pavilion were just as radical. Le Corbusier designed some of the furniture himself, including the steel cupboards and tubular steel-framed tables. His approach to furnishing the space reflected a belief that industry had refined certain objects to their optimum form, for example, laboratory porcelain and glassware, the English club armchair and the Thonet bentwood chair. They all represent Le Corbusier's perfect standardized solution to the problems of comfortable sitting, living and entertaining. The interior also reflects Le Corbusier's interest in painting, featuring works by Léger, Ozenfant and Le Corbusier himself, as well as sculptures by Laurens and Lipchitz.

Finally, the interior does not just show new forms of enclosed space. Le Corbusier wanted to integrate the occupier with nature – the Pavilion also incorporates the garden.

rno Goldfinger was born in Budapest, studied in Paris and came England in 1934 as a refugee. He built this house in Hampstead r his wife, the painter Ursula Blackwell, and their three children. It as the centre house in a terrace of three, overlooking Hampstead's mous heath. For its design Goldfinger moved away from white oncrete to a more sophisticated amalgamation of Modernist pproaches to material, space and furniture. He also referred to aditional English forms of housing: Willow Road was a Modernist ersion of a Georgian terrace.

From the tiny entrance hall the visitor climbs a tightly coiled spiral aircase to the main floor, which contains the most significant

rooms. Here the dining room, studio, living room and kitchen are designed as zones within a single volume of space which wraps around the staircase in a "C" shape forming distinct areas which can be closed off by folding screens. There is a sense of progression from the entrance into these spaces. The house constitutes a fascinating record of the taste of British progressive architects in the 1930s. Goldfinger designed most of the furniture, some of which is reminiscent of the work of Charlotte Perriand and Le Corbusier. Other more quirky and Surrealist-inspired details include the fireplace set into a convex screen and mounted within a projecting frame which appears to float in front of the main wall surface.

DATE: 1937–39
Hampstead, London, England

DESIGNER: Erno Goldfinger
(born 1902)

Casa Devalle

DATE: 1939–40

Turin, Italy

DESIGNER: Carlo Mollino
(1905–73)

In the 1930s, Carlo Mollino set out to extend the Modernist agenda. Mollino made trips to see the work of Antonio Gaudí in Spain and knew the work of Alvar Aalto, both of whom he deeply admired. He was a man of diverse talents – a poet, writer, sportsman, iconoclast and non-conformist. A deeply private individual, the complex strands of Mollino's personality express themselves through a range of buildings, interiors and furniture, all of which continue to exercise an important influence on design.

One of Mollino's obsessions was drawing and photographing nude women. His interiors extend the theme of the body, exploring open curving space and the idea of organic movement.

Mollino had studied the Modernist idea of opening up the interior space of the home but, unlike Mies van der Rohe or Le Corbusier, he did not focus on the placement of objects as sculpture. He filled his interiors with texture: drapes, cushions and screens creating sensual surfaces. This is one of Mollino's personal photographs of the bedroom of Casa Devalle, showing it as the ultimate erotic experience. Here, veiled curtains wrap a bed against velvet walls, a theme extended to Mollino's buttoned-lips sofa – his homage to Dali's original design. Mollino has deliberately blurred the erotic distinctions between masculine and feminine, combining hard industrial doors and walls with sensual surfaces and flowing fabrics and everywhere the extensive use of mirrors reflects and breaks up the space and contributes to the overall feeling of erotic tension.

Casa Malaparte

The Italian architect Adalberto Libera designed this house for the poet and aesthete Curzio Malaparte who, disillusioned after his imprisonment by the Italian Fascist government, needed a spiritual retreat. The house, completed in 1942, was a highly personal reflection of Malaparte's poetic life in which metaphysical and surrealist elements pushed Italian rationalism to a new intensity. Libero was part of the Gruppo Seven, founded in 1927 by Italian architects whose combination of Modernism and the classical tradition was adopted as the official Fascist architectural style.

The design of Casa Malaparte – sited on a spectacular cliff top overlooking the sea on the island of Capri – plays with the conventions of what a house should be. There is, for example, no obvious entrance. The approach – a winding rocky path cut out of the cliff – leads to a widening staircase that shifts to a vast rectangular roof terrace projecting out to the sea. Beneath the roof, two floors of rooms present a sequence of spaces that progress from land to sea, and from the public – the sitting room is enormous, resembling an Italian piazza – to a series of private symmetrical rooms. These spaces are pure white and rectilinear with parallel bedrooms on either side of the main axis of the house. However, the last room overlooking the sea remains private, accessible only from Malaparte's bedroom. This dramatic study spans the width of the house with a window looking onto the Mediterranean.

DATE: 1938–42
Capri, Italy

DESIGNER: Adalberto Libera
(1903–63)

Danish National Bank

DATE: 1971
Copenhagen, Denmark

DESIGNER: Arne Jacobsen
(1902–71)

This interior is one of Jacobsen's last works. Completed in 1978, seven years after the designer's death, the design for the Danish National Bank shows all the maturity and confidence of a master designer. Born in 1902, Jacobsen grew up with the ideas of the Modern Movement. Although his native Denmark was relatively isolated, with its own traditions of neoclassicism, as a young man Jacobsen had first-hand experience of the new. In 1925 he visited the Paris Exposition and saw for himself the work of Mies van der Rohe and Le Corbusier.

Jacobsen became well known in the 1930s for a style of architecture that merged the Danish vernacular with Continental Modernism. Together with architect Gunnar Asplund, he explored a "Scandinavian" design aesthetic, revealed in Jacobsen's work for Arhus Town Hall in 1937.

In the postwar period, Jacobsen continued this assimilation in his design for the main building of Denmark's National Bank. The building is enclosed by two glass façades stretched between two enclosed gables. The customer enters the lobby of the bank via a low entrance space. The lobby itself extends twenty metres (65 feet) high through all six storeys of the building where the walls and floor are covered in Norwegian Porsgrunn marble. Jacobsen's practice was largely confined to his homeland, but he completed two interesting buildings in Britain during the 1960s: St Catherine's College, Oxford, and the Danish Embassy in London.

Habitat

DATE: 1964
London, England

DESIGNER: Sir Terence
Conran (born 1931)

The designer and entrepreneur Sir Terence Conran was responsible for a revolution in retail design during the 1960s. In 1964, when he opened his first Habitat shop in London's Fulham Road, he brought the concept of the total lifestyle to a mass market. His aim was simple: recognizing that the young affluent consumer in the 1960s was being offered little to appeal to new lifestyles and aspirations, Habitat presented a solution to the interior design and decoration of the home. Habitat not only sold furniture but wallpapers, curtain fabrics, crockery, lighting and kitchen equipment. With its white painted walls and red quarry tiles, the shop's design suggested the effect its customers were encouraged to achieve in their own interiors.

Goods were informally stacked on the floor or grouped on industrial shelving, creating a relaxed environment that people found sympathetic. Habitat produced its own designs as well as stocking a range of what Conran identified as design classics – for example, the reissue of Marcel Breuer's Cesca chair from the 1920s. Also innovative was the production of a mail order catalogue which expanded Habitat's market to include the whole country. The catalogue was designed to look fresh, modern and appealing and it proved an immediate commercial success.

Mr Freedom

DATE: 1968–69
London, England

DESIGNER: Jon Wealleans
(born 1949)

Jon Wealleans designed this clothes boutique for Tommy Roberts on London's Kensington High Street, then a centre for the new Pop culture of swinging London. Wealleans had recently visited Disneyland and the west coast of America. His design was a fusion of theme park, neon, rock'n'roll and the inspiration of new wave Italian design. Filled with oversized soft sculptures and pictures of Mickey Mouse, it was London's first retail Pop interior.

The shop reflected the instant and immediate qualities of Pop, including murals borrowed from Roy Lichtenstein, like a continually changing stage set with Wealleans supplying drawings for objects

such as a giant coat hanger which were designed and installed with a week. Mr Freedom became more than just a shop. People used as a meeting place and it included a café. It was chaotic but mad people smile. A typical example of 1960s naiveté, the business wa totally disorganized and the shop ultimately closed. For a whil however, Mr Freedom and the clothes of Pamela Motown and Ji O'Connor dressed the likes of Peter Sellers and Elton John, ar contributed to the mythology of Swinging London. The shop's c status also attracted buyers from a new enterprise in Milan – Fioruc – who bought up the stock to take home in suitcases.

The Factory

DATE: 1964
East 47th Street, New
York City, USA

DESIGNER: Billy Linich (aka
Billy Name) (born 1940)

e Factory was Andy Warhol's famous New York studio. The nverted Manhattan warehouse functioned as a studio, a film set d the setting for Warhol's infamous parties. The Factory was about style in the 1960s, pioneering the reclamation of industrial space d the idea of interior design as art installation. Warhol attracted any of New York's fringe community, among them Billy Name, who is to become an integral figure in the life of The Factory, cumenting, organizing and contributing ideas, notably for the nous Cow wallpaper. Warhol gave him a camera and made him the oup's photographer. The resulting grainy black and white photographs have become the essential documentation of Factory life. Name had set himself up in his own apartment as a hairdresser and many of The Factory crowd used it as a meeting place. Warhol liked the way Name had decorated the space with silver foil and when shortly afterward Billy Name moved into The Factory, he set about covering the walls in the same way. It was exactly the kind of unplanned event that Warhol enjoyed. The idea of anti-design, of do-it-yourself, ran against the manicured and lavish interiors for which New York was then famous and the silver interior has come to express the spirit of Pop design.

Joseph Shop

DATE: 1988
Sloane Street, London, England

DESIGNER: Eva Jiricna (born 1939)

Eva Jiricna was born and educated in the Czech Republic. She left her home country in 1968, shortly before the Russians invaded Prague, to take up a post at the architectural office of the now-defunct Greater London Council. She is best known for her sophisticated and understated work for the Joseph fashion shops. Her interest in architecture has always had an engineering bias, with a concern for materials and structure. It was this aesthetic which attracted the attention of Joseph. Regarded by many as a fashion retailer of international significance, Joseph's ability to spot and nurture talent is well known. For his chain of shops he chose Jiricna to create a cool, industrial modern space as the backdrop for the more extravagant world of fashion. The focal point for the shop is the staircase. Walls and fixtures are painted grey which allow the skeletal steel and glass staircase to stand out as the most important element. Jiricna's staircases are intended to appear as though they are floating, thus all the structural elements are reduced to a minimum – the glass and perspex strips sit on circular panels which rest on a horizontal truss connected to the glass-panelled balustrade. The quality of this beautiful detailing makes this staircase more than a piece of engineering – its sculptural effect has been widely imitated in shops throughout the world.

Imagination
Offices

DATE: 1989

London, England

DESIGNER: Herron Associates

Imagination, run by Gary Withers, is one of Britain's most prestigious design companies. In the late 1980s, the company wanted to expand into larger premises and bought two buildings connected by an alleyway behind London's busy Tottenham Court Road. It was an awkward site with two red-brick blocks running parallel, but Ron Herron's solution was masterful, opening up the dead central space by roofing it over with a skin of translucent plastic fabric. The result is a soaring white atrium, criss-crossed by a network of lightweight, semi-transparent bridges of steel and aluminium. Walls which were once external are now inside and opened up to public view. They are painted white to lighten the space and to stress their new role as interior walls.

For the Imagination offices, Herron has used interior design to revive an old building by opening up these previously hidden facades. At the same time he has acknowledged the past life and memory of the building while adding something completely new.

Royalton Hotel

DATE: 1988
West 44th Street, New York City, USA

DESIGNER: Philippe Starck (born 1949)

The Royalton was more than a new hotel design: it marked the revival of the hotel as a social focus for "happening" people – a place for the designer generation of the 1980s to stay and be seen. Before Starck, the hotel was a necessity, but it was not hip. Now, people not only stayed in the Royalton, they socialized in the bar and restaurant. It became a meeting place, more like a bar or club than the traditional exclusive and business foyer of the hotel.

Starck transformed this space with his typical concern for customized detailing. He introduced new designs for the lighting furniture, toilets and the restaurant. He dispensed with the reception desk as the traditional focus of the hotel foyer and introduced informal seating arrangements and steps, which layered the space and provided an intimate atmosphere in which guests could meet and be seen.

Barney's

DATE: 1994
Beverly Hills, Los Angeles, California, USA

DESIGNER: Peter Marino (born 1949)

Barney's has a long-standing reputation for being the most stylish of Manhattan's big stores, a view that was enhanced by the redecoration of its Fifth Avenue branch in 1994. With its policy of promoting leading edge fashion Barney's has redefined the idea, not just of the clothes shop, but the department store itself. With such an approach, Barney's challenges the established New York giants, Macy's, Saks and Bloomingdales, targeting a more youthful and style-conscious clientèle. Part of Barney's expansion programme included opening a store in America's richest and most prestigious shopping area, Beverly Hills in California. The store was lavishly fitted, with no expense spared, from the lift interiors to the floor finishes, to create a "new look" department store for the 1990s.

The inspiration for the store was the Alphonso XIV hotel in Seville, Spain. The Spanish influence permeates the design. The exterior combines brick, stucco and limestone, while the roof is covered with Spanish tiles. The main feature of the store is a central open staircase, which affords the customer glimpses of every level and of other shoppers. The staircase and ground floor are fashioned from a Spanish stone called "Blanco Macael". Other flooring is made from wood from France.

Kidosaki House

DATE: 1982–86
Tokyo, Japan

DESIGNER: Tadao Ando
(born 1941)

Tadao Ando is one of Japan's most celebrated architects. Although much of his work, including this house, can be found in Tokyo, his practice is based in Osaka away from the pressures of city life. The Kidosaki house is a typical example of his philosophy. Located in a quiet suburb of Tokyo, Ando's design provides a home for three families, each with separate living spaces within the main volume of the house. The house itself is a perfect twelve-metre cube surrounded by a wall that runs along the perimeter of the site. The living room looks out through floor-to-ceiling windows onto a courtyard, which introduces an element of nature within the cityscape.

The interior is beautifully simple. Ando's concern is to reduc form to its essentials. He uses light to articulate and highlig form, reflecting both modern design and also traditional Japanes ways of living. Ando is part of what the architectural critic Kenne Frampton described as "Critical Regionalism", the combination Modernism with the vernacular and rural traditions of design. On of the key themes in Ando's interiors is a rejection of the chaos modern metropolitan life. His solution is to create haven-lik interiors, often hidden away surrounded by walls and garden that offer the occupant a peaceful refuge.

Throughout his life Carlo Scarpa failed to receive much recognition as an architect, but he has since been acclaimed by architects and designers all over the world for his use of formal experimentation and sensitive detail. He offered a model for interior designers because his architecture deals with intervention, the conversion of existing buildings. Many of these projects included museums, the best-known being the Museo Correr and La Foscari Palace, both completed in the mid-1950s in Venice. Scarpa's work showed how it was possible to achieve a creative interweaving of tradition and innovation respecting the original building without allowing the past to overwhelm the new. This approach has become increasingly significant.

In 1955 Scarpa began work on the extensions to the Museum Canova to redisplay the work of this master of late eighteenth-century white marble sculptures. Scarpa's achievement was the design of an exhibition space which used unusual light sources by cutting into the space windows and openings which ingeniously spotlit Canova's masterpieces. Scarpa also worked on the Castelvecchio Museum in Verona and as design consultant for the prestigious Venice Biennale international modern art showcase.

DATE: 1955–57
Possagno, Italy

DESIGNER: Carlo Scarpa
(1906–78)

Nicole Farhi Showrooms

DATE: 1990s
London, England

DESIGNER: Din Associates

Din Associates was founded in 1986 by Rasshied Din and John Harvey. The partnership has become best known for its stylish yet classic work in the fashion retail world. Din and Harvey have an open attitude to the projects they undertake, endeavouring to enhance the qualities of the existing space while overlaying the new function. Their creative exploration of materials, details and technology ensure an innovative solution to each of the projects they work on.

Also included in the design team for this wholesale showroom space for the fashion designer Nicole Farhi was Lesley Bachelor. The result was a showroom as much about the Farhi's personality as it is her minimal fashions. Farhi and Din have enjoyed a close

working relationship that has resulted in the design of her menswear store in Covent Garden, her flagship store in Bond Street and her home in central London. For the latter, the brief was to produce a classic, timeless interior that reflected Farhi's "Frenchness". The interior successfully combines the drama of scale, proportion and play of light alongside simple materials such as crossed steel trusses, bleached oak, natural honey coloured paving slabs, white walls and pale green paint work. The resulting interior evoked the atmosphere of a London arcade and nineteenth-century conservatory. The use of painted surfaces, simple mouldings and cast steel columns was an approach to interior design that has been much imitated both in retailing and in the domestic environment.

Apartment London

John Young is a partner in one of Britain's most distinguished architectural practices, the Richard Rogers Partnership. Designed as an apartment for himself and his wife, this project is a monument to Young's fascination with technology. Practically every element in the apartment is manufactured from industrial materials: the structural elements are the architecture. The main living space consists of an open-plan "L" shape forming a single living, cooking and work space. The area is single height except for the short arm in the L, which is double height and contains a mezzanine level that functions as a sleeping area. The space is articulated by the furniture and by the use of staircases all of which, in Young's hands, become works of art as well as an exercise in engineering.

The living room is dominated by a suspended staircase, the truss of which is painted Day-Glo yellow. The banister steel is made from wire suspended between narrow steel balustrades in contrast to the teak treads. Connected to the mezzanine is a bathroom, a pod of glass bricks with a glass roof and a sunken cedarwood Japanese bath tub. The spiral staircase, which wraps around the exterior, also gives access to another pod-like form, the glass observatory on the roof of the building. In this interior functionalism becomes a form of high art – every possible feature is pared back to the structure and made into a memorable interior through its spaciousness and simplicity of materials.

DATE: 1989

Hammersmith, London, England

DESIGNER: John Young (born 1944)

The Graan-Silo Squat

DATE: 1991
Westerdoksdijk 51, Amsterdam,
The Netherlands

Not all interiors in this section are designed by professionals. In 1989 a group of people occupied an 1896 derelict silo in Amsterdam, with the intention of converting this huge industrial space into their own "village" of homes. This project was documented by the art and design analyst David Carr-Smith and he provides a rare insight into this unique project.

Converting this hostile industrial environment into habitable living space resulted in an astonishing transformation. To construct their two-level apartments, Mark Horner and Brian Zaetinck had to dismantle sixteen vertical metres of steel installations, install dra[...] and power, lay wooden floors and salvage fittings from the skips[...] demolished city apartments and consumer refuse. Their wo[...] reveals an inventiveness and resourcefulness that blends domes[...] needs with the sheer grandeur and danger of the space, whe[...] steel pillars and girdered walls can be seen alongside the carpe[...] and domestic objects of the home. It delivers a simple messa[...] that some people have the creativity and resourcefulness to desi[...] their own living spaces.

Chiat Day Offices

DATE: 1993–96
New York City, USA

DESIGNER: Gaetano Pesce
(born 1939)

Chiat Day is a large international advertising agency with offices in Europe and America. It has become well known for its pioneering work in developing the concept of the new paperless office, turning the traditional working environment into a series of spaces that can accommodate a variety of activities instead of being, to quote Jay Chiat, "waste dumps of dead paperwork". What Chiat Day wanted was a total rethink of the way offices were organized and designed, exploring a new and experimental "non-territorial" office etiquette. Staff were no longer given designated spaces; rooms were flexible with walls and floors saturated with data-power ports so that people could hook up to the system anywhere within the office.

But electronic technology is only part of the answer. The success of such a bold move relies on the role of the designer in the manipulation of this new spatial diversity. For its New York offices Chiat Day commissioned Gaetano Pesce, one of Italy's leading architects, widely admired for his visionary and forward-thinking attitudes. Pesce's solution was to take the rather mundane building shell and reconfigure the plan to create imaginative treatments of the internal partitions. He introduced a number of idiosyncratic details including the vivid floors, made of pigmented resin, poured to a thickness of seven millimetres over a concrete slab. In the thirty minutes it took to set, written messages and whimsical drawings were imprinted by hand. Pesce also used diverse wall finishes such as padding and thick felt and "brickwork" made from casts of television remote controls, and, in keeping with his interest in iconography, silhouetted doorways that recall advertising campaigns for important clients. A large staff locker room replaced the individual office desk and here Pesce introduced muted lighting to create a sense of privacy along with wooden cabinets to dispel the old image of uniformity usually associated with the locker room.

Prada New York Epicentre

DATE: 2001
New York, USA

DESIGNER: Rem Koolhaas
(born 1944) and OMA

In 2000 Prada, one of the world's most sought after luxury fashion brands, commissioned the Office for Metropolitan Architecture (OMA) to create three flagship stores in the USA, and commissioned OMA's conceptual division, AMO, to research new retail concepts. The results helped to define a new design sector, "experience design", which connects with the consumer and offers something more than selling, an environment.

The Prada New York Epicentre occupies the ground floor and basement of the former Guggenheim SoHo building. Approximately a quarter of the space is taken up by an undulation in the floor across the width of the building, resembling a huge wave that steps down and rolls up again to connect the ground floor with the basement. This can be used as an experimental display or exhibition space; an event platform rotates out from the smoo side of the ramp, allowing the space to be used as an auditoriu for lectures or performances. A wallpaper mural running the ent length of the store allows for a simple change of interior theme.

AMO worked with IDEO to research and develop new technolog staff have hand-held wireless devices, while in the changing roor customers can change the glass walls from transparent to opaqu at the touch of a button; the rooms also contain a touch-scree giving access to the Prada database of images, colours and siz available of the clothes they are trying on.

The conceptual development of all aspects of the Pra shopping experience by OMA and AMO adds exclusivity and allu to the brand and ensures it stays at the top of the fashion marke

Avant-garde fashion designers Viktor Horsting (born 1969) and Rolf Snoeren (born 1969) graduated from the Academy of Arts in 1992. The following year they set up Viktor & Rolf and moved to Paris, using their trademark theatricality and subversive tactics to draw attention to their work. In 1998 they presented their first haute couture collection in an off-schedule, underground performance during Paris Fashion Week. Performance and spectacle is at the heart of Viktor & Rolf's fashion shows, alongside accomplished cutting and draping skills which they use to create new and extravagant silhouettes. In 2000 they learnt to tap dance so that they could take to the stage during their show's finale and in 2002 their Babushka collection was presented using a single model, standing on a plinth wearing ten outfits which were placed on top of one another as the show progressed.

The design for their flagship store had to match the theatricality of their clothes and designers Siebe Tettero, who also works as a curator at the Central Museum, Utrecht, and Sherrie Zwail of SZI Design were given the brief of upside-down. The design style of the boutique had to be strong for visitors to recognize it upside-down and it had to fit within the character of the Viktor & Rolf brand, so neoclassicism was chosen. The entire store appears as if it is inverted – the ceiling is parquet flooring, while crystal chandeliers spring from the floor. Chairs are screwed to the ceiling and a central corridor is impassable due to upended archways which are now used as waiting seats. Following a limited edition collection produced for German fashion retailer H&M in autumn 2006, Viktor & Rolf are now placing themselves firmly within mainstream fashion and moving away from the haute couture of their early work.

DATE: 2005
Milan, Italy

DESIGNER: Siebe Tettero & SZI Design

Letchworth Bedroom

DATE: 1905

DESIGNER: Ambrose Heal
(1872–1959)

MANUFACTURER: Heal and
Son, London, England

Heal's was and is one of the best known furniture shops in London. Under the directorship of Ambrose Heal, the company allied itself to progressive design. Heal learnt his trade as an apprentice to a furniture workshop in Warwick. When he joined his father's business in 1893 he was allowed a small area in the shop to show his own designs. His work was heavily influenced by the Arts and Crafts Movement, but far from being an amateur designer, Heal quickly attracted international interest in his designs, exhibiting them in Paris and London.

In 1905, Ambrose Heal was asked to design a range of furniture for the Letchworth Exhibition. The furniture would be displayed in a cottage designed by FW Troup. Letchworth was one of the ne "Garden Cities" that were springing up over Britain, and the furnitu was intended to appeal to the middle-classes who inhabited su leafy suburbs.

Heal's designs were beautifully made and linked to a vernacu tradition of furniture making which had so inspired the Victorian desig reformers. His furniture emphasized simple and rational forms with surface decoration and plain finishes. These qualities, in spite of t name, place the Heals range alongside radical continental design. T Cottage Furniture range, which was shown to the public in 19 through an illustrated catalogue, summed up his approach.

Shaker

DATE: nineteenth century USA

Original Shaker furniture and reproductions now command high prices and have attracted a dedicated following. The Shakers were originally an English nonconformist sect founded by Ann Lee in Manchester. In the late eighteenth century, in search of religious freedom, Mother Lee and a group of followers emigrated to the East Coast of America where they established a series of communities. The Shakers rejected all modern inventions, living a life of refined austerity which they translated into their furniture and household objects. Shaker craftsmen encapsulated their moral beliefs in spare and simple interiors and furniture – ladder back chairs, tables and boxes – which owed something of their aesthetic to late eighteenth-century English furniture. What they added was an idiosyncratic element of invention, introducing ideas such as fitted furniture and the distinctive rails on which they hung clothes and chairs.

Shaker communities dwindled during the course of the twentieth century and today very few remain. However, Shaker style has remained influential to twenty-first-century designers. Their furniture rejected decoration and used the language of form to express moral purity. It is not difficult to see why they attracted the admiration of so many modern designers.

Red and Blue Armchair

DATE: 1918

DESIGNER: Gerrit Rietveld
(1888–1964)

MATERIAL: painted wood

The visual impact of the Red and Blue Chair has ensured that it remains a standard image in any history of twentieth-century design, and with the Schröder house it has become a metaphor for the Modern Movement.

Rietveld was a member of De Stijl (the Style), one of the most coherent groups within the Modern Movement. Although Gerrit Rietveld was a key player in De Stijl, his work remains rooted in the craft tradition in which he trained. Until 1911, when he opened his own cabinet-making business in Utrecht, his early years were spent as an apprentice cabinet-maker to his father.

His approach changed dramatically in 1918 when he came into contact with the early members of De Stijl. Their search for a universal form of expression led them to experiment with primary colours, basic geometric shapes and abstracted pu forms. The most recognizable expression of these aims ca be found in the paintings of Piet Mondrian. This work was a inspiration to Rietveld, who took literally the De Stijl messag that "the new consciousness is ready to be realized everything, including the everyday things of life".

Rietveld developed the ideas of De Stijl in a three-dimension form, the most famous expressions of which were the celebrate Red and Blue chair of 1918, and the Schröder House built six yea later in Utrecht.

It is simplistic but nonetheless true to describe these designs three-dimensional Mondrian paintings. However, it is worth pointir out that his work remains more interesting on a visual level than a design solution for the needs of the twenty-first century.

Cesca Chair (B32)

Marcel Breuer started his career at the most famous design school of the twentieth century, the Bauhaus in Germany. Enrolled in 1920, Breuer spent most of his time in the cabinet-making workshop. Almost immediately his work was recognized as highly original. The story of how he discovered bent tubular steel has become part of the mythology of the Modern Movement. Legend has it that he purchased an Adler bicycle and was so inspired by its strength and lightness, he determined to apply the same techniques to furniture. Although other designers experimented with a single, curved chair shape that did not use traditional legs, it was Breuer's B32 and B64, nicknamed the Cesca Chair in the 1960s after Breuer's daughter Francesca, which became that decade's most-famous cantilevered design.

Breuer did not train as an architect and only started to design buildings after he left the Bauhaus in 1928, when he moved to Berlin.

While his architectural projects during this period were restricted to interiors and competition entries, they were as radical as any in the avant-garde. Breuer was unusual in that, unlike Gropius and Mies van der Rohe, his furniture preceded his architecture. In this way it can be seen as a rehearsal for his buildings. Streamlined, continuous metal furniture that flowed seamlessly became the perfect expression of the Modern Movement and informed Breuer's interiors and structures. In 1937, at the invitation of Walter Gropius, he taught architecture at Harvard. It was there that Breuer became an important bridge between Europe and America. Partly due to his early workshop training, Breuer proved a popular and practical teacher. In this sense Breuer became more important for his influence on a key generation of American architects – among them Philip Johnson – than for his own buildings.

DATE: c.1926

DESIGNER: Marcel Breuer (1902–81)

MATERIAL: chrome-plated steel, wood and cane

MANUFACTURER: Gebrüder Thonet, Frankenberg, Germany

Fauteuil, Modèle Petit Confort

DATE: 1928

DESIGNERS: Le Corbusier (1887–1965), Pierre Jeanneret (1896–1967), Charlotte Perriand (born 1903)

MATERIAL: chrome-plated steel and leather upholstery

Le Corbusier's furniture – or "equipment" – must be understood as an extension of his architectural aims of this period. When Le Corbusier realized that his clients could not buy furniture that would complement the flowing space of his houses, he developed a range of a furniture – machines for sitting in – to co-exist with machines for living in. Placed in the interiors of houses such as the Maison Cook (1927), the Villa Church (1927–28) and the Villa Savoye (1929) this furniture became discrete sculpture, articulating the free-flowing space of the interior, and rendering the house a totally designed entity.

The furniture was not the work of Le Corbusier alone. He worked in collaboration with a young furniture designer, Charlotte Perriand, who had been experimenting with tubular steel as a material, as well as with his cousin and partner Pierre Jeanneret. It is to these three that the furniture should be attributed, and some to Perriand alone – a fact recognized only recently.

The "confort" armchair was made in both small and large versions. The prototypes had sprung rear legs with feather-filled cushions. It is now reproduced in modified form by the Milanese company, Cassina.

1925, Eileen Gray and Jean Badovici designed a house – the
lla E.1027 near Saint Tropez – which featured furnishings that
ad been made in her Paris workshops. Gray exploited
ew materials, such as the tubular steel used for the table
own here. It was originally designed as a bed table with the
g foot pushed under the bed for ease of use with adjustable
bletop height. It was later used as an occasional table for the
ing room.

The E.1027 Table relates to the cantilever chair experiments of the 1920s in that it also explored the idea of a table without conventional legs exploiting the streamlined possibilities of tubular steel. Gray, however, did not share the machine age preoccupations of many of her contemporaries in the European Modern Movement. Her driving force was less concerned with industrial techniques than with a search for visual perfection. The table was put into production again in the late 1970s.

DATE: 1927

DESIGNER: Eileen Gray
(1879–1976)

MATERIAL: tubular steel and
acrylic glass

MANUFACTURER: Atelier
Eileen Gray–Galerie Jean Desert,
Paris, France

Stacking Stool "L" Leg

DATE: 1932–33

DESIGNER: Alvar Aalto (1898–1976)

MATERIAL: plywood

MANUFACTURER: Artek, Helsinki, Finland

Aalto's great achievement was the production of designs that were simultaneously ahead of their time and timeless. Designed as fixtures for his buildings, the furniture reflects exactly the same aesthetic as the architecture – they remain part of the same vision.

The beauty of his plywood furniture meant that it became more than just furniture – it was appreciated and collected as sculpture for the modern interior. In this context, for example, his plywood kitchen stools were specified as seating for Manchester's Hacienda nightclub in the 1980s, by designer Ben Kelly, and for kitchens, restaurants and homes all over the world. Aalto's designs have found a place in the modern domestic interior and inspired countless imitations in stores such as Ikea.

Aalto's choice of natural materials – such as wood – and his simple use of curves reflects both an interest in organic forms and the need for a human and humane aesthetic.

In 1925 he married the architect Aino Marsio, his most important collaborator. It was Marsio who ran the Artek Wooden Furniture company, which marketed Aalto's designs that found almost immediate commercial success around the world.

Ant Chair

rne Jacobsen's achievement as an architect was to fuse the traditions
f his native Denmark with those of mainstream Modernism. In
ommon with many Scandinavian architects of his generation,
acobsen also concerned himself with the design of the interior and its
xtures. Most of his designs for silverware, textiles and furniture were
te specific but their appeal to a wider audience was immediate.

In 1952 he designed The Ant, a light, stackable chair, the seat and
ack of which were moulded from a single piece of plywood supported
y a tubular steel frame. The chair was designed for the Fritz Hansen
rniture factory, which had experimented with steam-bent plywood for
number of years. The Ant was Jacobsen's contribution to the
nguage of modern, industrially manufactured furniture and it inspired

a series of successors from 1952 to 1968 whose common elements
were the continuous seat and back. These chairs marked an important
turning-point in Jacobsen's career and they mark his shift from a
distinguished Danish designer to a figure of international importance.

The 3107 Ant Chair, pictured here, produced as the Series 7,
was designed for the Rodovre Town Hall as a stacking chair. it is
now manufactured in many different versions and numerous
colours, and remains the most sold chair in Denmark. With their
new materials and organic forms these chairs were original and
fresh, sensual and even sexy objects. It is no coincidence that the
photograph of the naked Christine Keeler posing on a fake Ant
chair has become a legendary icon of the Swinging Sixties.

DATE: 1955

DESIGNER: Arne Jacobsen
(1902–71)

MATERIAL: moulded plywood
and chrome steel

MANUFACTURER: Fritz
Hansen, Denmark

Superleggera Chair

DATE: 1955

DESIGNER: Gio Ponti (1891–1979)

MATERIAL: tinted ash and cane

MANUFACTURER: Cassina, Meda, Italy

Gio Ponti was a true Renaissance man. Not only was he active as a teacher and writer, he was also a gifted painter and designed products, lighting and furniture. Even in the context of so many talented Italian designers, Ponti remains a unique individual, remarkable for his integration of ceramics, furniture, theatre design, town planning and graphics with architecture.

During the 1930s he had worked with Cassina, one of Italy's most respected furniture manufacturers, and this relationship continued in the postwar period. Cassina wanted a light, versatile chair that would suit the smaller apartments of the 1950s where space was at a premium, so Ponti produced a seminal design, the Superleggera chair of 1955. For this he was inspired by the tradition of light wooden chairs, used by local fishermen he had seen as a child. He had worked on versions of this vernacular design as early as 1947. His final work for the Superleggera produced a classic but modern chair that proved extremely popular with Italian consumers. In 1957 it won the prestigious Compasso d'Oro prize. Ponti's trademark combination of tradition with modernity can be seen in Milan's Pirelli Tower (1956), where modern concrete is capped with a cantilevered roof in the shape of a cardinal's hat.

s not surprising that this simple and spare table was designed a garden designer and a sculptor who had worked in the 20s as an assistant for Alexander Calder. This table became mu Noguchi's best-known design and received international blicity for its minimalist aesthetic that fitted so well into the lture of the 1950s. It was designed using two identical ements for the base, one of which was inverted and glued to the other. Interestingly, it was this same quality of minimalism that caused Noguchi many problems and inspired the imitations that dogged his career as a designer. In fact it was a copycat design of an earlier piece that prompted Noguchi to produce this table. As soon as it was designed it sold in huge quantities, helped by the fact that Herman Miller were able to promote this table as knock-down furniture.

DATE: 1945

DESIGNER: Isamu Noguchi (1904–88)

MATERIAL: ebonized birchwood and glass

MANUFACTURER: Herman Miller Furniture Company, Michigan, USA

P40 Reclining Armchair

DATE: 1954

DESIGNER: Orsaldo Borsani
(1911–85)

MATERIAL: metal and
upholstery

MANUFACTURER: Tecno,
Milan, Italy

One of the most striking designs of the decade, this chair relies on an engineering aesthetic – with its adjustable seat and back, and flexible armrests, it resembles an aircraft seat. The chair was influenced by the techniques used in the automobile industry: foam rubber, then a new material from Pirelli, was used to pad the seat, the footrest was retractable and the chair could be adjusted into 486 different positions. Tecno, the manufacturer, started life as the

Atelier Varedo, run by Gaetano Borsani, a progressive 192□ designer, who won a silver medal at the Monza Triennale of 192□ Borsani opened his first shop in Milan's prestigious V□ Montenapoleone after the war. He later established Tecno, whi□ was run by his two sons, designer Orsaldo and financial direc□ Fulgenzio. Tecno concentrated on the design and production □ furniture for offices and factories, including Olivetti.

Eames Storage Unit 421-C

DATE: 1949–50

DESIGNER: Charles Eames
(1907–78) and Ray Eames (1916–88)

MATERIAL: plywood, varnished
steel, fibreglass, masonite, and rubber

MANUFACTURER: Herman Miller
Furniture Company, Michigan, USA

In 1941 Charles Eames married Ray
Kaiser and together they became
America's most important furniture
designers.; their work dominated
postwar design not only in the US but
internationally, and their experiments
with new materials, particularly
plywood and plastic, established an
aesthetic that came to express the
spirit of the 1950s. The Eames
Storage Unit (ESU) is closely linked to
the house the Eames built for
themselves in California (p. 62) using
steel-frame prefabricated units with
infill units painted in bright colours.
These units can be placed in the
Modernist tradition of using
standardized, industrial techniques for
domestic furniture. The idea was that
by using prefabricated parts, the user
could assemble virtually limitless
combinations according to practical
needs and personal taste. In its
catalogue the manufacturer Herman
Miller illustrated the various options
which the range made possible, but
this early experiment was difficult to
market. The self-assembly element
proved difficult and required skilled
installation, a DIY concept which
1950s people found unappealing.
Although the Eames design inspired
many later copycat versions, the ESU
was not a commercial success in its
own right and was discontinued.

Generally, however, the Eameses
were fortunate in acting virtually as
in-house designers for Herman Miller,
whose respected design profile meant
that Eames furniture was painstakingly
produced and marketed, featuring
then, as now, in books, magazines
and high-profile interiors.

Action Office

DATE: 1964

DESIGNER: George Nelson
(1907–86)

MATERIAL: aluminium, steel,
wood, plastic and leather

MANUFACTURED: Herman
Miller Furniture Company,
Michigan, USA

Herman Miller was America's most prestigious postwar furniture company. Their ambitious agenda for furniture design included a research department established in 1960 to introduce a new approach to the design of office furniture. George Nelson, the company's director of design from 1946 to 1966, was given the brief to design a new system of modular units that could be adapted to the different requirements of people and work. The Action Office consisted of a chair on wheels, different tables, and stackable shelf sections accompanied by a variety of accessories. The common component was the aluminium base, which acted as a support for the different units, including the option to use two as the support for a larger conference table. In the 1960s Nelson was a pioneer is developing office systems that suited the new flexible work environments of the large company or small office. Although it was later promoted in a more simplified form, the Action Office established a new standard for the design of office furniture and the system proved extremely popular.

ere had been earlier experiments with inflatable designs, for ample emergency rafts for aeroplanes. Blow, however, was the time that inflatable furniture was made popular and available, nks to new plastic technology which used electronic welding by io frequency to seal the chair seams. It was a collaboration ween four architects designing their first piece of furniture. The plicity it received did much to establish Zanotta in the 1960s as ompany with fresh, exciting ideas .

The aesthetic of Pop design led to a quest for furniture that was eap, witty, fun and disposable. Inflatable furniture was an obvious ension of these ideas. The chair was bought as a flat pack kit ich was inflated at home – when moving, it was simply deflated d folded flat.

Visually, the styling is reminiscent of the Modernist chairs of the 1930s, notably those of Eileen Gray. It also connects with the inflatable Pop art experiments of Claes Oldenburg. The Blow chair became one of the instantly recognizable icons of the decade, appearing in films of the period to express the new spirit of the times, and in endless design magazines.

The Blow was an impractical piece of furniture. It was easily damaged, and so came equipped with its own repair kit. However, it is important to remember that it was relatively cheap to buy and intended to have a short lifespan – when it was beyond repair it was simply replaced.

Although revived as a design classic in the 1980s by Zanotta, the real impact of plastic, inflatable furniture was for fun – play items for the beach and swimming pool.

DATE: 1967

DESIGNERS: Jonathan De Pas (1932–91), Donato D'Urbino (born 1935), Paolo Lomazzi (born 1936), and Carlo Scolari (born c.1930)

MATERIAL: transparent PVC plastic

MANUFACTURER: Zanotta, Nova Milanese, Italy

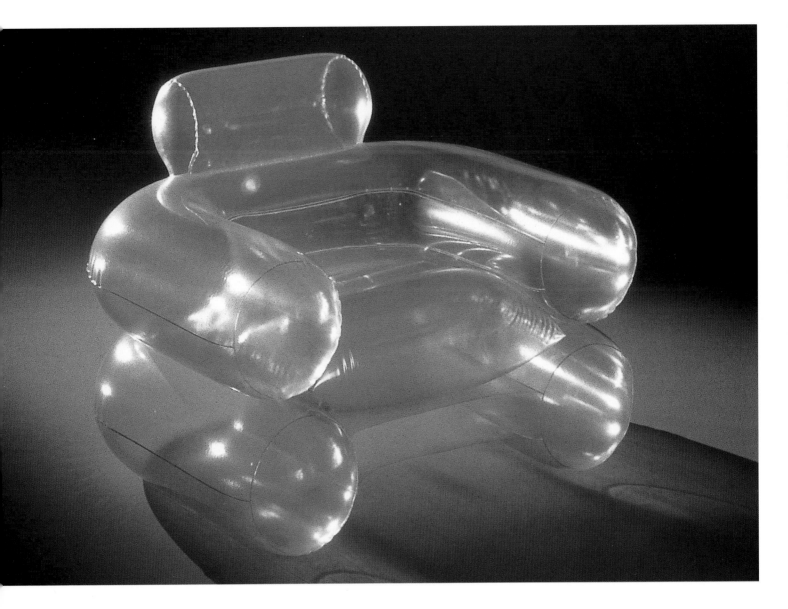

4867 Chair

DATE: 1965

DESIGNER: Cesare "Joe" Columbo
(1930–71)

MATERIAL: plastic

MANUFACTURER: Kartell, Milan,
Italy

Joe Columbo has become a legendary Italian designer, arguably the most original and inventive of his generation and his early death has contributed to this reputation. His creativity was incredibly versatile, perhaps the result of training both as a painter and an architect in Milan. The 4867 was Columbo's first experiment with new technology: it was the first chair made of ABS plastic to be injection-moulded in one piece, although a hole in the back was needed to remove the chair from the mould.

Kartell was founded in 1949 by Giulio Castelli to produce household objects using the newly patented plastics. Castelli's father had been involved in the early Italian plastics industry and Kartell used this experience to design functional objects, such as plate racks and kitchen pails, but commissioning leading designers to work on the aesthetics. The 4867 chair was Joe Columbo's response to a new material which could be curved in three dimensions and allowed the designer the freedom to create fresh, different shapes.

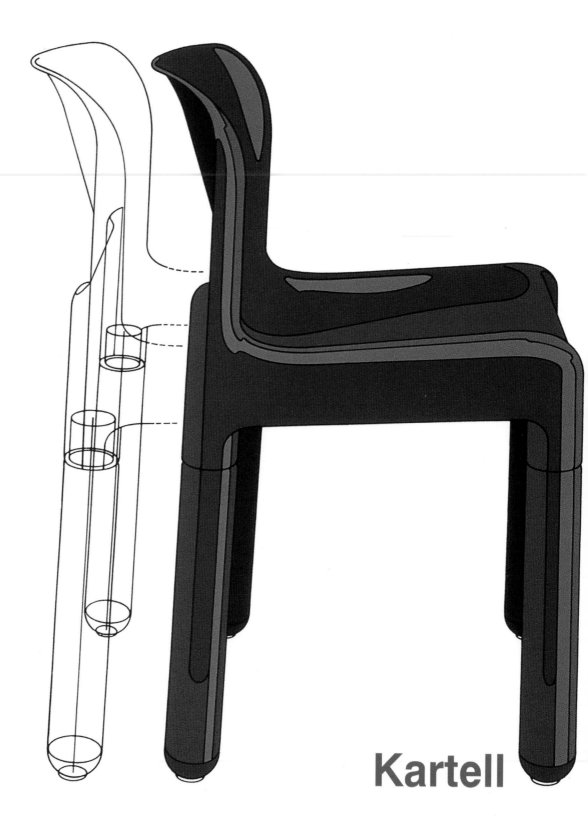

Kartell

AEO Armchair

DATE: 1973

DESIGNER: Paolo Deganello (born 1940)

MATERIAL: painted metal, fabric covered upholstery and steel manufacturer: Cassina, Meda, Italy

In 1972 the Museum of Modern Art in New York held an exhibition called "Italy: The New Domestic Landscape". If indeed there was any doubt, this exhibition established Italian design as the most innovative and creative in the world. During the 1960s Italian design established a reputation for radical, leading edge work and many young designers had formed design groups of which Archizoom Associati was one of the best known. They acted less as conventional design practices than as think-tanks, producing prototypes, art installations and events. With typical Italian pragmatism, the more mainstream companies did not ignore these activities and often worked in collaboration with young designers.

This experimental chair, designed for Archizoom Associati, is such a collaboration, investigating structure and form. Piero Daganello divided the chair into separate elements: an organic plastic base, in which was placed the iron frame covered with stretch cloth supporting a soft cushion. The back is a loose canvas cover which slips over the frame. AEO stands for Alpha and Omega – the first and last letters of the Greek alphabet. The chair was designed to sell as a flat-pack.

Cab Chair

DATE: 1976

DESIGNER: Mario Bellini (born 1935)

MATERIAL: enamelled steel, leather upholstery

MANUFACTURER: Cassina, Meda, Italy

Mario Bellini ranks alongside Sottsass, Branzi and Magistretti as one of Italy's most important postwar designers. Bellini not only enjoys a prestigious reputation for the quality of his furniture and products, but also his writing. From 1986–91, Bellini was editor of *Domus* magazine, arguably the world's best-known design publication. In 1987, his international status was confirmed when the Museum of Modern Art in New York City awarded him the rare distinction of a one-man show.

The experience of working for Olivetti influenced the design of one of Cassina's best-selling chairs, the Cab. Here a flexible leather skin sheaths a simple metal frame in a way that recalls the casing of a typewriter.

Bellini's career spans architecture and product design – exemplifying the Italian tradition for designers to train originally as architects. This seamless relationship between the two professions is expressed in the Bellini quote: "To be a good furniture designer, you have to be an architect. Everything meaningful that's been designed has been by meaningful architects."

Carlton Sideboard

1981, Ettore Sottsass, one of Italy's best-known designers, launched a new design group in Milan. Rather tellingly, it was called Memphis – the home town of Elvis Presley, the king of American music, and the sacred capital of the Egyptian Pharaohs. Memphis was an immediate success. Set against the prevailing late-1970s mood for "classic" and "good taste", Sottsass and his collaborators produced something exciting, fresh and new. Their furniture used a new palette of colours and materials, mixing plastic laminates with expensive wood veneers in bright reds, blues and yellows. These objects evoked the wit and fun of children's toys, and used references to the past, reworking the coffee bar era of the 1950s. Memphis challenged basic assumptions: for example, why should the shelves of a bookcase be straight, or the legs of a chair identical?

Sottsass drew on his own experience of the 1960s. He commented that much of his inspiration came from watching girls on London's Kings Road and his fascination with the monuments and structures of ancient cultures. The Carlton Bookcase is one of the most famous of the Memphis objects. Like so much of Sottsass' work, the piece combines his interest in Indian and Aztec art, 1950s popular culture, and his roots in 1960s Pop.

DATE: 1981

DESIGNER: Ettore Sottsass (born 1917)

MATERIAL: wood and plastic laminate

MANUFACTURER:
Memphis, Milan, Italy

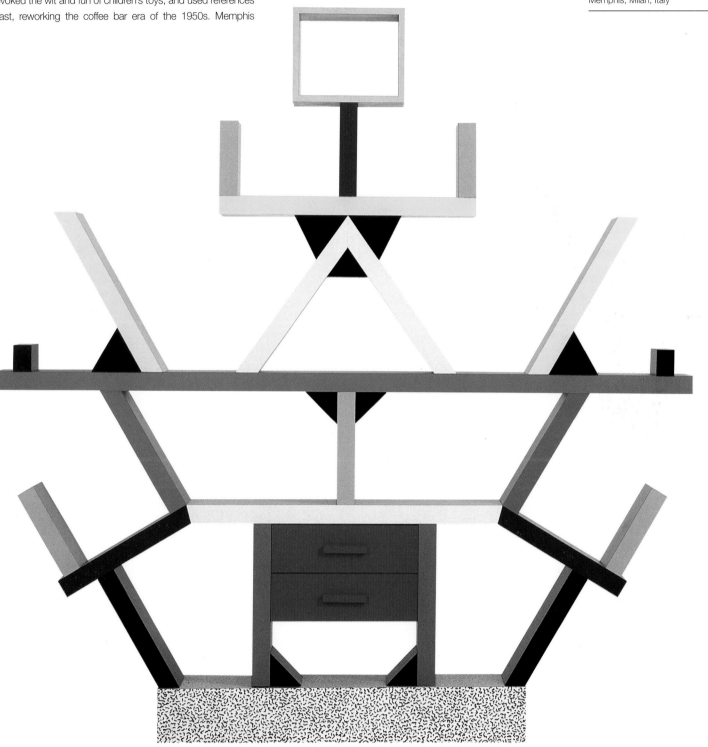

Nomos Table

DATE: 1986

DESIGNER: Foster and Partners, London, England

MATERIAL: glass and chromed steel

MANUFACTURED: Tecno, Milan, Italy

Nomos uses the high-tech components of engineering construction for this furniture system designed by Foster and Partners for the Italian furniture company Tecno. Sir Norman Foster's office is well known for its daring technical structures and Nomos started life as a table design for Foster's own office and for the Renault factory in Swindon, England. The basic idea was simple: a top resting on a metal frame with a central spine, two lateral brackets and four inclined shaft legs. The effect is not unlike the backbone and ribs of the human body. It is an inventory of precision components that can be combined to create total environments for groups of varying sizes, self-sufficient even to the extent of providing built-in and background lighting. Using different leg configurations, the ta height can be adjusted and the system can expand horizontally well as vertically, it can also accommodate a variety of surfa finishes from glass to wood, marble, metal and plastic.

Nomos was designed to cope with the rapid changes information technology and includes a built-in vertebrae-l conduit to carry cabling from desk terminals, allowing the flc space underneath to remain free. Although the range w designed as a high perform-ance office system, many people lik its aesthetic so much that it was used as a domestic table in context of the home.

e Aulenti remains a rare phenomenon: a female designer. ined as an architect in Milan, she made her greatest impact as exhibition designer but worked on other projects including a laboration with Richard Sapper in 1972 on a proposal for new an transportation systems, presented at the 1979 Milan XVI ennale. Working from the 1950s she enjoyed a quiet profile, mired for her furniture designs and commissions for interiors d showrooms for Knoll, Fiat, Olivetti, and Pirelli. Then she was chosen to design the new Paris museum Musée d'Orsay, which was sited in an old railway station. The brilliant success of this project placed her in the international design spotlight. Gae Aulenti's work reveals a complex sensibility, wishing to make contemporary objects rational, yet also accessible and human. The coffee table is one of her most famous designs using industrial components. The wheels form the base for a more traditional glass table top.

DATE: 1980

DESIGNER: Gae Aulenti (born 1927)

MATERIAL: glass, metal and rubber

MANUFACTURER: Fontane Arte, Milan, Italy

S Chair

DATE: 1987

DESIGNER: Tom Dixon (born 1959)

MATERIAL: metal and wicker

Tom Dixon was part of a group of young British designers in the 1980s who, inspired by the do-it-yourself aesthetic of Punk, started working with recycled materials and welded metal. These designs crossed the boundaries of sculpture, design and craft and became known as "creative salvage", a name Dixon chose for his first design company.

Largely self-taught as a designer, Dixon might have remained part of an interesting, if marginal, design trend. However in the late 1980s he crossed over from one-off furniture into more commercial design. The S Chair is an example of this change, combining Dixon's idiosyncratic vision with a more accessible version of his earlier work.

Dixon based the distinctive organic curve of the chair on a sketch he made of a chicken and for the S chair he worked on over fifty different prototypes. These were made using many different materials, including rush, wicker, old tyre rubber, paper and copper, which Dixon produced in his studio called SPACE. In 1987, the well-known Italian furniture company Capellini bought the design and put it into mass production; since then it has been acquired by many leading international museums including the Victoria and Albert Museum in London and the Vitra Museum in Germany. In 1994 Dixon opened the SPACE shop as an outlet for his designs and as an exhibition venue for new talent. In 1996, he launched a new product range called Eurolounge.

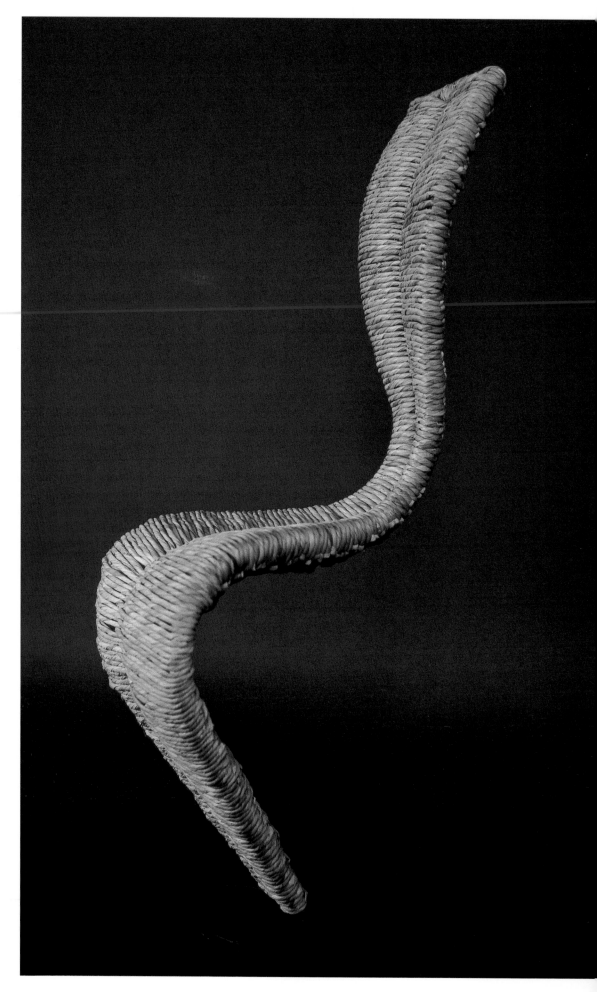

Well Tempered Chair

Born in Israel, Ron Arad moved to London in 1973, studied at the Architectural Association and in 1981 opened a furniture shop in Covent Garden. Called "One Off", the showroom became a significant part of the new British design wave of the 1980s and established Arad as Britain's most creative designer–maker. His early work used industrial materials and recycled parts, notably the famous Rover chair, which placed the car seat into a tubular steel frame. His showroom attracted many other designers with whom he collaborated or whose work he sold, including glass furniture by Danny Lane and metal furniture by Tom Dixon. Arad was therefore at the centre of new and exciting developments in London.

Always an inventive maker, Arad worked extensively in his metal workshop, welding large pieces together to make installations and furniture. Here Arad has reduced the traditional armchair to simple folded forms which challenge the conventional idea of comfort and use. Unlike many of his contemporaries in the 1980s, Arad made the significant jump into the international arena. His work was profiled in many leading museums, including the Pompidou Centre in Paris, and his annual exhibitions at the Milan Furniture Fair attracted a great deal of favourable attention. Leading Italian manufacturers, including Driade, Vitra and Poltronova, have commissioned him to design furniture for limited production.

DATE: 1986–93

DESIGNER: Ron Arad (born 1951)

MATERIAL: high grade sheet steel and thumb screws

MANUFACTURER: Vitra AG, Basel, Switzerland

Sofa

DATE: 1988

DESIGNER: Jasper Morrison (born 1959)

MATERIAL: wool upholstery and wood frame

MANUFACTURER: Sheridan Coakley Products, London, England

Jasper Morrison is now widely regarded as one of the world's leading furniture designers. His work in the 1980s marked a new direction away from the complexities of Postmodern design towards simple, classical sculptural shapes that established a cooler and highly individual style.

In 1982 Morrison graduated from Kingston University before moving on to the Royal College of Art in London. He opened his own design studio in 1987. Morrison designed a series of pieces for British company Sheridan Coakley before quickly attracting the attention of manufacturers abroad, including Vitra and Capellini. also worked for the popular Swedish retail store Ikea.

Morrison's series of sofas, using brightly coloured stretch upholstery, typically in oranges and purples, fitted perfectly with taste for spare, simple interiors in the late 1980s and early 199 Additionally, Morrison has applied the same aesthetic to ot objects, including sculptural door handles for the German comp Franz Schedier GmbH and a simple wine rack made from brigh coloured plastic.

Powerplay Armchair

ank Gehry can be placed in the great tradition of American
dividualist architects that includes Frank Lloyd Wright. His
her trademark is the use of everyday materials in distinctly
n-everyday ways – an approach which inspires his furniture
esign. Once again, the influence of the Pop aesthetic is
portant here. For Gehry, furniture should include the elements
of surprise and challenge. The Powerplay chair reflects these
ideas, and can be read as a cheeky reworking of his earlier
design, the Wiggle – a cardboard version of the Rietveld Zig-
Zag chair, which demystified a Modernist icon by using such a
cheap everyday material. With the Powerplay Chair, Gehry uses
bent wood.

DATE: 1992

DESIGNER: Frank Gehry (born 1929)

MATERIAL: high-bonding urea, laminated and bent maple wood strips

MANUFACTURER: Knoll Associates, New York City, USA

W W Stool

DATE: 1990

DESIGNER: Philippe Starck
(born 1949)

MATERIAL: lacquered aluminium

MANUFACTURER: Vitra AG,
Basel, Switzerland

Philippe Starck is now one of the best-known contemporary designers in the world. His office has produced a number of high-profile commissions, including work on the private apartment for former French President François Mitterrand in the Elysée Palace and the fashionable Royalton Hotel in New York City, which has become a standard for the new metropolitan meeting place.

In the early 1980s, however, the project that brought him to public attention was a small Paris café near the Pompidou Centre called Café Costes. What was so interesting about the project was the fact that Starck designed all the fittings, including a three-legged chair, which became an international best-seller and has come to signify modern design in restaurants and venues all over the world.

Since then he has gone on to design many well-known objects, including his Juicy Salif Lemon Press for Alessi and the WW Stool, part of a series of designs that use anthropomorphic forms. The WW is a reference to the German film director Wim Wenders for whom he designed this office chair, defining the idea of a stool as a sculptural and growing form which resembles the roots of a living plant.

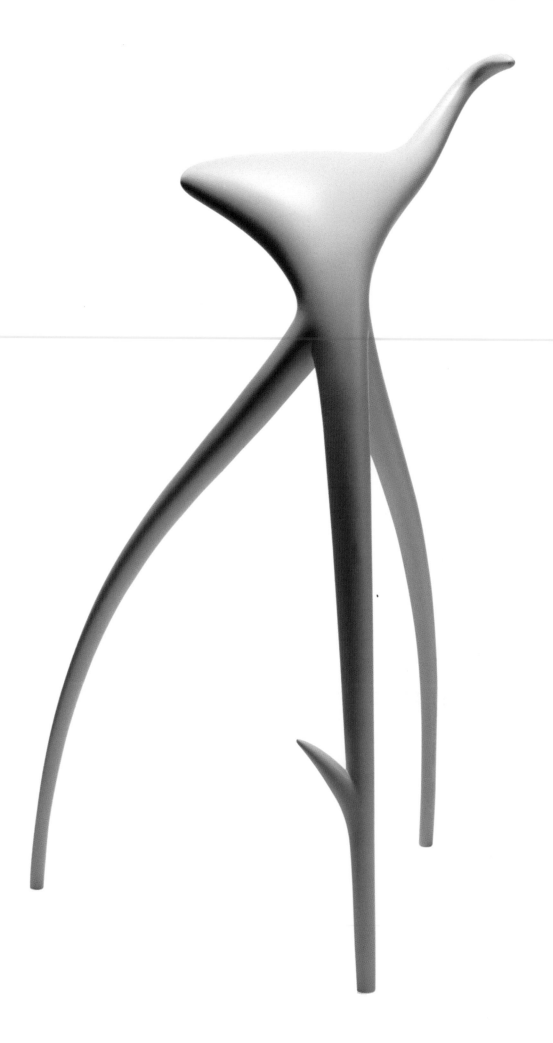

Sardine Collector's Cabinet

DATE: 1995

DESIGNER: Michael Marriott
(born 1963)

MATERIAL: MDF, sardine tins,
wing nuts

MANUFACTURER: Space UK,
London, England

In 1996 the Crafts Council in London put on an exhibition called "Recycling: Forms for The Next Century". As the title suggests the show explored the new interest in alternative design, in the reuse of materials and the search for a design future that took on board concerns for the environment and a less aggressive use of raw materials. This exhibition highlighted the work of Michael Marriott, a graduate from the furniture department of the Royal College of Art, whose quirky and fun objects caught the imagination of many people. His cabinet used a medium-density fibreboard structure to house used sardine cans as the drawers. This witty, simple and elegant solution suggested another agenda for design that looked back to the 1960s alternative tradition of Victor Papanek and the Whole Earth Catalogue.

In his work Marriott exploited the tradition of found objects. For him, found materials produced not only beautiful accidental effects but also established familiarity with the object. He recognized a culture with a wealth of wasted resources, and that he could capitalize on such materials with interesting qualities. So far the results have included a table using an old oil drum, castors and chipboard top, and a wall light using a traditional glass lemon squeezer, plywood and shelf brackets.

Smoke

DATE: 2002

DESIGNER: Maarten Baas
(born 1978)

MANUFACTURER: Baas
and den Herder (self-production),
Netherlands

Maarten Baas is part of a second generation of Dutch designers, following in the footsteps of Droog Design and established names from the 1990s such as Marcel Wanders and Hella Jongerius. Baas made a significant impact on the design industry with his graduation show in 2002 at the Eindhoven Design Academy. Smoke, one of his final year pieces, caught the attention of the international design press and expressed the radical and conceptual spirit of contemporary Dutch design philosophy. The Smoke series were pieces of iconic furniture, which had been carefully burnt until they were black, preserving their structural strength, and then painted with clear epoxy resin to protect and finish them. By burning these pieces Baas posed questions about perceptions of beauty, perfection and the care of precious objects. His Smoke Armchair

and Chandelier were taken into the collection of Dutch manufactu Moooi to be mass-produced, but he continues to produce one-works from his Eindhoven studio. Although these are not alwa produced in limited editions, each piece is unique due to its har made manufacture.

In 2004, the influential New York design gallery owner Murr Moss commissioned him to produce a series of limited editi Smoke pieces called "Where There's Smoke". Twenty-five of t most iconic design works of the last 100 years were burnt for t collection, including works by Rietveld, Sottsass and Eames. Th almost sacrilegious burning of great design works to produ something new and unmistakeably authored by Baas w controversial within the design world.

Tom Vac

n Arad is famous for his inventive and playful use of materials d his interdisciplinary approach to design practice. After more n thirty years, he remains one of Britain's best-known designers furniture and products and more recently of architectural mmissions for a design museum in Israel and a factory in Italy for gis. After studying architecture at the London Architecture sociation Arad set up "One Off" in 1981 with Caroline Thorman, o remains his business partner. In this Covent Garden workshop produced bespoke metal furniture for customers, held exhibitions d did much to build a new sense of creative British design. Arad also a highly influential design educator, pioneering cross-sciplinary design practice and research. He is also well known for ited edition design works for international design galleries such as the Gallery Mourmans, in Maastricht, Holland, which push the boundaries of production technology. In addition he has designed for volume production for leading manufacturers such as Driade, Moroso and Kartell.

The Tom Vac chair has its origins in a project, commissioned by Domus magazine, to create a sculpture in the centre of Milan. Arad designed a Domus Totem: a stack of 100 vacuum-formed aluminium chairs created from a mould. The aluminium chairs – Tom Vac – used in the sculpture were later sold in a limited edition of 500 before Vitra offered to produce an injection-moulded plastic Tom Vac (1999), which is still in production today. The Tom Vac expresses Arad's technical inventiveness and his ability to refresh and expand the boundaries of design.

DATE: 1997

DESIGNER: Ron Arad (born 1951)

MATERIAL: aluminium, stainless steel / injection-moulded plastic

MANUFACTURER: Vitra, Germany

Cork Chair

DATE: 2007

DESIGNER: Jasper Morrison
(born 1959)

MATERIAL: recycled wine-bottle corks

MANUFACTURER: Vitra, Germany

Jasper Morrison is widely regarded as one of the world's most directional designers today. British born and trained at Kingston University and the Royal College of Art, Morrison came to prominence in the late 1980s. His client portfolio is both international and mainstream and he is one of the few British designers to achieve this standing.

The Cork Chair is the result of a longstanding collaboration with Vitra, for whom Morrison began working in 1991. Since gaining the European rights to produce and distribute Ray & Charles Eames and George Nelson furniture in 1956, Vitra has maintained a high design profile and is respected internationally for its quality of manufacture and the vision of its director Rolf Fehlbaum. The Cork chair is part of

the Vitra Edition 2007, a collection of strictly limited edition furnit inspired by Fehlbaum's mission to develop pieces created by wo class designers without the considerations of cost, manufacture a the constraints of the market. For his Vitra Edition, Morrison ch to take a new look at an old material, cork, a relatively unfashiona design material with associations with 1970s' flooring tiles a wedge-heeled platform shoes. In its design, the chair uses a 196 bucket shape which cleverly plays on the material's retro qualiti while the use of cork – a sustainable and natural material which harvested without harming the tree – reflects contemporary conce about the environment. In addition, Morrison uses recycled bo stoppers rather than new cork.

The Crate

Jasper Morrison's Crate re-produced an overlooked everyday object (a traditional wine crate) in a more valuable material (Douglas fir). It provoked an ongoing debate about the design validity of this approach: some accused Morrison of arrogance for not producing something new, while others supported his celebration of the everyday, apparently rejecting the consumerism and extravagance that new design work often fuels. Morrison argued that he could not better the simple, generic wine packing crate that he used as a bedside table. He observed that "objects made outside the design world tend to perform better than designer ones" and went on to celebrate the ordinary in an influential touring exhibition, called "Super Normal", of ordinary objects (potato peelers, paper clips, etc.) which he organized and curated with Naoto Fukasawa, Japan's foremost product designer. In 2007 the piece was developed into a series called Crate Furniture 2007.

British company Established & Sons, founded in 2004, launched the Crate collection at the Salone del Mobile, Milan in 2005. Established & Sons are a relatively new and innovative UK design manufacturer, leading the emerging market for limited edition design objects. In addition to Morrison, they have launched limited edition furniture by Zaha Hadid and Amanda Levete of Future Systems at premiere events including Design Miami, an annual design and art fair launched in 2005 to coincide with Art Basel Miami Beach.

DATE: 2006

DESIGNER: Jasper Morrison (born 1959)

MATERIAL: Douglas fir

MANUFACTURER:
Established & Sons, UK

PART 5

Lighting

Until the invention of electricity, the industrialized world relied on oil lamps or gas for lighting. Electricity – instant and clean – changed all that and introduced lighting as an integral and important design area.

HANGING LAMP

Since the start of the twentieth century, lighting design has always been closely related to the development of bulb technology. The tungsten bulbs most of us still use in the home are virtually the same as those Edison and Swan invented in 1879, using a coiled tungsten filament as light source, surrounded by a mixture of gases that slow the process of oxidization that will eventually end the bulb's life. Tungsten lights range from clear, candle bulbs to crown-silvered versions for use in reflector lamps. They are cheap and flexible, and the average life span is about a thousand hours; however, they are not energy efficient, with only six per cent of their energy emitted as light and the remainder emitted as heat.

By the 1880s one of the first electric lighting systems for the home had been introduced by Lord Armstrong at Cragside in Northumbria, in the North of England. By 1900 electric lighting had spread to such an extent that a growing industry producing light fittings had begun to develop, but the overall design aim was the same: to reduce the light emitted and conceal the bulb.

One of the best-known lamp-producing companies was Tiffany, which by 1905 employed over 200 craftsmen to produce light fittings that were designed in stained glass. These shades and table lamps have come to represent one of the most important contributions to Art Nouveau style. Other important pioneers included William Arthur Smith Benson, arguably the first modern lighting designer, whose London shop and catalogue sold light fittings made not by hand but with industrial techniques.

More radical solutions were also being explored and in the early 1920s and 1930s the Modern Movement introduced new attitudes to lighting design. Early signs of change came, most notably, from Peter Behrens for the German company AEG. Behrens' early lights rejected the naturalism of Art Nouveau, and instead concentrated on industrial concerns, simple mass-produced forms using industrial materials. Designers at the Bauhaus also started to look at light bulbs not simply as a means to produce light but as objects with their own aesthetic appeal.

TIZIO TABLE LAMP

These designers did not want to hide the bulb but wanted it to lead the design. Designers produced tube lighting arranged as formal sculptures and introduced some of the most innovatory advances in the design of industrial lighting into the house. These included the use of opaque and frosted glass in simple globe forms, integrated switches and the use of aluminium for reflectors. At this date they relied heavily on lighting developed for the factory and the office which could be adapted for use in the new home.

Technical developments after the War included the widespread use of fluorescent tubes, which, although introduced in 1938, were based on the nineteenth-century research of a German scientist called Heinrich Gessler. They quickly become the main form of lighting in shops and offices. Fluorescence works on a completely different principle from tungsten, using an electrical discharge. At the end of each tube, electrodes send out electrons, which react with mercury vapour to create ultraviolet light. This is turned into visible light by a coating of phosphor on the inside of the glass tube. The advantage of such lights is that they are cheap to buy and run,

BAY TABLE LAMP

TREFORCHETTE

installations are easy to maintain, there is a large choice of sizes and shapes, and the tubes are energy effective. However, such lights have their drawbacks – they are difficult to control and toxic materials are present, so all tubes require special disposal. Tungsten halogen bulbs were originally used in car headlights and then shop lighting display. They came in two types, mains voltage and low voltage, which was introduced in the 1980s. Halogen bulbs work in the same way as a conventional bulb except for the addition of gas and this gas helps to regenerate the tungsten. The advantage is that the light is stronger and it allows the designer to use smaller bulbs and therefore a greater flexibility of light fittings. The disadvantage is that they are delicate and more sensitive, and the short lifespan of the bulbs, which produce a large amount of heat, gives low energy efficiency.

During the 1960s and 1970s lighting manufacturers took advantage of the new reflector bulbs to develop single spot systems or track lighting. They were an immediate commercial success and dominated certain aspects of the market until well into the 1980s. The 1980s and 1990s saw important new lighting developments with the introduction of halogen and mini-fluorescents. Both these technologies have inspired designers such as the German Ingo Maurer and caught the public imagination, showing new possibilities in lighting design. Low-voltage versions of the halogen are small and popular for interiors because they offer strong directional lighting, and low-voltage lighting is safe to touch. They are easy to control and energy efficient but they need a transformer, which must be incorporated into the design or into the plug. Current new directions on the market include the appearance of a range of low-energy bulbs, brought about by a new public concern about energy conservation.

LIGHTCOLUMN

Tiffany Lamp

DATE: c.1910

DESIGNER: Louis Comfort Tiffany

MATERIAL: stained glass, lead and bronze

MANUFACTURER: Tiffany Glass Company, New York, USA

Tiffany and Company was founded in 1837 and became a fashionable New York department store specializing in decorative silverware. It quickly achieved an international reputation for the quality of its products, opening branches in London and Paris. In 1885 Louis Comfort Tiffany, the founder's son, established his own enterprise, the Tiffany Glass Company in New York. A hugely successful studio, it marketed his trademark architectural stained glass and other decorative objects for the home.

By 1900 Tiffany had developed what was to become one of the most famous Art Nouveau products: a series of oil, then electrical, lamps. Originally the lamps had been developed as an economical use for the offcuts of coloured glass from the stained-glass workshop. The coloured-glass lamps produced a warm, glowing light and turned Tiffany lamps into an art form in their own right. Though expensive, they quickly became popular. Using rich, iridescent colours, the decoration drew on the Art Nouveau concern for naturalistic form, insects, flowers and the swelling shapes and abstracted forms of the body. Tiffany glass fitted perfectly into the architecture and interior design of the new century.

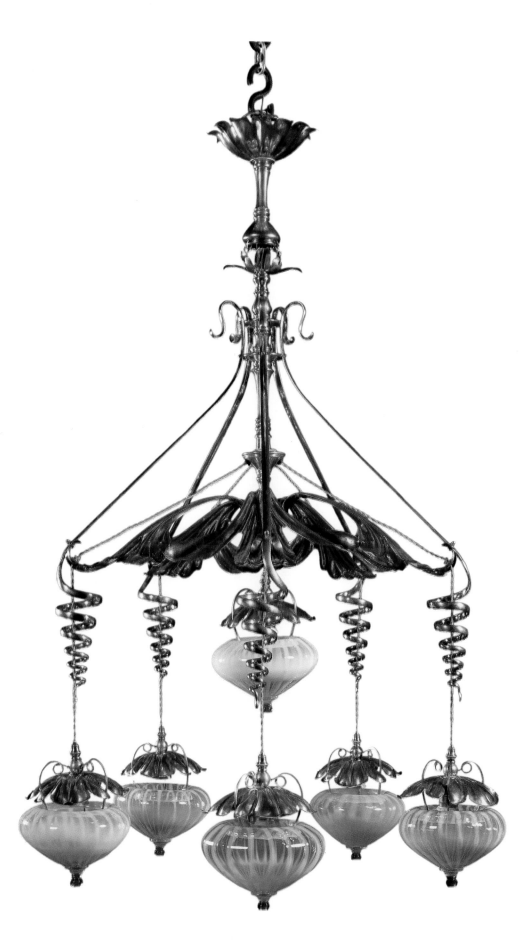

Ceiling Light

DATE: 1890s

DESIGNER: William Arthur Smith Benson (1854–1924)

MATERIAL: brass and glass

MANUFACTURER: Benson and Company, London, England

William Arthur Smith Benson was arguably the first person to design modern electric light fittings for the home: it was an achievement appreciated by his contemporaries both in his home country and abroad. When, in the early 1900s, the famous German critic Hermann Muthesius published *Das Englische Haus*, his study of avant-garde British design, he dedicated the last pages of the book to images of Benson's electric lights. From the 1870s Benson had been at the centre of the British Arts and Crafts movement when, as a student at Oxford, he had met members of the William Morris circle, including the painter Burne-Jones. Benson designed wallpapers, furniture and lighting for William Morris, and, after Morris's death in 1896, became a director of William Morris and Company. Morris inspired him to set up a metal workshop in Hammersmith, West London, and later a larger factory in Chiswick, where Benson not only designed lighting but also furniture.

Alone among the Arts and Crafts designers, Benson was prepared to use machine production, and introduced the innovation of marketing his lights using his own catalogue and opening a shop, Benson and Co in Bond Street, in which to sell them. He was a natural inventor, patenting his ideas and working on many products including Thermos jugs. In 1914 he became a founder member of the Design and Industries Association, which was set up to pioneer new standards of design in British industry.

Bauhaus Table Lamp

DATE: 1923–24

DESIGNER: Karl J. Jucker and Wilhelm Wagenfeld (1900–90)

MATERIAL: clear and opalescent glass, brass and steel

MANUFACTURER: Bauhaus metal workshop, Dessau, Germany

This design was one of the most simple and successful lamps to come from the Bauhaus metal workshop, then under the direction of László Moholy-Nagy. It was designed by two students, Willhelm Wagenfeld and Karl Jucker. Wagenfeld became one of Germany's best-known industrial designers, applying the Bauhaus principles of Modernist forms and materials to lighting design and glassware for the home. Nothing is known about Jucker's career after 1925. The only surviving information about his work documents a number of his innovative student designs for light fittings from 1922 to 1925. The two students' collaboration on the lamp, however, attracted a great deal of interest almost immediately. It was shown at the Leipzig Trade Fair in 1924 and published the following year in a book of new work from the school. The lamp looked startlingly modern and industrial: the shade was borrowed from existing factory lighting and steel tubing concealed the wiring. However, it represented a paring down of quite conventional Art Nouveau shapes. The industrial effects were achieved by laborious hand production, which meant that it was never available as a mass-produced, cheap, modern product for the home.

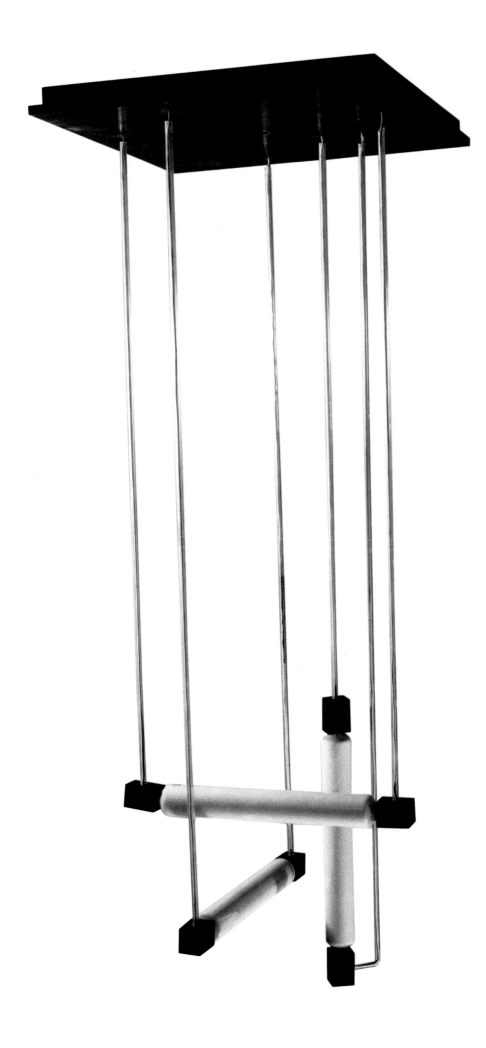

Hanging Lamp

DATE: 1920–24

DESIGNER: Gerrit Rietveld
(1888–1964)

MATERIAL: glass and wood

In 1920, Rietveld experimented with a version of this hanging lamp for a doctor's clinic in Maarssen, one of the earliest interiors inspired by the Dutch De Stijl Movement. Constructed using standard light bulbs and electric wiring, various versions of this minimalist design appeared. Different versions using three or four lights were used in the Schröder House (see p. 50) and the office of Walter Gropius at the Bauhaus (see p. 53).

The light fittings that appeared at Bauhaus in around 1920 do not hide technology, but incorporate it into the design. Using tungsten bulbs, and with its radical shape, the lamp was available in different combinations incorporating the same basic elements – the bulb and two square wooden fixings.

Other designers also found the aesthetic of tubular tungsten bulbs appealing – Max Krajewski's 1927 installation at the Bauhaus and Eileen Gray's tube light of the same year employ the same design vocabulary.

Hanging Lamp

DATE: 1926

DESIGNER: Poul Henningsen (1894–1967)

MATERIAL: opal glass and brass

MANUFACTURER: Louis Poulsen & Company, Copenhagen, Denmark

The end of the 1920s saw the emergence in Scandinavia of a new type of lighting. Experiments in the design of lamp fittings concentrated greater emphasis on the quality of light, rather than simply designing around the bulb. Poul Henningsen trained as an architect but quickly attracted international attention with the design of a new range of light fittings. Reflectors of different sizes were combined so that the lamps would give off direct and indirect light simultaneously without any glare. These ergonomic quali[ti]es made them popular as dining table lights. They appeared in [the] Danish Pavilion for the 1925 *Paris Exposition des Arts Décorat[ifs]* where they were awarded several prizes. They were soon specif[ied] and used by Modernist architects and designers all over the wo[rld], as well as attracting a popular market in Scandinavia. They rem[ain] in production: a modern classic of design.

Arco Floor Lamp

Arco lamp, designed in the early 1960s, is another collaboration ween the Castiglioni brothers, Achille and Pier Giacomo. ough designed to light the dining table and therefore adjustable hree different heights, it was more generally used as a floor and proved to be extremely popular. It has since become a sic of its time and has come to define the radical, bold and y style of the Castiglioni brothers.

Both men were inspired as students by the work of Marcel champ and the tradition of the "found object" – a theme which Achille was to explore for the rest of his career. Light bulbs, transformers and – for his famous chair – tractor seats provided him with sources of inspiration. This approach to design, Achille explained, gave his work "resonances of previous artefacts so that there is an almost ready-built relationship with the user".

The Castiglioni brothers were extremely fortunate that their original approach to design was supported by a series of committed Italian manufacturers prepared to spend the time and money on product development.

DATE: 1962

DESIGNER: Achille (born 1918) and Pier Giacomo Castiglioni (1913–68)

MATERIAL: white marble base, stainless steel stem, polished aluminiumreflector

MANUFACTURER: Flos, Brescia, Italy

Boalum Lamp

DATE: 1969

DESIGNER: Livio Castiglioni
(1911–79) and Gianfranco Frattini
(born 1926)

MATERIAL: PVC plastic
and metal

MANUFACTURER:
Artemide, Milan, Italy

Made from industrial translucent plastic tubing held in place by a series of metal rings into which light bulbs were fitted, the Boalum is the typical Pop design. It expressed radical new form and relied on the consumer to define the object's shape. The consumer could hang it vertically or arrange it as a piece of sculpture on the table or floor. Theoretically the user could purchase more units and decide the length of the light based on units, each of which was 2 metres (6½ feet) in length.

Boalum showed that designs using industrial components need be hard and aggressive: here was an object that was glowing animal-like. It gave off a soft and gentle light more reminiscent Japanese lantern than the glare of a laboratory or factory. The de combined the talents of two of Italy's famous designers. Although L Castiglioni worked independently, he was part of the trio of fam brothers who included Achille, also well known for his lighting desig This was Livio's only collaboration with Gianfranco Frattini.

Parentesi Lamp

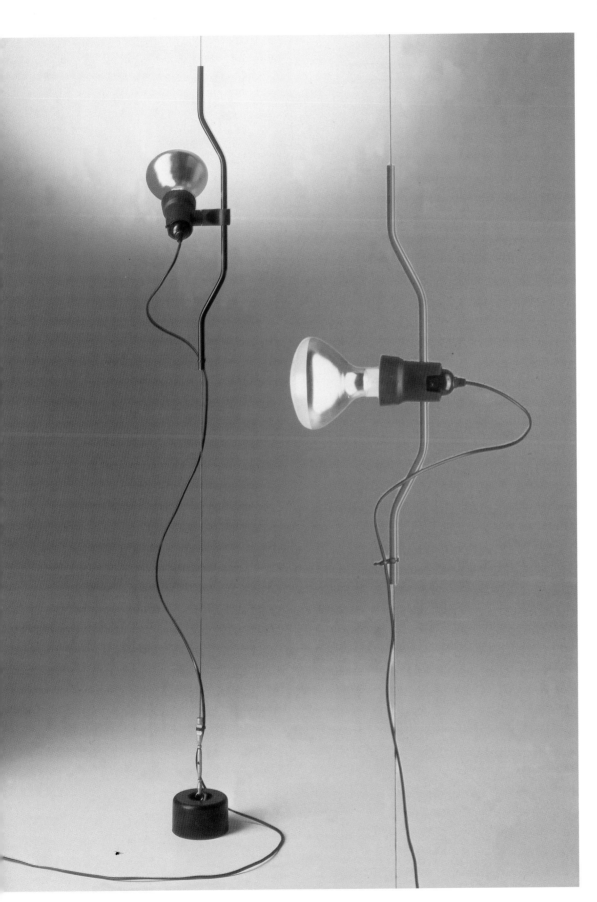

DATE: 1970

DESIGNER: Achille Castiglioni (born 1918) and Pio Manzù (1939–69)

MATERIAL: stainless steel with spotlight

MANUFACTURER: Flos, Brescia, Italy

Achille Castiglioni's unique and fresh vision found expression in a series of seminal light designs that he continued to produce in the 1990s. Parentesi, designed in 1970, is one of his best-known lights and for this design he collaborated with Pio Manzù. Manzù had trained at the well-known Ulm School of Design and then worked for the Fiat Design Centre, producing the original concept drawings for the Fiat 127 car. Tragically, he died in a car accident in 1969 and the lamp was completed by Castiglioni. Manzù, however, was probably responsible for the Parentesi's reflector bulbs, which had previously only been used as automobile lighting. Hitherto, light fitting manufacturers had taken advantage of the new reflector bulbs and used them largely for single spot fittings or for the newly developed track systems. Characteristically simple and stylish, Parentesi used tensioned wire suspended from the ceiling. It was a direct-light lamp with flexible movements and a light intensity adjuster.

Luminator

DATE: 1955

DESIGNERS: Achille Castiglioni
(born 1918) and Pier Giacomo
Castiglioni (1913–68)

MATERIAL: steel

MANUFACTURER: Gilardi e
Barzaghi, Milan, Italy

The Castiglioni brothers designed several of the lights in this section. They came from an artistic family: their father was a classical sculptor and the three sons, Pier Giacomo, Achille and Livio, all studied architecture at Milan Polytechnic. They made a unique contribution to Italian design in general but to lighting design in particular. The collaboration from 1945 between Achille and Pier Giacomo was to prove especially fruitful.

In the postwar years of 1950s *"ricostruzione"*, or reconstruction, the light fitting assumed a special significance in the Italian quest to rebuild the economy. Italian industry needed to produce low-tech objects for export for which the added value of design and style could command high prices. The Luminator was an immediate success. Manufacturing costs were low: apart from a simple three-legged stand, the only other feature was a wire that flowed from the base of the tube with a simple control switch. The result was an elegant uplighter that was widely exported.

The Luminator was also the first domestic light to exploit the latest tungsten bulb with a built-in reflector on top. The lamp's visual appearance, with its simple vertical steel tube supported on a slim tripod, reflects this technical inspiration. But the Castiglionis produced an object which was much more than a clever technological innovation: the Luminator helped to define the qualities of postwar Italian design with its use of stylish and expressive sculptural form combining good looks with function and structure.

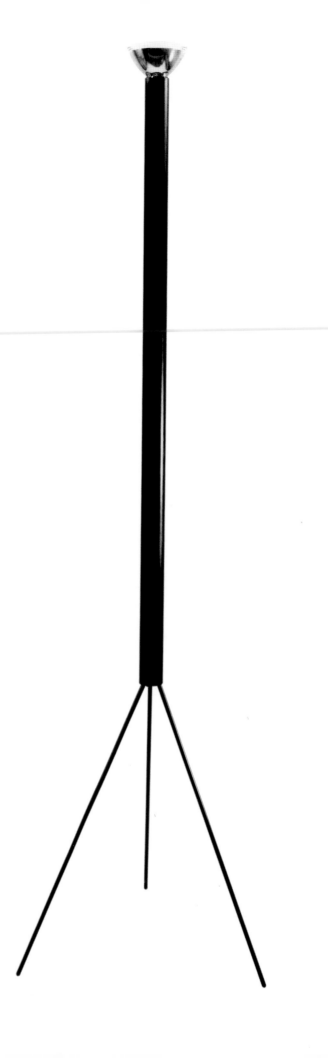

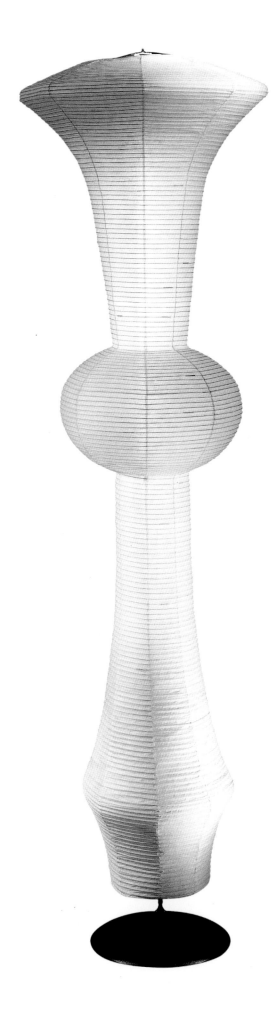

Model H

DATE: shade 1954, base 1962

DESIGNER: Isamu Noguchi
(1904–88)

MATERIAL: mulberry bark paper,
bamboo and steel

MANUFACTURER: Ozweki
and Company, Gifu, Japan

Isamu Noguchi's original training as a sculptor informed the design of both his furniture and his lighting. With this floor lamp he explores the lamp shade as both a sculptural form and as a modern reinterpretation of the traditional Japanese paper lantern. In 1951, Noguchi travelled to Japan, and studied such lanterns constructed from a framework of bamboo covered with paper. Called *chochins,* these lanterns were traditionally unornamented and used to diffuse candlelight. Inspired by their simplicity, Noguchi explored ways in which he could use them in a contemporary context and adapt them for electric light. Like the original Japanese chochin, Noguchi's lights were designed to be collapsible, reflecting a widespread trend towards the purchase of consumer goods in flat packs. Using a mulberry bark paper, his lights could be folded into an envelope. Over twenty-five years he produced a whole series of designs based on the paper shades, which he called Akaris. In the 1960s he produced versions using fluorescent lights and devised a standing lamp using a flat metal base to support the shade.

Noguchi's ideal was to produce floating sculptural forms that reflected the inspiration of modern designs but were inspired by the vernacular craft traditions of Japan. Although his designs were notable for their simple and be§autiful effects, they were always produced as expensive limited edition lights. In the 1960s his work was quickly imitated in countless less expensive forms.

Gibigiana
Lamp

DATE: 1981

DESIGNER: Achille Castiglioni (born 1918)

MATERIAL: metal reflector with mirrored surface, aluminium support with enameled metal

MANUFACTURER: Flos, Brescia, Italy

Wit and humour form a key part of Castiglioni's approach to design, expressed here by a shape that evokes an animal or bird. The Gibigiana is an adjustable table lamp. It produces reflected light and incorporates a dimmer. The lamp also demonstrates successful use of the relatively new technology of the halogen bulb that reflects light against a mirror and concentrates it on a particular spot – a function conveyed in the lamp's unusual name, which is the Italian expression for light reflected from a surface.

The angle of reflection is controlled by a circular dial on the "head" of the lamp, while the intensity of the light is controlled by a lever which runs up and down the base. The Gibigiana sought to combine a quirky appearance with a high specification, quality finish not normally associated with this kind of domestic product.

Tizio Table Lamp

Richard Sapper trained as an engineer in Munich and began his career working for Daimler. He went on to apply these technical skills to consumer products and later worked with many blue-chip companies including Artemide and, since 1980, IBM. Sapper is responsible for many twentieth-century design classics. In the 1960s he worked on ground-breaking products for the television and radio manufacturer Brionvega, which made the company world-famous. His approach promoted the idea that the technological function of a product should determine its appearance, and the Artemide Tizio lamp follows this principle. It is classic Sapper: finished in matt-black aluminium, the lamp has a formal beauty that incorporates balanced, lightweight engineering forms to produce an elegant shape with arms that move smoothly and offer a number of different, stable positions. It is also a technical success in that it uses a low-voltage halogen bulb, which gives a concentrated light source.

The Tizio became one of Artemide's best-selling designs and won the *Compasso d'Oro* prize in 1979.

DATE: 1972

DESIGNER: Richard Sapper (born 1932)

MATERIAL: ABS plastic and aluminium

MANUFACTURER: Artemide, Milan, Italy

Ya Ya Ho Lighting System

DATE: 1984

DESIGNER: Ingo Maurer (born 1932)

MATERIAL: glass, ceramic, metal and plastic

MANUFACTURER: Design M Ingo Maurer, Munich, Germany

Such was the originality of Ya Ya Ho that it turned the German designer Ingo Maurer into an overnight success. The light became his signature piece and it was hailed as one of the freshest and most original lighting designs of the decade. Ya Ya Ho stretched out fine wires of low-tension cabling onto which were attached halogen lamps, counterbalanced to create the effect of a sculptural mobile. The clip-on miniature light sources can be arranged by the consumer at will, a flexibility reminiscent of the famous lighting icons of the 1960s, including the Boalum light (see p. 164).

Maurer exploited the 1980s development of the halogen family of bulbs and the new mini fluorescent lamps. Initially, halogen technology was rather primitive, and indeed rather dangerous, until the introduction of transformers. Maurer wanted to promote a situation where lighting could be reduced to a series of simple components offering a wide variety of designed forms and lighting effects, using low-voltage lighting sources that enable the consumer to touch and move the lights freely.

Birds, Birds, Birds

DATE: 1992

DESIGNER: Ingo Maurer (born 1932)

MANUFACTURER: Design M Ingo Maurer, Munich, Germany

During the 1980s, Ingo Maurer created a sensation with a series of lights that combined state-of-the-art technology with an approach that brought lighting closer to installation art than design. German-born Maurer had worked in America for several years and began his career as a lighting designer in the 1960s. His work during this decade explored themes of Pop Art, experimenting with scale, decoration and the recycling of found objects. The ideas and theories of this seminal decade were to emerge in a different form twenty years later when his projects in the 1980s established him as an international designer. When it was shown at the annual Arteluce exhibition in Milan, international critics began to compare Maurer's work to other original lighting designers such as the Castiglioni brothers. They admired the way that Maurer introduced a playful, almost throwaway approach to design, which used new technology but did not allow it to dominate the final result.

Maurer works with a team of designers who include electronics engineers and has worked on a range of domestic lights.

Treforchette
Table Lamp

DATE: 1997

DESIGNER: Michele de Lucchi
(born 1951)

MATERIAL: PVC shade and
table forks

MANUFACTURER: Produzione
Privata, Italy

Produzione Privata is an experimental range that produces objects from the combination and assembly of simple, pre-existing components. This is a new and limited edition range of objects, which comes from the studio of one of Italy's best-known designers, Michele de Lucchi.

In the 1980s, de Lucchi established himself as a designer of international importance with his work for Studio Alchimia and, more famously, for the Memphis group under Ettore Sottsass. During this period his work on experimental, but essentially one-off, pieces was balanced by his career as an industrial designer for a series of high-profile Italian companies, including Kartell, Artemide and Olivetti. Produzione Privata is a return to more intimate and small-scale experiments, which reflect de Lucchi's interest in the twentieth-century idea of the found object. This concept was developed in the 1920s by Marcel Duchamp, who exhibited wine racks and urinals as art pieces. In his design for Treforchette, Michele de Lucchi is searching for a new direction that assembles ordinary objects in an unexpected way. He has used a simple circle of PVC for the shade, which is supported by two "ready made" metal cutlery forks. His intention is to rediscover in this way the potential of the ordinary and the everyday.

Lightcolumn

DATE: 1995

DESIGNERS: Philips Corporate
Design

MANUFACTURER: Philips,
Eindhoven, The Netherlands

In 1891 Philips and Company was
established in Eindhoven, The
Netherlands, as a light-bulb factory.
Although the company quickly
diversified into products such as
radios, they remain leading
exponents in the field of lighting
technology. Lightcolumn exploits
improved technology to disperse
and adjust the intensity of the light
source and create a light that
evokes natural light. Developed by
Philips as a series of decorative
components it uses organic,
sculptural structures to blend with
their surroundings. Each choice of
components creates a different
lighting effect. The intention was to
enable urban planners to provide an
environment with a more modern
feel with "natural" lighting.

Garland Light

DATE: 2002

DESIGNER: Tord Boontje (born 1968)

MATERIAL: etched metal

MANUFACTURER: Habitat, UK

Tord Boontje's intricate and delicate organic designs have caught the imagination of contemporary consumers. His approach is focused on materials and techniques that sit on the borderline between craft and design. He orginally studied industrial design at the Design Academy, Eindhoven before completing a Masters at the Royal College of Art, London in 1994 where he later taught Design Products. He founded Studio Tord Boontje in 1996 and moved his practice to rural France in 2006.

Boontje's work ranges from early low tech experiments such as the tranSglass series of glasses and jugs made from used bottles, to later work such as his Blossom chandelier for Swarovski. In 2000, after the birth of his daughter, his direction changed to explore nature, decoration and decorative layers. Boontje combined these elements with the latest manufacturing and material technologies; he was an early pioneer of processes such as laser cutting when it was considered prohibitively priced for the mass market. Using these processes he created the Wednesday light, suspending a wreath of flowers and leaves on a light bulb. Habitat commissioned an affordable version for their new collection and the result was his most famous design, the Garland light, which uses a sheet of stainless steel photographically etched with a series of flowers. Using a clip, it can be wrapped round a hanging light bulb to form a garland. Retailing at a modest price, it is both available to the mass market and a classic design product, included in the permanent collections of the Victoria and Albert Museum in London and the Museum of Modern Art in New York.

Solar Tree

DATE: 2007

DESIGNERS: Ross Lovegrove
(born 1958)

MATERIALS: metal, photovoltaic
cells, LEDs, plastic

MANUFACTURER: Artemide,
Italy, in collaboration with Sharp Solar,
Germany

The work of British product designer Ross Lovegrove was defined in 1989 by his hugely popular Ty Nant water bottle, with its distinctive cobalt blue colour and original sculptural shape. In the twenty-first century Lovegrove has continued to develop his aesthetic of sculptural and forward-thinking designs, working with new technology to realize concepts for international companies such as Moroso and Luceplan. The Solar Tree was commissioned as a result of a design project initiated by the Museum for Angewandte Kunst (Museum of Applied Arts) in Vienna. MAK is an unusual client, one of the world's greatest collections of design which supports contemporary initiatives.

The challenge was to investigate alternative designs and technologies for street lighting, which consumed 10 per cent of Europe's electricity in 2006, equating to 2000 billion KWh and carbon emissions of 2,900 million tonnes. Lovegrove's solution was the Solar Tree, which brings natural forms into the urban environment. The Tree has tubular branches diverging from a central stem. On top of each branch is a disc containing 10 solar lamps, each powered by 36 solar cells. In 2007, the prototype lights were installed in Vienna for four weeks, passing a crucial test phase in which they continued to produce light overnight even when the cells had not received direct sunlight for up to four days. Lovegrove developed the concept for the Solar Tree with Artemide, a leading lighting manufacturer with a reputation for innovation, and Sharp Solar, the world's largest producer of photo-voltaic cells.

PART 6

Homeware

SOUP LADLE

Throughout history, products for the home have reflected both the culture of a society and the technology of an age. Social and technological developments brought about by the Industrial Revolution, for example, had a significant effect on the way tableware was manufactured and used. The rise of the middle class increased the demand for good quality tableware, while the introduction of mass-production techniques allowed factories to manufacture to a standardized quality and design.

In the nineteenth century Victorian values of display and the availability of cheap servants enabled formal rituals of eating and organized leisure to develop in the home. Each activity and area in the home was clearly separated – for example, the kitchen and the parlour – so objects were designed for their particular place and purpose. The new requirements of twentieth-century society broke these traditions.

In the last one hundred years, developments in material technology, together with changes in social patterns, have further influenced the look of products. The relaxation of dining rituals, the growing desire

GLASS TEAPOT

for convenience and practicality, and the introduction of new materials such as stainless steel, heat resistant glass and synthetic plastics have all led to designs that are multi-functional, more durable, easier to clean and, in some cases, disposable.

There was another important shift in attitudes to homeware which derived from the reform of kitchen design. Now the kitchen was as precisely calculated and equipped as a scientist's laboratory; the principles of factory organization could be applied to the family home. This involved the careful integration of areas for preparation, cleaning and cooking, with work surfaces and appliances positioned at the same height. The most influential of these models was the so-called "Frankfurt Kitchen", used for standardized houses built to replace the slum areas of the city after World War One. It was intended to improve hygiene and facilitate the work of the housewife, but also to upgrade her status: the housewife was no longer a domestic maid but a manager.

PASTA SET 9092

Modern Movement designers looked to mass production to improve the design and quality of products for the home. Leading designers no longer saw their remit within the context of traditional craft products but within the factory, using cheap industrial materials to best effect. The glassware designed by the husband and wife team Alvar Aalto and Aino Marsio-Aalto is one such example. Aino Aalto directed her talents to pressed glass: a cheap material whose production flaws she sought to conceal with the use of simple, curved bands and basic shapes. Tableware was designed using easy to clean, simple shapes that could be bought in single pieces to build up the set requirement, breaking

GRAVES KETTLE

the long tradition of buying ceramic services in large sets. In this context the pioneer Bauhaus School is particularly important. Here students were encouraged to design objects with a new modern agenda and to consider always the question of its potential for mass production.

Almost every category of object for the home was redesigned in this way. In Italy, for example, items such as the Moka coffee maker were designed to make the transition from kitchen cooker hob to table, the Caccia cutlery set was produced to offer an alternative to traditional, high-maintenance use of silver for knives and forks. New materials also began to make an impact: in the 1920s heat-resistant glass was used for cooking and storage, designed again to be flexible as oven-to-table ware and fridge-to-table. Plastic was another key material. In the postwar period it began to replace glass in the design

ODEON CUTLERY

of storage containers, most famously by the Tupperware company; other key materials were ceramics for bowls and metal for kitchen implements such as salad servers and spoons.

While many leading designers worked to produce rational and functional mass-produced objects, other designers continued to work in the more traditional areas of craft and decoration. The famous Marion Dorn geometric rugs of the 1930s are a good example of this, as are the decorated patterns of Eric Ravilious and Susie Cooper, which made Wedgwood ceramics so distinctive. The Scandinavian countries in particular led the way in creating well-designed objects for the home. The quality of Scandinavian glass and tableware attracted international admiration in the postwar period and this work is typified by the architect Arne Jacobsen's designs for objects, ranging from coffee pots to simple taps.

GINEVRA CARAFE

The rise of the designer decade in the 1980s brought home-ware into even sharper focus. Nowhere is this better illustrated than in the products from the Italian company Alessi. They quickly recognized that people now wanted objects for the home that represented many functions. They wanted the products of named designers like Michael Graves and Philippe Starck and items that were not only functional but pieces of sculpture – true objects of desire. A new and affluent section of society sought a market that would provide them with Jasper Morrison wine racks in bright plastic and Ettore Sottsass wineglasses alongside an ever increasing choice of cheap tableware and cutlery designs sold by modern retail shops such as Ikea. Consumers have learnt to negotiate the old and the new within the home.

Soup Ladle

DATE: 1879

DESIGNER: Dr Christopher Dresser (1834–1904)

MATERIAL: silver-plated steel and ebonized wood

MANUFACTURER: Hukin and Heath, Birmingham, England

Christopher Dresser was unique among nineteenth-century designers. He has come to be seen as an important pioneer of modern industrial design, producing simple, functional items for mass production at a time when contemporaries such as William Morris and John Ruskin were advocating a return to craft production, based on the model of the medieval guild.

Trained as a botanist, Dresser studied at the South Kensington School of Design where he established himself as a star pupil and later taught. His design rationale was derived from his study of nature, producing a language of geometric pattern and form that could be applied to industrial design. His interest in Moorish patterns and Japanese art led him to develop a geometric, simplified visual grammar that he applied to startlingly modern and functional silverware such as teapots, toast racks and soup tureens. Dresser published his ideas in a se of books on design that were influential both in the Uni Kingdom and abroad.

Although the majority of Dresser's output was conventional nineteenth-century standards, some of his metalware featu astonishingly original shapes that predated the work of the Bauh by almost thirty years. His designs represent important archety in the development of twentieth-century Modernism. His w combined the latest in materials technology, such as electroplating of metals, with the most up-to-date manufactu techniques. His minimalist designs had no contempo counterparts in Victorian England – many of his uncompromis forms would not be matched until the 1920s.

Design for a Rug

Archibald Knox is probably best known for his turn-of-the-century metalware designs for Liberty's, the famous London department store. His talent as an architect and designer was, however, much more widespread and he is recognized as one of the great exponents of the British Arts and Crafts movement.

In common with his contemporaries, Knox explored the Celtic traditions of his native Isle of Man. This can be seen in his use of complex flowing patterns. However, his style was much more than simple revivalism and although still inspired by the glowing colours and the flowing, sinuous forms of Celtic decoration, Knox went on to create a language of ornament that saw an increasing simplification and refinement of forms.

Designed in 1900, Knox's watercolour sketch for the rug shown here still appears fresh and timeless. Such work positioned Knox not only as a leading Arts and Crafts designer but as a practitioner who helped to establish a new direction in design for the next century.

DATE: 1900

DESIGNER: Archibald Knox

(1864–1933)

Cutlery for Lilly and Fritz Waerndorfer

DATE: 1904

DESIGNER: Josef Hoffman (1870–1956)

MATERIAL: silver

MANUFACTURER: Wiener Werkstätte, Vienna, Austria

The architect and designer Josef Hoffman was a leading member of the Vienna Secession, a group of avant-garde designers who were opposed to established and academic forms in architecture and design.

In 1903, together with Koloman Moser and Fritz Waerndorfer, Hoffman founded the *Wiener Werkstätte* (Vienna Workshop) and remained its artistic director until 1931. The *Werkstätte* was inspired by the British designer C. R. Ashbee's Guild of Handicrafts and Hoffman was strongly influenced by the English Arts and Crafts Movement, particularly Charles Rennie Mackintosh and Glasgow School.

Hoffman's furniture and metalwork designs are strictly based geometric and rectilinear shapes, giving them an austere and eleg simplicity, in radical contrast to the florid forms prevalent in Art Nouve that dominated progressive design at the turn of the century.

Hoffman is viewed as one of the founding fathers of twentie century design and his work remains a source of inspiration contemporary designers.

Electric Light Bulbs Fabric

the immediate aftermath of the Bolshevik Revolution of 1917
ny Russian artists rejected the bourgeois practice of art and
dged their skills to serving the Soviet state. Their designs were
nded to symbolize the new Soviet society and to help foster the
nsition to a new way of life.

n the first few years after the Revolution, much emphasis was made
the State on the need for new imagery and products to convey the
ology of the Revolution to the ordinary people. The desperate
nomic situation meant there was little industry and no money to
d grand architecture. Inevitably Russian Constructivist designers
ned their attention to graphics, textiles and ceramics to express their
on of the future. The most famous members of the group included
_issitsky, Vavara Stepanova and Liubov Popova. However, virtually
biographical information has survived on Strusevich.

The work of the Constructivists was characterized by bold
abstract motifs that found their way into the design of theatre sets,
tapestries, rugs, wallpapers and fabric designs. The visual language
of Constructivism was largely based on the use of multiple flat planes
derived from the Cubism of Picasso and Braque. However, the
Constructivists almost always insisted on an abstract and logical
application of line and colour, and – the key element – the underlying
suggestion of the Revolution's ideology.

The design carried a message to the people, represented here
in the use of light bulbs as the repeat pattern illustrating the
electrification programme of the Soviet Five Year Plan of 1928–32.
The use of industry and technology as imagery symbolized a break
with the decadent, bourgeois ornamental traditions of the
nineteenth century.

DATE: 1928–30

DESIGNER: S Strusevich
(active 1920s)

MATERIAL: printed cotton

MANUFACTURER:
Sosnevsk Amalgamated Mills,
Ivanava, Russia

Glass Teapot

DATE: 1932

DESIGNER: Wilhelm
Wagenfeld (1900–90)

MATERIAL: glass

MANUFACTURER: Jenaer
Glaswerk Schott and Genossen,
Jena, Germany

Although Wagenfeld went on to design electrical products for Braun in the 1950s, he is best known as a designer of glassware and ceramics. He studied at the Bauhaus – where he later taught – and remained a lifelong advocate of the principles of uncluttered simplicity and functionalism in design which the school fostered. Wagenfeld was teaching at the Berlin Kunsthochschule (art college) when he developed the tea service. It remains one of the purest expressions of Wagenfeld's industrial aesthetic, in which every aspect of the relationship between form and function is figuratively and literally transparent. Working with the same heat-resistant glass used to ma test tubes, his brief was to design glassware, such as the tea (shown here with a later cup and saucer) that could be used both the kitchen and on the table. His pioneering use of new mater brought Bauhaus ideals to the mass-market. Despite his unflinch devotion to Modernism, Wagenfeld nonetheless enjoyed a success career in German industry during the Third Reich. After the war opened his own design workshop where he continued to produ work for leading clients until 1978.

Kubus Stacking Containers

The Kubus range of stacking glass containers demonstrates the Bauhaus principle that design could be reduced to pure geometric form that would lend itself to mass production and, therefore, a mass market. When in 1935 Wagenfeld was appointed the artistic director of Vereinigte Lausitze Glaswerke, he became responsible for the introduction of Modernist ideals into inexpensive pressed glass products. Based on a rectangular module, his Kubus containers remain the best-known of hundreds of design he produced for the company. They were designed for use straight from the fridge to the table and when not in use could be stacked together to form neat geometric shapes for ease of storage. Because it is non-porous and easy to clean, glass is ideally suited for kitchen use. The Kubus range included ten separate refrigerator storage containers, seven boxes and three jars, all with air vents and interchangeable lids.

DATE: 1938

DESIGNER: Wilhelm Wagenfeld (1900–90)

MATERIAL: pressed glass

MANUFACTURER: Kamenz Glassworks, Vereinigte Lausitze Glaswerke, Weiswasser, Germany

Savoy Vase

DATE: 1936

DESIGNER: Alvar Aalto
(1898–1976)

MATERIAL: blown glass

MANUFACTURER: Karhula
Iltala, Karhula, Finland

The famous Karhula glass manufacturer in Finland launched a competition to find new glassware designs to show at the Finnish section of the 1937 Paris International Exhibition. Alvar Aalto's design won first prize. Aalto submitted a series of drawings called *Eskimoerindens Skinnbuxa* (Eskimo leather pants) and his curving forms broke the glass design tradition of symmetrical form.

Sometimes known as the Savoy, because they were used in the well-known Stockholm restaurant of the same name, the interior of which Aalto had designed, the vases were an immediate success and have remained in production ever since. Aalto developed a unique architectural style based on irregular and asymmetric form and the imaginative use of natural materials.

The organic and non-rational form of the Savoy vase can be seen as a rejection of the geometric formalism adhered to by the majority of Aalto's contemporaries. Its fluid form is similar to that of Aalto's bent laminate birch chair designs from the same period, and calls to mind the free-form shapes of Surrealist painting.

no Marsio was the wife of the famous Finnish architect Alvar alto. Like the wives of many other designers, her distinguished ork has often been overshadowed by that of her more famous usband. Marsio was, nonetheless, a distinguished designer in er own right who also played a key role in Alvar's career, working his office from 1924 until her death in 1949. Together they set Artek, a company to market their designs. Marsio enjoyed a ng and successful collaboration with the glass manufacturer arhula, beginning in 1932 when she won a design competition ponsored by the company to create a range of cheap, mass-

produced pressed glass. Originally called Bölgeblick, the name of a café in the 1930 Stockholm Exhibition, the range included a pitcher, glasses, bowls, dishes and a creamer. It used thick glass made in three-piece moulds that left clear seams down the side. The distinctive "stepping rings" were not an original idea: in 1930 the Swedish designer Edvard Hald had used a similar technique for his Orrefors Glass Works bowls.

Aino Aalto's glass went into production in 1934 and two years later won a gold medal at the Milan Triennale. The range, still admired for its simple practical forms, has enjoyed enduring success.

DATE: 1932

DESIGNER: Aino Marsio-Aalto (1894–1949)

MATERIAL: pressed glass

MANUFACTURER: Karhula Iltala, Karhula, Finland

Rug

DATE: 1932

DESIGNER: Marion Dorn
(1896–1964)

MATERIAL: wool

MANUFACTURER: Wilton Royal
Carpet Factory Limited, United Kingdom

During the 1930s, Marion Dorn's rugs and textiles were the preferred choice of leading British Modernist architects who wanted interior furnishings sympathetic to their work. It was Dorn's rugs that appeared in Syrie Maughan's famous White Room at The Savoy Hotel, and in the foyer of Oswald P. Milne's redecorated Claridges Hotel, both in London.

Trained as a painter, Dorn's output was prolific. She designed fabric for the London Underground seats as well as fabrics, wallpapers and furniture. She was also commissioned to work on the great ocean liners of the period, including Cunard's *Queen Mary*. During the 1930s, she completed over one hundred rug designs for Wilton Royal, which led to her being described in the *Architectural Review* magazine as "the architect of floors". Her long and fruitful collaboration with Wilton concentrated on handmade rugs, usually produced in limited editions. Dorn's rugs were used in the new Modernist interiors to define particular spaces, often placed at key points with furniture arranged around the rug or left in isolation as a decorative feature. The patterns were generally bold geometric shapes but her use of colour was restrained, employing tones of white, cream, black and brown.

DATE: 1938

DESIGNER: Eric William Ravilious (1903–42)

MATERIAL: earthenware

MANUFACTURER: Josiah Wedgwood and Sons Limited, Etruria, Stoke on Trent, England

Although Eric Ravilious died tragically young while on a flying mission as a war artist during World War Two, the impact of his graphic style was an enduring influence in the immediate postwar years.

Ravilious was an illustrator and wood engraver who had been taught at London's Royal College of Art by the leading British artist Paul Nash. Like his fellow student, Edward Bawden, with whom he painted the murals in the canteen at Morley College in London, Ravilious provided illustrations for a number of publishing houses during the 1930s, most notably Jonathan Cape. His simple but pleasingly decorative style was well suited to industries that were attempting to raise the standards of modern design in 1930s Britain.

In 1936, Ravilious was commissioned to design a Regency Revival dining table and chairs for Dunbar Hay and Company, a shop established by Athole Hay and Cecilia Dunbar Kilburn (Lady Semphill) that marketed works of applied art. It was through Lady Semphill that Ravilious was introduced to Tom Wedgwood in 1935. For the next few years Ravilious designed Wedgwood's most successful printed ceramics, some of which would retain their popularity well into the 1950s.

American Modern Table Service

DATE: 1937

DESIGNER: Russel Wright
(1904–76)

MATERIAL: glazed earthenware

MANUFACTURER:
Steubenville Pottery, East
Liverpool, Ohio, USA

More than any other American designer, the work of Russel Wright has come to represent an image of informal living in the 1940s. He started his career as an apprentice to Norman Bel Geddes but unlike his contemporaries, who applied their talents to transport and products, Russel Wright concentrated on the design of homeware – particularly tableware. His American Modern service, designed in 1937 and in production from 1939 to 1959, was a huge commercial success. It sold over eighty million pieces making it one of the most popular tableware sets ever designed. The American Modern also signalled a more widespread change in American design. Wright rejected the popular machine aesthetic in favour of sculptural, organic forms for his ceramics. In the 193 the work of Surrealist painters, such as Salvador Dali, and t sculpture of Jean Arp was widely exhibited in New York. Their u of biomorphic shapes had a gradual impact on design. At t same time the leading American architect Frank Lloyd Wright w shifting direction towards a more natural architectural for exploring traditions and roots of American visual culture. Americ Modern brought these new ideas to the public – the shape of t water jug, for example, was compared to a traditional eighteent century coal scuttle, while other pieces defined the new colour a organic style of the period.

Vase with Horses

sie Cooper was a unique designer in many respects: a rare
imple of a successful female designer, she was not exclusively
"art" potter but designed primarily for mass production.

She was born in Burslem in the heart of the Staffordshire
teries. Her first job was as an assistant designer for A. E. Gray
: she soon began producing and decorating her own pieces. In
29, she opened the Susie Cooper Pottery, which produced a
mber of hugely popular decorative pieces in her own distinctive
lized version of Modernism. Her factory, Crown Works in
Burslem, became part of Wedgwood & Sons Ltd.

Although she worked initially as an art potter, Cooper's career
took a different turn into the mass market after the war. Turning her
attention to bone-china tableware during the 1950s, her modern
colours, clear lines and graphic patterns inspired by nature
captured the spirit of the times.

Her achievement as a designer focused on her ability for form,
natural forms which are reflected in her signature use of plants and
animals in her decoration.

DATE: 1938

DESIGNER: Susie Cooper
(born 1902)

MATERIAL: unknown

Prestige 65 Pressure Cooker

DATE: 1948

DESIGNER: unknown

MATERIAL: plastic handles and metal body

MANUFACTURER: Platers and Stampers Limited, London, England

Prestige 65's simple and stylish design proved very popular when it was launched in 1949. Made from polished steel with black plastic handles and incorporating a cooking trivet to release the steam on the lid, it looked modern, practical and extremely durable. In the 1950s pressure cookers enabled the housewife to cook a variety of foods quickly and cheaply, fulfilling something of the function of today's microwave oven. In practical terms the pressure cooker meant that you did not have to heat the oven to cook only a single item or to prepare food in different pans on the hob, since it was fitted with three separate areas for cooking individual foods. In theory, using the Prestige 65 allowed the cook to prepare complete family meal using a single cooking utensil; and the 195 saw the publication of a number of specialist cookbooks suggess appropriate menus.

Using high pressure steam also had another advantage: cook vegetables in this way was quick and healthy since it preser nutrients and vitamins. A pressure cooker was therefore not on functional and practical household object but was contributing the health and wellbeing of the consumer – a factor which prov an extremely strong selling point.

Cornish Kitchenware

DATE: 1927

DESIGNER: unknown

MATERIAL: earthenware

MANUFACTURER: T.G. Green and Company, Church Gresley, Derbyshire, England

rnish Kitchenware, adapted in the 1920s from traditional blue-ped ware, made its first appearance in the 1927 T.G. Green alogue. Made from white earthenware dipped into blue glaze, the ge was introduced to provide work for the factory's turners, ose jobs were then under threat because of the widespread onomic slump. T.G. Green, anxious not to lose its skilled workforce, ed Cornishware as a way of exploiting their expertise. Originally nsisting only of utilitarian jars and jugs, it was extended to include leware such as mugs, plates and teapots. Aimed at the middle-ome mass market, the range offered functional, cheap tableware for breakfast and informal meals. The title "Cornish" was a marketing strategy used to evoke farmhouse and country associations, while the use of blue reinforced the fresh feel of the dairy.

Cornishware's distinctive blue and white bands owe something to the Continental development of well-designed, mass-produced Modernist tableware at this time. It became a British design classic, and early examples are avidly sought by collectors and featured in museums. In 1967 Royal College of Art graduate Judith Onions redesigned many of the Cornishware shapes and its commercial success continues.

Victory V

DATE: 1941

DESIGNER: unknown

MATERIAL: printed cotton

MANUFACTURER: Calico Printers Association, England

This novelty fabric was part of a series of patriotic prints produced during the Second World War under the auspices of the Utility scheme, a programme of design controlled by the Government to produce consumer goods for the civilian population.

During this period everyone from the Queen to the ordinary citizen was issued with ration coupons, which they were required to produce when purchasing goods. It was a simple but fair system, aimed at tackling the severe shortages in the shops. Any imported material was strictly rationed, including dyestuffs, which may account for the dark brown of this fabric. With a distinctly patriotic theme it used Winston Churchill's famous Victory salute as a pattern repeat designed in various forms, including falling bombs, RAF fighter planes and an "X-ray image" of women's hands – a technique which probably owed something to the Surrealist photographic experimentation of Man Ray in the 1930s.

Crystal Design

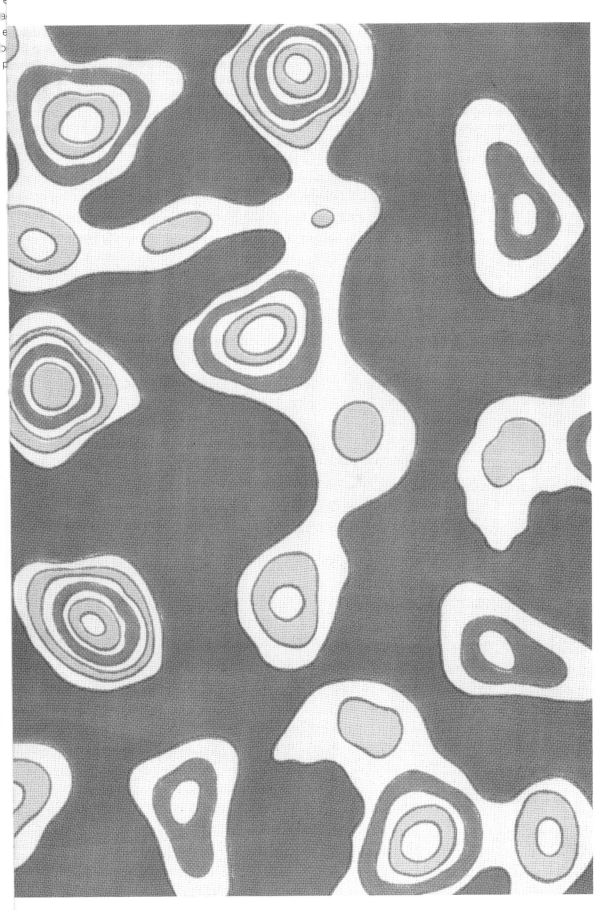

DATE: 1951

DESIGNER: S.M. Slade

MATERIAL: Celanese

MANUFACTURER: British Celanese, United Kingdom

This pattern comes from a *Souvenir Book of Crystal Patterns* from the 1951 Festival of Britain. It represents an interesting design experiment. This famous festival, held on London's South Bank, was intended to promote British achievements and trade in a national and international context. Part of the brief was to feature the radical scientific work undertaken at that time in Cambridge on the structure of crystals. This research lent itself to a commission inviting designers to produce patterns for the home for carpets, curtain fabric and laminates using the distinctive forms and shapes of crystals revealed under the microscope. The fabric shown here exploits the contour type of diagram and fits perfectly with the prevailing current taste for bright colours and the freeform outlines of organic shapes.

These designs proved extremely popular with the consumer and were widely imitated in a whole range of carpets and fabrics for the 1950s home.

Terrazzo Fabric

DATE: 1943

DESIGNER: Josef Frank
(1885–1967)

MATERIAL: printed linen

MANUFACTURER: Svenskt
Tenn, Stockholm, Sweden

In the years after World War One, Josef Frank emerged as one of Austria's leading avant-garde architects, building apartment blocks, houses and offices using modern styling and techniques. In 1927 he came to the attention of Mies van der Rohe who invited him to take part in a Deutsche Werkbund exhibition; but his career was to be cut short in the 1930s, when Nazi domination made his position as a Jew untenable.

In 1933 he and his Swedish wife emigrated to Stockholm where he worked for Svenskt Tenn, Sweden's leading interior design company. Along with his Scandinavian contemporaries, Frank helped establish a distinctly Swedish approach to Modernism – an approach to design that was less hard line, that used nature and vernacular as sources, and developed sculptural, organic shapes.

Although Frank spent the war years in America, he maintain contacts with Sweden. In 1944 he sent Estrid Ericson, Svenskt Tenn founder, a series of fifty new designs for her fiftieth birthday. Among the was Terrazzo. This is an unusual design in that Frank's sources we mainly derived from nature, using flowers, birds or animals. The patte here is made up of polished stones with a background of terrazzo – Italian floor finish using pieces of marble. Although the patterned ston appear to be random they make up a repeating geometric patte which acts as a surface net to hold the design together.

Cylinda Line Tea Service

DATE: 1967

DESIGNER: Arne Jacobsen (1902–71)

MATERIAL: stainless steel

MANUFACTURER: A. S. Stelton, Denmark

Arne Jacobsen was foremost among Denmark's modern architects. This range of utility objects in stainless steel conformed entirely to Modernist principles of beauty through honesty to materials and method of manufacture, while at the same time being inexpensive and available to the mass of the populace. The Cylinda Line series – all based on the form of a cylinder – was developed with Stelton over a three-year period. The range included saucepans, ice tongs, ashtrays and coffeepots.

Pasta Set 9092

DATE: 1985

DESIGNER: Massimo Morozzi (born 1941)

MATERIAL: stainless steel

MANUFACTURER: Alessi, Crusinallo, Italy

Established in the 1930s, the Italian company Alessi enjoyed a reputation for good quality metalware that continued into the postwar period. In 1983 they launched a new and hugely successful series of products for the home called Officina Alessi. They saw an opportunity to expand their range and to exploit the growing interest in design in the 1980s. Alessi commissioned leading international architects and designers to produce specially designed, distinctive products exploiting Alessi's traditional expertise in the use of stainless steel, brass, copper and silver. In some ways the choice of Massimo Morozzi was typical of the Alessi approach in that previously Morozzi was a leading Italian avant-garde designer,

producing radical and experimental work that did not make him t[...] obvious candidate for a pasta set. Alessi, however, had a talent f[...] exploiting this kind of creative edge and they also recognized t[...] food revolution of the 1980s. Internationally, people were expe[...] menting with new authentic regional foods and pasta, whic[...] although always widely enjoyed, required specialist cookin[...] equipment. Morozzi's set consists of a multi-purpose boiling u[...] and steamer, a colander with handles and a lid with a hollow kno[...] for steam to escape. Not only did it succeed in cooking larg[...] quantities of pasta efficiently – it also made a stylish contributi[...] to the new "designer kitchen" of the 1980s.

Whistling Kettle 9093

Michael Graves is one of the leading theorists and architects of postmodernism, a movement in architecture and design that has sought to invest buildings and objects with a narrative content. Implicit within the movement's ideas is a critique of the international style and the sober and allegedly impersonal character of Modernism.

Graves studied architecture at Harvard University and has taught at Princeton since 1962. Although he has designed relatively few objects and his architectural output remains small, he has become an influential spokesman for an approach to design that advocates bold use of colour and pattern and witty references to popular culture. In this respect he broke away from his original allegiance to Modernism and it is significant that when the Italian Memphis group produced their first collection in 1982 it featured the work of only one American: Graves. This brought him to the attention of Alessi.

The Graves kettle was one of Alessi's first, and most successful, experiments with Postmodernism. With its simple form and restrained use of materials, the kettle is essentially a straightforward modern piece of design. However, Graves gives it a humorous twist with the addition of a blue plastic bird mounted on the spout that sings when the water boils.

DATE: 1985

DESIGNER: Michael Graves (born 1934)

MATERIAL: steel with polyamide handle

MANUFACTURER: Alessi, Crusinallo, Italy

Arizona Carpet

DATE: 1984

DESIGNER: Nathalie du Pasquier (born 1957)

MATERIAL: wool

MANUFACTURER:
Memphis, Milan, Italy

Nathalie du Pasquier was part of the Memphis group working in Milan in the early 1980s that helped to change the design map. The Postmodernist agenda, which had been gaining ground throughout the 1970s, had reintroduced colour and decoration as important themes in architecture. However, in the world of design, the dominant taste remained for classic simple shapes in neutral colours. Memphis was part of a radical change that brought bright colour and patterns back into fashion, echoing the Pop aesthetic of the 1960s. The Arizona carpet illustrated here is typical of these designs.

Trained as a painter, du Pasquier was still a young woman wh[] she joined Memphis. Her early designs for laminates, fabrics a[] carpets created a tremendous impact. Her use of bold form and palette of the brightest colours helped to establish pattern as[] priority for interiors in the 1980s.

Du Pasquier worked in collaboration with her partner and fell[] founder member of Memphis, George Sowden. Together they produc[] a whole series of patterns designed for carpets, wallpapers and textil[] called Progetto Decorazione. One successful commercial project w[] the laminate designs produced by the Italian company Abet Lamina[]

Ginevra
Carafe

DATE: 1997

DESIGNER: Ettore Sottsass (born 1917)

MATERIAL: glass

MANUFACTURER: Alessi, Crusinallo, Italy

Ettore Sottsass is the grand old man of Italian design. His work spans over forty years and in each decade he has produced a fresh and original vision that manages to express the period. The Ginevra range of glasses and carafe is no exception. It fits perfectly into a 1990s direction for simple classic shapes in which Sottsass cast his master's eye for balance and detail. Sottsass has worked in glass over many decades. In a series of famous experiments for Memphis in the 1980s, he took a traditional Italian craft and used glass as a plastic material combining bright colours with simple forms reminiscent of a child's play with plasticine. Sotsass' versatility in glass is illustrated here by his superb redefinition of the classic carafe.

Mr Mause Hanger

DATE: 1990s

DESIGNER: Sebastian Bergne

MATERIAL: bristles and galvanized mild steel

MANUFACTURER:

D-House, Fedra b.v., Italy

In 1998, powerhouse:uk showcased Britain's brightest designers. During the exhibition the work of Sebastian Bergne was brought to the attention of a much wider public.

After studying at the Royal College of Art in London, Bergne opened his own studio in Battersea and attracted a number of important commissions from clients that included Vitra. One of the themes running through Bergne's work is the reinterpretation and use of existing production technology. The Mr Mause clothes hanger uses bottle brush technology to effectively pad hanging garments. The hanger was a quirky, surprise success, combining visual pun and functionality. The design of Mr Mause worked perfectly because the technology of the bottle brush is cheap – a similar level to the wire coat hanger. In combining materials in this way, and offering them in a variety of bright colours, Bergne has created an object whose perceived value is very much higher than that of its constituent parts.

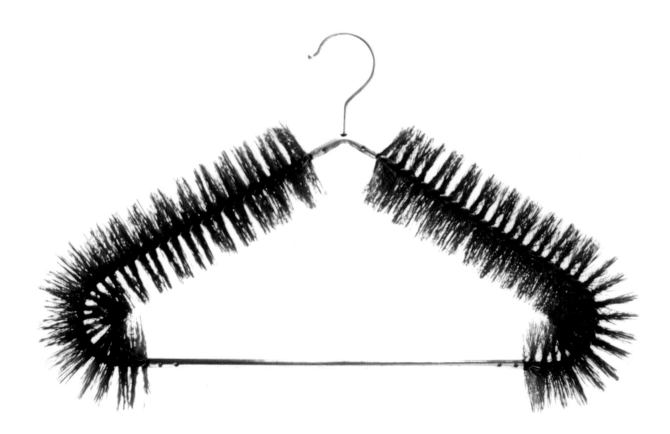

Wine Rack

DATE: 1994

DESIGNER: Jasper Morrison (born 1959)

MATERIAL: plastic

MANUFACTURER: Magis, Treviso, Italy

[Ja]sper Morrison is a British designer best known for his stylish, [m]inimalist furniture, but he has also produced a series of objects for [the] home, including this new version of the wine rack.

Previous designs had relied on traditional vernacular form, [wit]h wood and metal supports, sometimes scaled down for kitchen work surfaces. Jasper Morrison took the simple but obvious step of producing the wine rack in plastic. Using simple geometric forms, he made it an accessory for the modern home, producing it in flat pack form in a series of bright modern colours.

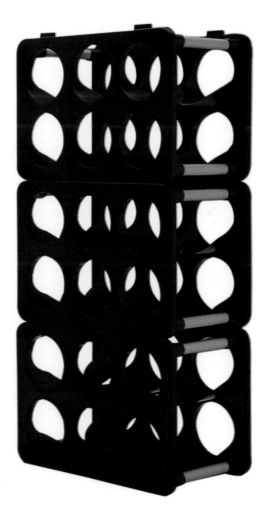

Glasgow Toile

DATE: 2004

DESIGNER: Timorous Beasties

MATERIAL: Screen printed paper

Timorous Beasties are part of a growing number of Scottish designers with an international profile, creating awareness of Scottish design over the last decade. Based in Glasgow, Alistair McAuley (born 1967) and Paul Simmons (born 1967) founded Timorous Beasties in 1990 after meeting at the Glasgow School of Art. The company name comes from the Robert Burns' poem "To a Mouse" and both are proud of their Scottish heritage, which is often referenced in their work.

Initially the company sold wallpaper and textile designs to other companies before starting their own range. At the outset their work featured fantastical and contemporary interpretations of nature, plants and insects, known for their hyper-reality. Timorous Beasties went on to develop a contemporary graphic style, which explores hard-edged, urban social and political issues, as illustrated by the Glasgow Toile fabric and wallpaper.

At first glance, the Glasgow Toile looks like a typical 1770s Toile de Jouy with its scenes of pastoral romance, but when it is examined more closely a nightmarish interpretation of a contemporary Glaswegian urban landscape is revealed. A drug addict shoots up in a graveyard and a young man urinates against a tree, while an alcoholic drinks from a can of beer in a park set against a background of Glasgow landmarks. Timorous Beasties have updated the content for our times, while using the same printing and drawing techniques as the original Toile.

Non Temporary

During the 1990s Droog Design was the dominant new movement in the design world, with a reputation for producing witty, subversive products. When Hella Jongerius graduated from the Design Academy, Eindhoven in 1993, Droog chose one of her products for their collection and they continued to produce virtually every product she designed for a number of years after that. Jongerius's work combines a traditional craft sensibility with an intellectual rigour and is characterized by an incongruous approach to materials, techniques and function, such as the embroidered porcelain in the Embroidered Tablecloth (2000) project.

Jongerius now manufactures many of her products through her studio, JongeriusLab. She produces small batch productions as well as one-off and experimental works which are commissioned in collaboration with design galleries such as Gallerie Kreo, Paris. In recent years Jongerius has become internationally recognized, one of few female designers to achieve this status, and has designed products for Vitra, Nymphenburg and Artecnica as well as the Ideal House at imm Cologne (2005).

The Non Temporary range employs the traditional, hand-crafted techniques and motifs used for centuries by ceramic manufacturer Royal Tichelaar Makkum, to imbue the objects with something familiar to the user. Earthenware bowls, dishes and plates are made from the Friesian marine clay found near Makkum's factories and decorated with glazing and painting. The traditional decorative motifs are shifted on the surface of the ceramic so that the glaze designs are offset and overlap, creating a contemporary twist on traditional tableware. In doing so Jongerius aims to challenge contemporary consumerist culture by designing a product that the user will identify with and love so much that they will use it for years.

DATE: 2004

DESIGNER: Hella Jongerius (born 1963)

MATERIAL: ceramic

MANUFACTURER: Royal Tichelaar Makkum, Netherlands

Wall-Mounted CD Player

DATE: 2002

DESIGNER: Naoto Fukasawa
(born 1956)

MANUFACTURER: Muji, Japan

Fukasawa is one of Japan's most prominent industrial designers and has worked with numerous international companies such as B&B Italia, Driade and Magis. Fukasawa was head of American design company IDEO's Toyko office before he established Naoto Fukasawa Design in 2003. He has become known for his own brand of contemporary modernist minimalism exemplified by his simple, pared down to the essentials work for his company, Plus Minus Zero, as well as for products such as this wall-mounted CD Player for Muji. He has also collaborated on the Super Normal project with designer Jasper Morrison, which has resulted in several exhibitions and publication of *Super Normal; Sensations of the Ordinary* (2007).

Muji was founded in 1980 and supplies consumer driven daily necessities including clothing, household goods and food to a global market. The name translates into English as "no brand quality goods" which exemplifies its aim of providing new, simple products at reasonable prices by making the best use of available materials and considering the environment.

The wall-mounted CD player is compact and functional. The speakers are built into the body of the CD player and the power cable doubles as an on/off switch and works by giving the cord a gentle tug. The disc itself is not covered while playing and volume and search controls are situated on the top of the CD player. It was added to the Museum of Modern Art's collection in 2005 and received several other design awards including *Design Week* (2002) and a D&AD Gold Award (2002).

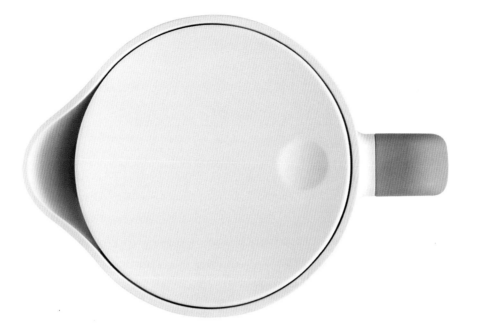

Morrison Kettle KF93

DATE: 2004

DESIGNER: Jasper Morrison (born 1959)

MATERIAL: polypropylene and stainless steel

MANUFACTURER: Rowenta, Germany

Resistance to the electric kettle in mainland Europe is traditionally connected with a culture of drinking coffee as opposed to tea, and in the USA stovetop kettles remain the popular household choice. The electric kettle therefore remains mainly a British product developed from our need for boiling water to make tea, although there is a growing Asian market. Rowenta has a long and respected design history and was founded in Germany in 1884. In the twentieth century Rowenta produced a range of early domestic appliances, including kettles. Its reputation as an innovative design company continues into the twenty-first century with a commissioned family of white objects from Morrison, which included an automatic cordless kettle, toaster and coffeemaker. The kettle's innovative technical features include a soft touch closing mechanism and a fully concealed heating element, which gives high resistance to corrosion and the build up of scale. The water level indicator is an energy-saving feature allowing the user to accurately measure the amount of water they wish to boil. Another Morrison feature is the well thought-out cord storage in the base of the kettle. The kitchen objects chosen for his Super Normal exhibition developed with fellow designer Naoto Fukasawa reflect this consideration of the needs of the user, fundamental to Morrison's work.

PART 7

Products

SWISS ARMY KNIFE

This section, called Products, deals with machines for the home, including washing machines, fridges, irons and vacuum cleaners. The domestic appliance industry is unique in that the pace of its growth was not governed so much by consumer demand as by the increasing availability of utilities in the home. With the widespread introduction of gas and plumbing in the nineteenth century, to be followed later by electricity, the character of the domestic house and domestic products was radically changed. The Victorian home contained many appliances, indeed there were countless and ingenious task-specific items on the market, including machines for the preparation of marmalade and meat mincers; however, they were hand-operated. The key domestic tasks of the nineteenth-century middle-class household – washing, ironing, cooking and the preservation of food – had relied on the availability of a cheap servant class. By the beginning of World War One, domestic service was no longer the only option in the job market for working-class men and women, so the attraction of new electrical appliances in newly servantless houses was obvious.

The development of electrical domestic appliances started from the 1880s, with simple basic items such as immersion heaters and flat irons. More importantly, they relied on electricity, which in Britain was made more widely available following the Electricity (Supply) Act of 1926, when the Central Electricity Board was empowered to create the first National Grid to connect supplies throughout the country. The appliance industries evolved from engineering plants but they relied on individual experimentation and

PYRAMID FRIDGE

development from pioneer individuals and companies. Manufacturers faced the problem of new methods of production, which required parts for machines that were standardized and interchangeable in order to make available goods for the mass market. Companies were driven by the need of consumers for products that would offer practical, functional solutions to the new lifestyles of the century. Bringing these products to a wider market was a slow process, with the creation of ever-smaller electrical motors to drive washing machines and food mixers and heat elements in kettles and irons. One important pioneer in this context was the designer Peter Behrens. His work from 1907, for the then most powerful electrical appliance company in the world, Germany's AEG, set a precedent. Under Behrens, AEG produced electrical goods that created a range of easy to use, simple and rational products that established the aesthetic for such items. It was Behrens' pioneering work that proved an inspiration to the Modern Movement's quest for the house as a machine for living in. The kitchen, for example, was now viewed as a laboratory where scientific principles could be applied to the

BRUTON ELECTRIC FIRE

organization of domestic tasks, including areas for the preparation and cleaning of food. Walls were often tiled, cookers were now made of enamel for easy cleaning and aluminium cooking pans replaced the old tradition of copper pots. The Bauhaus and its designers were quick to respond to these changes producing, for example, laboratory-like heat-resistant glass containers like the Kubus range that is featured in the homeware section. In the field of products, however, the world's most powerful economic power, America, led the way. Under the leadership of designers such as Norman Bel Geddes, Raymond Loewy and Walter Dorwin Teague, the profession of the industrial designer began to take shape and they quickly turned its attention to domestic appliances. These men set up professional offices that were modelled on those of the architect and the solicitor rather than the independent artist. They introduced the attractive idea of redefining the market using design. For them design meant restyling, providing a streamlined and modern outer casing for products whose engineering and machine function was already established but whose appearance was often antiquated and outdated. The Coldspot fridge is such an example; previously the fridge had been offered to consumers as a traditional larder with the cumbersome freezing equipment placed on top; now Loewy's Coldspot offered a sleek elegant form that could take its place with pride in the new kitchen. Irons, cookers and weighing scales quickly followed suit, using new materials and sculptural form to give these utilitarian objects a sense of quality and prestige.

MOKA EXPRESS

The Modernist rationale was continued in the postwar period by the German company Braun. It produced electrical goods for the home and used its business to foster an overall design strategy that stressed simple geometric shapes, no decoration and no colour, using white for the majority of products. From 1960, the Braun approach dominated the international styling of domestic products. Challenges to Braun's domination did come. During the 1960s pioneer companies like the Italian Brionvega promoted a vision of objects that used wit and humour more in keeping with the prevailing Pop aesthetic. Nonetheless the majority of electrical products of the period could be placed in the category of the white box. The early 1980s signalled an important shift in attitude. There had always been a market for products that used colour and decoration, but these had often been relegated by design purists to the category of bad taste. Now, influenced by the new attitudes of Postmodernism, manufacturers started to explore organic shapes while other companies like Zanussi introduced quirky detailing and colour into products such as fridges. In the 1990s the product designer was increasingly involved in more and more technically advanced products for the home. In the twenty-first century, environmental concerns are playing a key part in design and manufacturing decisions, with energy-efficiency to the fore.

SURFLINE IRON

DYSON

Hoover Junior

DATE: 1907

DESIGNER: unknown

MATERIAL: metal alloy and plastic

MANUFACTURER: Hoover
Limited, United Kingdom

In 1907 the Hoover company developed its first simple vacuum cleaner and quickly established an international market for the company's products. In 1919 the first Hoovers came to Britain, where they soon proved popular. Hoover pioneered new retailing methods and by the mid-1930s their vacuum cleaners, such as the model shown here, were regularly demonstrated in the home by travelling salesmen. Mass production methods made them cheaper to buy: by 1935 cleaners were a third of the price they had been in the 1920s and by 1949 forty per cent of British households owned one. Sales in the UK were so buoyant that the company decided to invest in a British manufacturing plant and in 1932 they built their flamboyant Art Deco factory in Perivale, West London. Designed by Wallis, Gilbert and Partners, it was intended to consolidate their modern image. The Hoover Junior was a cheaper version of the Hoover Senior. Both machines united all the working parts together under one covered section, making a neater, more streamlined design and thereby creating an association with progress and hygiene.

Electrolux Vacuum Cleaner

st produced in 1915, the cylinder vacuum cleaner, which
velled horizontally across the floor, was produced by Electrolux,
Swedish company dedicated to good design.

As part of the company's policy of hiring renowned designers,
xten Sason was engaged by Electrolux as a design consultant
and produced the more refined, sleek torpedo-like form for the
cleaner. Although a silversmith by training, Sixten Sason went on
to design some of the most distinctive industrial products of
the century, including the first Hasselblad cameras and Saab 96
and 99 cars.

DATE: c.1945

DESIGNER: Sixten Sason
(1912–69)

MANUFACTURER:
Electrolux, Sweden

Dyson Dual Cyclone

DATE: 1983

DESIGNER: James Dyson
(born 1947)

MATERIAL: moulded plastics

MANUFACTURER: Dyson
Appliances, United Kingdom

Since it was first produced for the mass market in 1993 the Dual Cyclone, which combines unconventional styling with technical innovation, has become a best-selling vacuum cleaner in the United Kingdom. Conventional cleaners use a filter bag, which traps dirt and dust while allowing clean air to re-enter the room. The effectiveness of such cleaners gradually reduces as the bag fills up, because the pores in the bag clog up with microscopic dust particles. James Dyson's cyclonic system, which uses the principle of centrifugal force, sucks up air and revolves it at eight hundred miles per hour through two cyclone chambers until the dust and dirt drop to the bottom of the transparent cylinder.

Dyson spent five years and over five thousand prototypes developing his first cleaner, a very Postmodern pink and lavender machine called the G-Force. At first he found little enthusiasm for it among European and American manufacturers, but in 1984 a Japanese company put it into limited production. In 1991 he sold his licence interests to the Japanese, which enabled him to fund the manufacture and marketing of the cleaner in Britain.

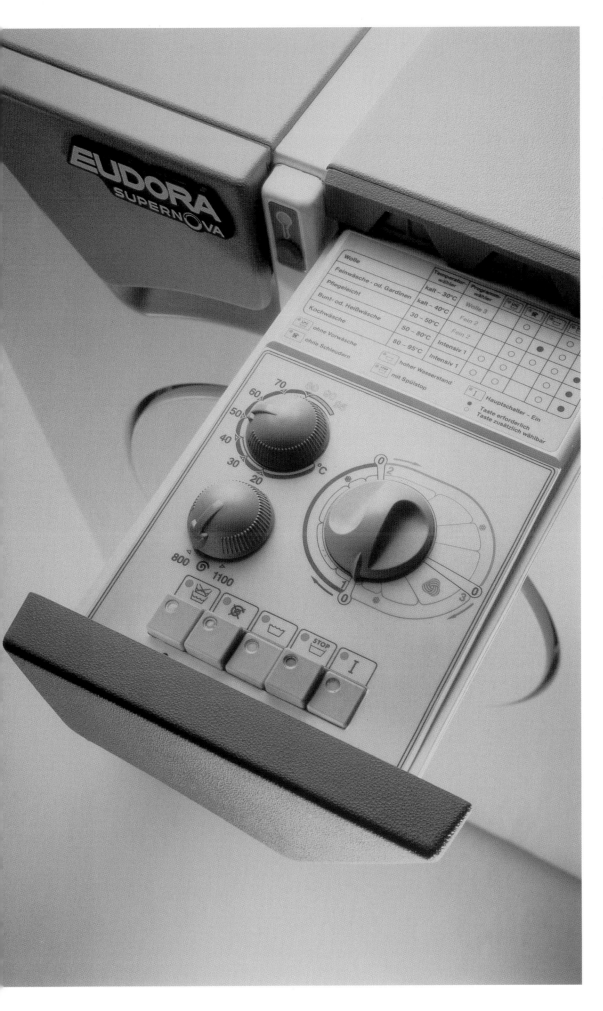

Supernova Washing Machine

DATE: 1989

DESIGNER: Porsche Design, GmbH, Austria

MATERIAL: steel and plastic

MANUFACTURER: Eudora, Austria

This domestic product defies the ubiquitous form of most large kitchen appliances commonly described as "white goods". Within two months of its launch the Supernova became the fourth best-selling washing machine in Austria. The traditional "TV screen" was replaced here by an operational control ring. The controls are housed in the right-hand panel of the machine, which mirrors the adjacent soap dispensing compartment, and the drawer principle protects the controls from soap and water. Heavy duty plastic panels protect the top surface from scratching. The product also includes an automatic sensor which recognizes the size of the wash load and supplies the precise amount of water required, saving electricity, detergent and water. Such ecosystems have now become a standard feature of washing machines.

Coldspot Super Six Refrigerator

DATE: 1934

DESIGNER: Raymond Loewy
(1893–1986)

MANUFACTURER: Sears
Roebuck Company, Chicago, USA

Raymond Loewy remains America's best-known industrial designer. Gifted with a legendary talent for self-promotion, his definition of good design was an upwards sales curve. In the 1930s this was appealing for manufacturers battling against the worst ever US recession. Loewy used design to produce distinctive modern objects for the home. He was famous for restyling, often providing a totally new casing concept for an existing machine. The Coldspot fridge is a classic example of this approach and remains one of Raymond Loewy's most enduring designs. It was commissioned for Sears Roebuck, a company that revolutionized mail-order retailing in the United States. Customers could simply order products by post and also benefit from attractive extended credit terms. The Coldspot was one of the first consumer products to use the sculptural lines of streamlining to market household goods. The fridge was no longer just a machine, but a thing of beauty, a piece of modern design. The Coldspot was one of the most enduring demonstrations of Loewy's prime concern with styling. It employs all the most sophisticated metal forming techniques, with rustproof aluminium shelving and a handle that responded to the lightest touch, and features a distinctive blue logo. It was a turning point in consumer products and signalled the beginning of the "objects of desire" trend.

Pyramid Fridge

DATE: 1987

DESIGNER: Roberto Pezzetta (born 1946)

MANUFACTURER: Zanussi, Italy

In the 1980s Zanussi introduced this fridge to challenge the prevailing dominance of white as the colour for domestic products in the kitchen. Colour is now established as a theme for the kitchen, giving "white goods" a front-rank presence and turning them into a point of reference in the home and the equal of furniture.

This decidedly Postmodern fridge, designed by Zanussi's in-house head of design, was not commercially successful, since its dramatic shape did not lend itself to the space constraints of modern kitchens.

Aga, New Standard Stove

DATE: 1922

DESIGNER: Gustaf Dalen
(1869–1937)

MANUFACTURER: Aga Heat
Limited, Sweden

For many, the Aga oven conjures up the definitive image of domesticity. The stove typifies values, preferably rural, that allow time for cooking and keep the kitchen at the heart of family life. Interestingly, when the Aga was first designed it was seen as leading-edge Modernist styling and technology. It was illustrated in many 1930s books that explored modern design, such as the important English critic Herbert Read's *Art and Industry* (1936).

The Aga was invented in 1922 by Gustaf Dalen, who, in 1912, had won the Nobel Prize for Physics for his Sun Valve. The Aga was not, however, put into production until the early 1930s, when it was licensed for manufacture in Britain. It offered a simple but highly

effective solution to the rather unpredictable performance of the th' widely used kitchen range. The design consisted of a cleve insulated iron box with two ovens of constant temperature. It work on the principle of heat storage with preset cooking plates for boili and simmering, topped by the Aga's distinctive hinged plates.

Originally only available in classic cream, in the 1960s and 197 the colour range was widened to include primary colours and d blues and greens. Although the design has been modified a most models now work on electricity, the Aga remains true to original cooking principles and as such maintains its appeal for t traditional consumer.

Oriole Electric Stove

During the 1930s American industrial designers published key books that set out their design agenda and also acted as a form of self-publicity. In 1932 Bel Geddes published *Horizons*, a classic of the period in which he published an image of the Oriole cooker. It was his object lesson in the principle of "form following function". To make it easy to clean, the burners were covered with flat panels, the oven doors were flush and corners were rounded. The material was vitreous white enamel, which, when dirty, could simply be wiped down. With an eye on new technology, Bel Geddes borrowed a device from the skyscraper construction industry, building a chassis of steel onto which the enamel panels could be clipped after installation, thus minimizing the problem of chipping the enamel surface. Standard Gas had an immediate success on their hands, with sales doubling and copycat versions appearing from rival companies.

The Oriole made large manufacturing corporations sit up and recognize the power of design to increase sales. Manufacturers of washers, fridges, vacuum cleaners and irons quickly followed suit with new products that were to transform the visual appearance of the home.

DATE: 1931

DESIGNER: Norman Bel Geddes (1893–1958)

MATERIAL: vitreous enamel

MANUFACTURER: Standard Gas Equipment Corporation, USA

Bruton Reflective Electric Fire

DATE: 1939

MATERIAL: chrome plate

MANUFACTURER: HMV,
London, England

To symbolize its qualities of modernity and efficiency, the designers of electrical products in the 1930s looked to reproduce features derived from Art Deco and streamlined automobile styling. The Bruton electric fire was typical of many designs of the period in that the extensive use of chrome had connotations of contemporary car styling. In addition, its use of a double parabola also improved the heat distribution and thus the efficiency of the fire.

The introduction of electric fires into the domestic market offered consumers their first experience of instant and portable heating in the home, and, although relatively expensive to run, were extremely popular supplements to coal fires, which were the standard form of heating before the widespread introduction of central heating in the postwar period.

ctric irons became the most successful of the early twentieth-ntury appliances. Early technology, in the form of an electric ment, was quite simple: irons were quick to heat and easy to keep t, clean and free of fumes and smell.

Nothing did more than the iron to increase the early demand for nvenient electricity supplies to the home and irons became the ntury's best-selling electric appliance. In the postwar period it as basic equipment for virtually every home. As a product, its velopment centred on the additions of technical extras, more iable thermostat control, water spray devices for steam and the ling of the product casing.

The German company Rowenta looked carefully at this market and positioned its range, the Surfline, very successfully. The iron combines the latest technology and lightweight metal alloys with a non-stick plate, but its success relies on the distinctive turquoise-blue plastic casing. This design feature gives the iron a contemporary Postmodern feel, which fits in with the taste for colour in the design of domestic products. It transforms an ordinary, dull, utilitarian product into a stylish design object for the home. The casing colour evokes the fresh and clean feel of the ocean, and also fulfils a useful function in that the housewife – statistics reveal that women still do most of the ironing – can easily see if the water level is sufficient.

DATE: 1994

MATERIAL: metal and plastic

MANUFACTURER:
Rowenta, Germany

Philips Toaster

DATE: 1996

DESIGNER: Philips Corporate Design with Alessandro Mendini (born 1931) /Alessi

MANUFACTURER: Philips, Eindhoven, The Netherlands

Philips is a world leader in the production of kitchen appliances and electronic technology. In 1995 they launched a series of products in collaboration with Alessi, a small, Italian, design-led company that manufactures kitchen and household products. The range included a coffee maker, juice extractor, kettle and toaster, all using distinctive plastic sculptural forms and in a range of contempora colours from green to pink and cream. The toaster uses a sens system that gives accurate control for light to dark brown toastin The bread carrier can be raised high enough to take out smallest piece of bread.

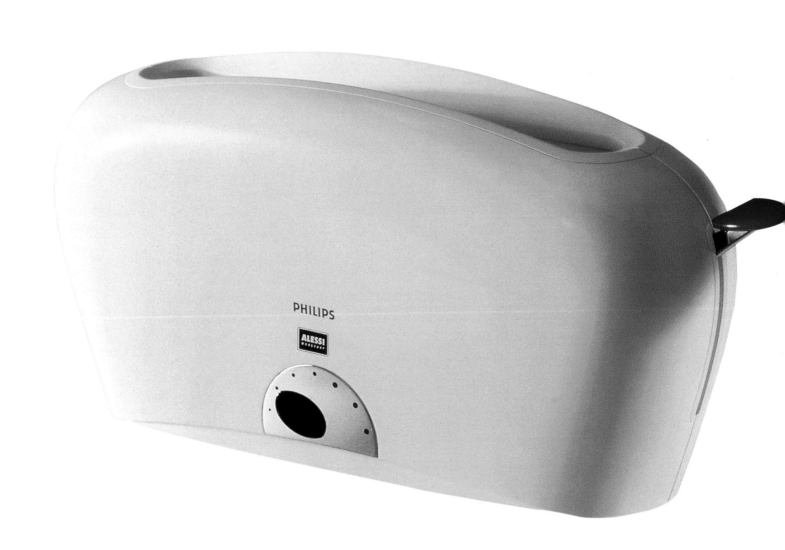

Hannibal Tape Dispenser

In 1998 Julian Brown received four international design awards for his tape dispenser, Hannibal. In December of the same year the American magazine *Time* included the object in its round-up of the best things of the year. It is a fitting tribute to a man who enjoys not only international fame but the warm admiration of his fellow product designers.

Brown started his career training as an engineer but switched to design and worked for a number of large practices before starting his own company, Studio Brown. Hannibal reflects his painstaking research and an empathy with product design that transforms what could have been an ephemeral throwaway object into a design that was seen by many to represent style and direction in the late 1990s.

Rexite had made high quality desk accessory ranges they had not yet addressed "nomadic work tools", products that deliver a secondary function but are not location specific. The elephant idea was not whimsy but the result of careful research and study, the shape of the trunk perfect for the requirements of the dispenser. Not only could you open the trunk but it also could be configured to close again and keep the tape "dust free" ready for the next use. Rexite also went to extreme lengths to maintain the highest quality of tooling and manufacturing detailing. Nowhere is this more evident than in the production of the stainless steel cutting blade. Under the naked eye exactly the design that Brown proposed, but under the magnifying glass, a triumph of metal engineering at a minute almost watch-like scale.

DATE: 1990s

DESIGNER: Julian Brown

MATERIAL: plastic

MANUFACTURER: Rexite

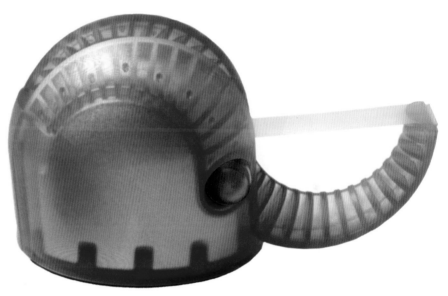

A7–1700 Kitchen Unit

DATE: 1996

DESIGNER: bulthaup in-house design team

MATERIAL: aluminium and steel

MANUFACTURER: bulthaup Gmbh, Aich, Germany

bulthaup is a German-based company founded in 1949 by Martin Bulthaup. The company developed from manufacturing kitchen buffets to the specialist supply of system furniture for kitchens, bathrooms and laboratories. Since the 1980s the company has concentrated on the kitchen. In 1982, bulthaup commissioned the German designer Otl Aicher (born 1922), to produce a book called *The Kitchen as a Place to Cook*. Aicher was at the heart of postwar German modern design. He studied at Ulm under Max Bill and worked for Braun, a company whose design creed was based on functionalism and simple forms. Aicher's aesthetic for bulthaup was first expressed in the company's development of a "butcher's block", a robust table of solid wood placed in the middle of the room. This became a trademark of the bulthaup kitchen with a simple stainless steel workbench that could be used independently or integrated into a range of units, cupboards,

and appliances bulthaup supplied. In 1989, this simple a functional design won a number of awards and bulthaup went to develop new products including a new kitchen extrac system in 1991. bulthaup, with their emphasis on design, hi quality materials and construction, quickly became the designe choice of kitchen. In 1992, they called their range System 25 series of multi-functional working areas, using units and surfac designed in wood, aluminium, and stainless steel. bultha pioneered the idea that the kitchen was the most important roo in the house and that the money, time and effort spent he should reflect this.

In 1994, bulthaup's product and research division develop technologically advanced water-based coatings for wood surfac in the furniture industry. bulthaup continue to remain leaders in ne technology and manufacturing techniques.

Robo-Stacker

DATE: 1994

MATERIAL: recycled washing machine drums, glass

MANUFACTURER: Jam, London, England

Astrid Zala, Jamie Ankey and Matthieu Paillard, three young designers with backgrounds in architecture and fine art, established Jam in London in 1994. The nature and outcome of their collaborative design work has been diverse and they describe their mission as "focused on the creative utilization of the material and technological innovations of today." In terms of product design, this means a recycling reuse agenda. The Robo-Stacker uses washing machine drums supplied by Whirlpool to make attractive general purpose storage units for the home. Jam collaborate with large companies. Whirlpool supply them with drums that have not passed quality control while Sony provided projectors and sound systems for a bed featured in a recent Crafts Council exhibition called Flexible Furniture. These companies enjoy the association with young leading-edge talent and the implications of recycling and reuse of products in another very different context. This has led to other commissions, including an installation made out of old television sets for the foyer of the Independent Advertising Association in London and a Chelsea bar for the Evian drinks company, where the decorative surface in the serving area is formed from bottle tops.

Whirlpool AquaSteam Washing Machine

DATE: 2007

DESIGNER: Alessandro Finetto
(Head of Whirlpool Design)

MANUFACTURER:

Whirlpool Europe, Italy

American and EC legislation has changed not only the design and production but also the disposal of traditional white goods for the home. Although legislation has driven manufacturers to think holistically about the whole lifecycle of a product, both in the way they manufacture such goods and in the amount of energy and water such machines use, consumers are also responding to the imperative to be more ecologically friendly. By cutting the amount of water and electricity needed to clean your clothes, Whirlpool's new AquaSteam model seeks to address market trends while adding a touch of twenty-first century technology. Whereas other washing machines use water which is then heated by the machine, the AquaSteam injects steam directly into the drum, boosting the temperature and transferring heat to the water more efficiently. "6th Sense" technology automatically adjusts the length of the washing cycle according to the soiling level of each load, thus saving water and cutting up to 30% off washing time, which saves energy. The large load capacity (8kg) also reduces the amount of loads needed, again saving water and energy.

he XO-1, also known as the $100 solar-powered laptop, is an mbitious project emerging from the One Laptop per Child (OLPC) organization, a charity that aims to sell laptops at one-third of the rice of the lowest machine currently on the market. The project ms to offer countries such as China, Brazil, India, Argentina, gypt, Nigeria and Thailand a solar-powered laptop, giving children nd adults alike the opportunities technology brings. The project as become part of a US$20 million research collaboration between rofessor Nicholas Negroponte at Massachusetts Institute of echnology and their ODM (original design manufacturer) Quanta omputer Incorporated, based in Tao Yuan Shien, Taiwan. Quanta a contract manufacturer of computer notebooks for international

companies including Dell and Hewlett Packard, founded in 1988 by Barry Lam, C.C. Leung and Michael Wang.

The laptops are powered by a hand crank and designed to use Linux, one of the best known free software programs, connecting to the internet through mesh networking, which allows maximum flexibility. Concerns about the viability of the project's long-term future have been raised, however. One serious issue is that consumers in emerging markets have rejected other cheap computers experiments. The XO-1 intends to address these concerns with a different approach to design. The early prototypes have a 7-inch screen, simplified keyboard and a flash memory instead of a hard drive.

DATE: 2008

DESIGNER: Yves Behar of fuseproject

MANUFACTURER: Quanta Computer Incorporated, Taiwan, China

Ford Model T

DATE: 1908

DESIGNER: Henry Ford
(1863–1947)

MANUFACTURER: Ford
Motor Company, Detroit, USA

When Henry Ford began building his first car by hand in 1893 there were only four petrol-powered automobiles in the United States. By the time of his death in 1947 more than sixty per cent of American families owned a motor car. This enormous growth in car ownership can largely be credited to Henry Ford's introduction of mass production techniques for the Model T in 1913.

The Ford Motor Company was established in 1903 and in 1908 Henry Ford launched a small and affordable car called the Model T. In 1913 Ford introduced the world's first moving assembly line for car construction. This was accompanied by a radical standardization of components, which allowed Ford to cut his costs dramatically by ordering materials in tremendous bulk.

By 1915 the Ford factory in Detroit could build a thousand vehicles per day. As a result of this high productivity Ford was able to lower the price of the Model T from $950 in 1908 to $360 in 1915, double his employees' wages and shorten the working day.

He used the complete standardization of his car to launch a se mocking advertising campaign, announcing that "you can buy Ford in any colour as long asit's black."

By the early 1920s, when this photograph was taken, Fo had captured half of the American car market and in 1925 began assembling Model Ts in Berlin. When production of tl Model T was halted in 1927 after nineteen years, fifteen and half million examples of the car had been built. This was remain the world's longest and largest production run of single model of car until 1972 when the record was broken the Volkswagen "Beetle".

In America the car has dictated many aspects of business ar culture, influencing urban planning, architecture and people lifestyles to a far greater extent than in any other country. Her Ford's impact on American life has been greater than that of ar other industrialist of the twentieth century.

hen the Deux Chevaux, or "two horsepower", was launched at e Paris Automobile Salon in 1948 it was met with a degree of dicule suffered by no other car before or since. Produced to mpete with the Volkswagen Beetle and the rival French "Auto du euple", the Renault 4CV, it was really contending to replace the orse and cart, which remained the dominant form of transport in largely rural France.

When Boulanger set out to design a car for the agricultural arket in 1939, he was given a demanding brief. The 2CV had to e capable of carrying a man wearing a top hat and carrying a asket full of eggs across a field without breaking any of his fragile argo. Less fancifully, it had to provide good head-room, excellent suspension and comfort, but in a truly small car that would be inexpensive to build and maintain.

The simplified, geometric bodywork facilitated minimum use of materials and ease of assembly in the immediate postwar period when resources were scarce. The lightweight hammock-style seats could be removed to provide additional storage space and the retractable canvas roof allowed the vehicle to accommodate long or bulky objects.

Despite its many detractors and the numerous insults it has collected, the 2CV has become a cult favourite. With a production run between 1948 and 1990 of more than five million units, it remains one of the most successful French cars ever.

DATE: 1939

DESIGNER: Pierre Boulanger (1886–1950)

MANUFACTURER: Citroën, France

Queen Mary Ocean Liner

DATE: 1934

CONSTRUCTED BY: John Brownand Company, Clydebank, Scotland

The *Queen Mary* is one of the largest sea-going vessels ever constructed and has had a romantic and illustrious history. The formidable task of building what was to be one of the largest and most luxurious ocean liners was given to John Brown and Company, which commenced construction of Job No.534, as the ship was originally called, in 1931. Later that year work was halted due to the Depression and it was not until March 1934 that building was recommenced. The new Cunard ship was finally launched in September 1934 by Her Majesty Queen Mary, who gave her name to the vessel.

With the outbreak of World War Two the *Queen Mary* wa forced to cease service for the Cunard Steamship Company as transatlantic passenger liner and was refitted in Sydney, Australia as a troopship. She became known as the "Grey Ghost", actin as an essential troop carrier. In 1943 she carried 16,683 peop on one voyage, the largest number ever conveyed on a ship. Th *Queen Mary* is now a floating hotel and tourist attraction in Lor Beach, Los Angeles, where she has been berthed for the la forty years.

Hudson J-3a

DATE: 1938

DESIGNER: Henry Dreyfuss (1903–72)

MANUFACTURER: New York Central Railroad, USA

the interwar years designers and architects in Europe and America re gripped by the possibilities of speed and power afforded by odern technology. Fast cars, aeroplanes and powerful locomotives came potent symbols of the "Machine Age" and the dizzying pace urban life. Ever increasing speed became an end in itself and signers began to look to the scientific principles of aerodynamics decrease the wind resistance and thus increase the efficiency of hicles. Streamlining, the practice of shaping an object to reduce ag, found its greatest expression in Henry Dreyfuss' locomotive for New York Central Railroad.

Dreyfuss began as a set and costume designer for theatre and ened his own industrial design bureau in 1929. He would quickly come one of the leading exponents of a rational and functional proach to design that was characterized by clean lines and bold, decorated statements in form.

During the 1930s in America streamlining developed into a superficial style as the sleek, rounded forms which served a genuine aerodynamic function in high-speed vehicles were applied to household objects as diverse as cameras, vacuum cleaners and refrigerators. This cosmetic styling of objects was often nothing more than a cynical marketing ploy designed to dress up old products as new.

Unlike his contemporaries, Raymond Loewy and Walter Dorwin Teague, Dreyfuss was largely opposed to this practice, which he considered a rejection of pure functionalism and ergonomic or anthropometric design. His measured and integral approach resulted in some of the most enduring classics of twentieth-century product design such as his telephone for the American Bell Company in 1933 that defined the basic shape of the modern telephone for more than fifty years.

Greyhound Bus

DATE: 1940

DESIGNER: Raymond Loewy
(1893–1986)

MANUFACTURER: Greyhound
Corporation, USA

In a country dominated by the ethos of individuality and with the highest percentage of private car ownership in the world, the Greyhound Bus system is a potent symbol of the democratizing force of affordable and accessible public transport. In novels, films and advertising it has become synonymous with freedom, escape and the pursuit of adventure across America's vast expanses.

The company began modestly in Minnesota in 1914, when a Swedish immigrant called Carl Wickmann set up an inexpensive transport service for mine workers. By 1921 the service could offer intercity connections and had its own fleet of buses, which were dubbed "Greyhounds" because of their sleek design and distinctive grey colouring.

Wickmann merged with Orville Swann Caesar in 1926, acquiring many smaller bus companies to become The Greyhound Corporation in 1930. The familiar "running dog" trademark was adopted and remains the company's logo to this day.

In the 1940s Greyhound employed one of the great pioneers of American industrial design and styling, Raymond Loewy, to redesign the fleet of buses, producing a vehicle which with its reflective and fluted aluminium bodywork is one of the greatest essays in American streamlining.

Routemaster Bus

The Routemaster, the classic red London bus, has become a symbol of Britain's capital throughout the world, along with the black taxi and Giles Gilbert-Scott's K2 telephone box.

Designed in 1954 to replace the existing trolley-buses, the Routemaster was once a familiar sight on London's streets. Its ungainly appearance attracted criticism from many sceptics and almost as soon as it entered service in 1959, its design was seen to be outdated, as legislation introduced in 1961 permitted buses of up to thirty feet in length. However, the Routemaster's basic design proved to be endlessly adaptable and extremely popular with Londoners. Early in its history there were already plans to phase out the Routemaster in favour of a crewless vehicle, and by the 1970s London Transport's "Reshaping Plan" set out a timetable for the elimination of all but the new driver-only buses. However, this project proved to be both inefficient and unpopular, and as a result the Routemaster remained a part of London's cityscape for nearly forty years more. In the twenty-first century, the iconic Routemaster was finally taken out of service because it did not conform to disability access requirements and required not only a driver but a conductor. This famous bus can only be seen as a vintage element at weddings and special events.

DATE: 1954

DESIGNERS: A.A.M. Durrant (1898–1984), Douglas Scott (1913–90)

MANUFACTURER: London Transport, London, England

Dursley-Pedersen Bicycle

DATE: 1893

DESIGNER: Mikael Pedersen
(1855–1929)

The turn of the century saw some of the greatest innovations in the design of the bicycle, which was fast becoming a universal means of personal transport. At the forefront of these developments was Mikael Pedersen, a Dane living in Dursley in England.

Pedersen's bicycle was a masterpiece of sophisticated engineering, which relied upon an ingenious frame structure, as shown below, to the right, held by the woman cyclist. The frame was constructed of fourteen separate thin hollow tubes, connected at fifty-seven points to produce twenty-one triangles. This structu the "space frame", afforded great strength with relative lightnes The saddle consisted of a leather "hammock" strung between t top part of the frame and the handlebars, giving a high degree suspension and so providing a relatively comfortable ride primitive roads and lanes at the turn of the century.

Many of Pedersen's pioneering developments have been tak up in recent years, especially in the field of frame design.

Harley-Davidson Motorbike

DATE: 1903

DESIGNERS: William
Harley (1871–1937), Arthur
Davidson (1881–1950),
Walter Davidson (1876–1942),
William Davidson (1880–1943)

MANUFACTURER: Harley
Davidson Motor Company, USA

ke the black leather jacket, the Harley-Davidson motorbike is nonymous with non-conformity, rebellion and danger. More than y other brand of motorbike, the Harley symbolizes the association speed and power with independence and sexual prowess.

The original Harley-Davidson was born at the turn of the century nen two childhood friends, William Harley and Arthur Davidson, tempted to build a motorized bicycle. Working on the project in eir spare time, they were soon joined by Davidson's brothers alter and William, the latter of whom was a skilled tool-maker. In 903 the four men constructed their first single-cylinder, three-orsepower bike, and happy with their creation set about building two more. Another three followed in 1904 and the Harley-Davidson Motor Company was born.

Their reputation for building resilient vehicles quickly spread and by 1910 their sales were guaranteed by a network of dealerships. The success of their bikes was primarily due to their reliability. By 1913 the first bike they built had covered an astonishing 100,000 miles without the need to replace any of its main components.

The growth of motorcycle racing in the 1920s and 1930s (this model is 1939) and the use of their vehicles by the military in virtually every continent during World War Two ensured that Harley-Davidson has become a household name.

Vespa

DATE: 1945

DESIGNER: Corradino
d'Ascanio (1891–1981)

MANUFACTURER: Piaggio,
Italy

The Vespa has become one of the greatest symbols of postwar Italian reconstruction. At the close of World War Two, like most European countries, Italy faced a transport crisis. During the war the entire Italian automotive industry had been converted to military production and had subsequently been reduced to rubble by the Allies. With raw materials such as metal and fuel in short supply and with a greatly lowered standard of living, a cost-effective and modern means of personal transport was required.

The Piaggio company had begun constructing aeroplanes in 1915; however during World War Two the factory was bombed. The company's president Enrico Piaggio decided to replace aeronautic production with building a vehicle that was cheap, reliable, easy to maintain and easy to drive in order to get the Italian nation back work. Piaggio's chief engineer Corradino d'Ascanio set abc designing a scooter that would be launched in 1946 as the Vesp which is Italian for "wasp".

D'Ascanio brought his experience of helicopter and aircraft engi design to bear on the Vespa's development. His design incorporate "stress-skin" technology with body and frame fused into a unified who This monocoque design, now a staple of the automotive industry, w virtually unique in civilian vehicle design in 1945. As this 1960s phc demonstrates, the Vespa's surprising and stylish looks have made it enduring favourite with young people, and have established it as one the most successful vehicles of the postwar period.

Ducati Motorbike

Renowned throughout the world as producers of some of the best high-performance motorbikes, the Ducati family business began in Bologna in 1926 as a manufacturer of components for the fledgling radio industry. Adriano Ducati's patents in this field quickly gained the company an international reputation.

Like those of so many other Italian companies, Ducati's factories were destroyed during World War Two and in the restructuring that followed, the company was compelled to broaden its product range. At a Milan Fair, Ducati presented a small auxiliary motor designed to be fitted to bicycles. This design laid the foundations for the company's move into motorcycle production, and with the

launch of the 175cc Cruiser in 1952, Ducati was firmly established as one of the world's leading manufacturers in the field.

In 1955 the company was joined by Fabio Taglioni who went on to produce some of the company's legendary designs, which were pushed to their limits in endurance races. Since then Ducati has continued to apply the engineering lessons of its racing successes to consistently innovative road bikes.

The M900 Monster, designed in 1993 by the Argentinian designer, Fabio Taglioni, ushered in a new era of top-class Ducati bikes. Its remarkably minimal bodywork gives full attention to its powerful engine and its lightweight trellis construction tubular frame.

DATE: 1993

DESIGNER: Fabio Taglioni (born 1920)

MANUFACTURER: Ducati MotorS.p.A., Italy

Porsche 356

DATE: 1948

DESIGNERS: Ferdinand
Porsche (1875–1951), Ferry
Porsche (1909–1998) and Erwin
Komenda (1904–66)

MANUFACTURER: Porsche,
Gmund/Stuttgart, Germany

Ferdinand Porsche was one of the greatest pioneers of automotive engineering and design. His first car, designed in 1900 for the Austrian manufacturer Lohner, was an electric vehicle driven by hub-mounted motors. The most important of his countless innovations include torsion-bar suspension and the rear-mounted air-cooled engine.

Before establishing his own auto-motive design consultancy in Stuttgart in 1930, Porsche had acted as chief engineer and designer for Austro-Daimler, Mercedes-Benz and Steyr, for whom he produced some of the most celebrated cars of the prewar period. During the 1930s his energies were split between the development of the Volkswagen and the design of revolutionary Grand Prix racing cars for Auto Union. World War Two found Porsche and his son Ferry designing military vehicles including an amphibious version of the Volkswagen and tanks such as the Tiger and the Maus.

The 356 was the first car to be manufactured by the Porsc[he] family under its own name and it was the fulfilment of Porsch[e's] dream to build a sports version of the Volkswagen. Using ma[ny] components from the "People's Car", including the rear-mount[ed] air-cooled engine developed by Franz Xavier Reimspiess, the 3[56] established the pattern of engineering excellence and aesthe[tic] elegance that the Porsche company maintains to this day.

When the 356 won its class at the twenty-four-hour endura[nce] race at Le Mans in 1951, it initiated a run of spectacular raci[ng] victories that few other marques have rivalled. Production [of] the 356 ceased in 1965 after the introduction in 1963 [of] the Porsche 911, designed by Porsche's grandson But[zi] which many see as the ultimate expression of the Porsc[he] design ethos.

LEADERSHIP

From Great Achievements...An Inspiring Tradition!

Cadillac's many and varied contributions to the cause of automotive progress have, over the years, represented one of the most important and inspiring traditions in all motordom. And certainly, that list of Cadillac's achievements has become all the more meaningful in the light of the current year. For in styling, in design and in engineering, this latest "car of cars" has added dramatic emphasis to the fact of

Cadillac leadership. If you have not yet inspected its magnificent new Fleetwood coachcrafting—or experienced its brilliant new performance —you should do so soon. Your dealer will be happy to introduce you to all the new models, including the distinguished Eldorado Brougham. CADILLAC MOTOR CAR DIVISION • GENERAL MOTORS CORPORATION Every Window of Every Cadillac is Safety Plate Glass   FORWARD FROM FIFTY

Standard of the World for more than half a century

Cadillac

DATE: 1959

DESIGNER: Harley Earl (1893–1969)

MANUFACTURER: General Motors, USA

Few products have been so heavily invested with the aspirations and dreams of a nation as the 1950s Cadillac and few designers have been so willing to pander to an entire generation's lust for superficial extravagance as Harley Earl.

Earl was born into a family of coach-builders in California that specialized in customized cars for Hollywood's first generation of affluent film stars. Early in his career Earl pioneered the now-universal practice of modelling a car's exterior form in clay, a technique that allowed for great sculptural freedom.

By the late 1920s, when Henry Ford's Model T had brought motoring to the majority of America's population, stylistic differentiation between car models was an important factor in attracting new buyers. In 1928 Earl was invited to head General Motors' newly formed Art and Colour section, to develop the styling of the company's vehicles. The age of the "dream car" was born and the success of Earl's Buicks, Cadillacs, Chevrolets, Oldsmobiles and Pontiacs soon established him as the most influential designer in the American car industry.

By the time he retired in 1959, more than fifty million cars had been produced to his designs. The Cadillac demonstrates his fascination with aeroplane design. With its elongated body, extended fins, rocket-like tail-lights and masses of chrome, it is the ultimate expression of the self-confidence and power of America in the 1950s.

Series II Land Rover

DATE: 1955

DESIGNER: David Bache (born 1926)

MANUFACTURER: Rover, Coventry, England

The Land Rover was developed in response to the Willys-Overland Jeep which, since its launch in 1940, had proved enormously successful as both an agricultural and military vehicle throughout the world.

The Land Rover was first unveiled to the public at the Amsterdam Car Show in 1948. Initially seen as a sturdy four-wheel drive vehicle to replace the horse and cart, the Land Rover was quickly adapted for use in the desert, the jungle, on Safari and in mountainous regions.

The vehicle has a steel frame chassis onto which can be bolted a variety of aluminium body panels to produce a car that is suited to a particular terrain. The body work has a simple form and is designed to be stripped with only the aid of a screwdriver and wrench.

Soon after joining Rover in 1954, David Bache set about redesigning the body work of the Land Rover and with his design of the Range Rover in 1970, he took the language of the large four-wheel drive vehicle a stage further, adding the attributes of luxury and style to that of rugged reliability.

David Bache was one of the few British car designers, along with Alec Issigonis, to achieve an international reputation and to exert a powerful influence on a generation of automotive designers – his Rover P10 of 1975 can be seen as the point of departure for Uwe Bahnsen's foresighted design of the Ford Sierra in 1982.

Mini

Like the skirt of the same name, the Mini has come to be seen as a cultural icon of the 1960s, a decade that saw a process of radical democratization in British social life, spurred largely by the growth of a new class of young, financially independent people. The resulting dramatic increase in car ownership led to the need for a small, dependable and modern car that conveyed an urbane and youthful image.

Alec Issigonis had already gone some way to revolutionizing the British motor car with his Morris Minor of 1948, but this car still owed much to the automotive styling of the 1930s and was in many ways similar to the Volkswagen Beetle and the Renault 4CV. The Mini represented a radical departure from all previous car design and

owed nothing to prevailing ideas in American or European engineering and styling. Issigonis produced an extremely small car that could comfortably seat four adults and was ideally suited to busy city streets. The large amount of space in the car's minimal interior was achieved by Issigonis installing the engine transversely, or sideways, a departure that was to influence much automotive design of the 1960s and 1970s.

With various modifications and new models, such as the Mini Cooper, shown here starring in the film *The Italian Job* (on the Fiat factory roof), the original Mini was in production for over thirty-five years. It is Britain's most successful and best-loved car, mainly due to its reliability and classic, timeless shape.

DATE: 1959

DESIGNER: Alec Issigonis (1906–88)

MANUFACTURER: Morris (British Motor Corporation), United Kingdom

Specialized Stump-jumper

DATE: 1981

DESIGNER: Mike Sinyard (born 1949)

MANUFACTURER: Specialized, Morgan Hill, California, USA

Since the mid-1970s the introduction of mountain and all-terrain bikes has brought about the greatest number of technological and design innovations in cycling history. The search for bicycles capable of greater speeds, combined with enormous strength and lightness, has created a thriving industry of companies devoted to producing specialized gears, pedals, tyres and above all highly sophisticated frames. It is particularly in the design of frames that materials technology has advanced at an astonishing rate, as designers have experimented with the use of carbon fibres, ultra-light alloys and metals such as aluminium and titanium.

The Specialized company was founded in 1974 by Mike Sinyard and by the late 1970s had established a reputation as one of the most innovative producers of mountain bikes. In 1981 following scores of impressive developments, particularly in the field of tyre technology, Specialized launched the Stumpjumper, the world's first mass-produced mountain bike.

In 1983 Specialized created the first professional mountain bike racing team and has achieved many successes. The lessons Specialized has learned in racing have contributed to countless innovations in its production of bicycles and accessories including helmets and water bottles.

Toyota Prius

DATE: 2008

DESIGNERS: Toyota Design Team

MANUFACTURER: Toyota, Japan

e Prius has achieved a remarkable brand perception for Toyota as h fashionable and green, making the Japanese car company a rket leader in this important sector. The car's distinctive rodynamic styling sends out a clear and immediate signal that the ver cares about the environment. It also helped that from 2004 llywood movie stars such as Cameron Diaz and Leonardo Caprio conspicuously drove the Prius both on and off screen. They ped make the car cool and American sales figures reflected this. Since its launch the Prius has sold one million vehicles and come the most popular "green" car. The car's 1.5 litre petrol gine charges a high performance battery, which in turn powers electric motor. When the car is in slow-moving traffic, it can run ently) on electric power and its CO_2 emissions of 104g/km

make it one of the greenest cars on the road. Travelling at higher speeds for longer periods, such as on the motorway, the car charges the battery while running on engine power alone; the energy lost during braking is recovered and also used to charge the battery. One of the most fuel-efficient cars on the market, its reaches a top figure of 65.7mpg (3.58l/100km). Due to its hybrid engine and lower emissions, the Prius is exempt from the London congestion charge, making it very attractive to buyers there and in other cities which plan to introduce similar schemes. Research into increasing the range of the hybrid in its all-electric mode via updated plug-in batteries is in progress. Toyota has invested heavily in the car's further research and development, supporting the continuing success of the Prius.

Smart fortwo

DATE: 2008

DESIGNER: Gerhard Steinie

MANUFACTURER: Smart GmbH/Daimler-Benz

Micro cars are designed to combat congestion in urban areas and to respond to user research that indicates most car journeys are under three miles distance, with only a single occupant. The Smart car placed the engine underneath the car's occupants to save space, making it short enough to be parked nose to kerb, and small enough for two, or even three, cars to squeeze into a conventional parking space. The original Smart car, now known as the "fortwo" was launched in October 1998 as a two-seater, and helped change motoring patterns with its stylish design and innovative marketing. It was designed by an interdisciplinary team led by Gerhard Steinie, a car designer with long experience in the industry. The original two-seater has now been joined by a roadster and a four-seater "forfour".

The project idea came from Nicholas Hayek, the CEO of Sw manufacturer Swatch whose stylish and cheap digital watch dominated design trends in the 1980s and '90s.

Swatch admired the tradition of iconic micro cars of t twentieth century such as the Fiat 500 and the UK Mini a wanted a twenty-first-century version aimed at the young market. It was a complex project to bring to the market, b eventually Swatch found a production partner in Daimler-Be and a purpose built factory in France called Smartville w completed in 1994. Smart production was modular, w interchangeable plastic body parts attached to a ridge Tridi frame and designed to be changed by the owner accordi to fashion.

Airbus A380

DATE: 2000–2007

MANUFACTURER: Airbus, Toulouse, France

he Airbus A380, popularly known as the Superjumbo, is the world's st double-decker, double-aisled four-engine passenger airliner with s upper deck extending the entire length of the fuselage. This extra ace offers Upper Class passengers a new experience in air travel cluding shopping, keep fit areas, bars and even showers.

The A380 was the first competitor to challenge the market hold the Boeing 747. Although it is estimated to have cost 11 billion uros to develop, it offers lower operating costs per passenger. ble to carry up to 850 passengers, it was designed for long stance flights with a range of over 15,000 kilometres (9,375 miles) d developed to alleviate the growing threat of gridlock facing ternational airports. The A380 was also designed to meet the rowing demands of international freight services.

The Airbus had been in development since the end of the last century; it undertook its maiden flight in 2005 and its first commercial flight in 2007, from Singapore to Sydney, Australia with Singapore Airlines. The challenges presented by the scale of the airliner proved immense: electrics for the cabins, for example, required over 500 miles of wiring.

Transportation of production parts was another challenge: the Superjumbo supply chain is a case study of shared international expertise, with major structural elements provided by France, Germany and the UK from suppliers including Rolls Royce, SAFRAN, United Technologies and General Electric. Airbus's production projections are for 45 Superjumbos a year by 2010.

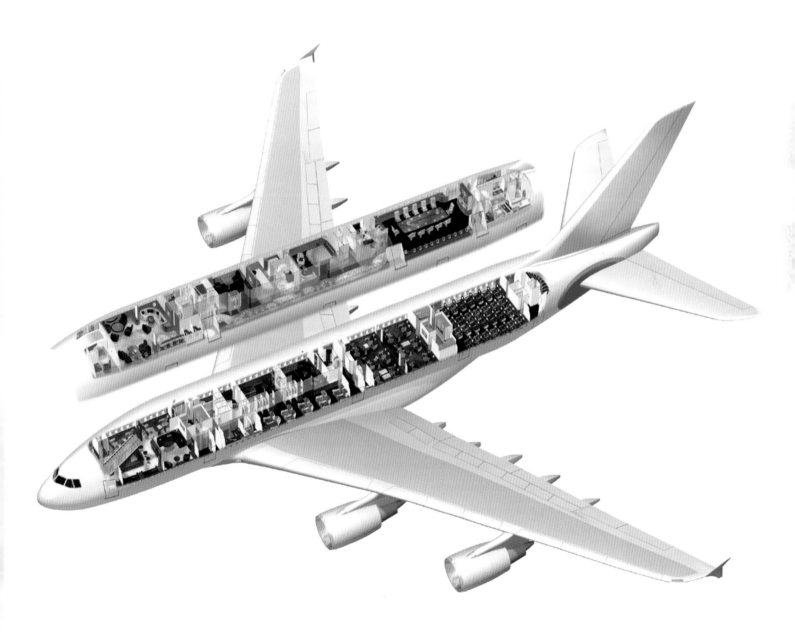

The Deer Cry

DATE: 1916

DESIGNER: Archibald Knox
(1864–1933)

It is not hard to see the links between Knox's brightly coloured hand-drawn type and the freeform experiments in hand-drawn lettering associated with psychedelia in the 1960s. What also makes this work so extraordinary is the direction Knox took towards abstraction in the letterforms, a direction that ran against the contemporary trend in the 1920s towards simplification.

Archibald Knox is an Arts and Crafts architect–designer best known for his work for the London department store Liberty's for whom he produced a distinctive range of metalware. Less familiar is his work as an illustrator and calligrapher. The best surviving collection of his work can be found in the museum of his home town Douglas in the Isle of Man. All of Knox's designs were inspired by Celtic art and nature, as is visible in this illustration for *The Deer Cry* from 1916. In his calligraphy this produced linear interlaced motifs and ornamentation. During the 1920s Knox produced a range of graphic work including illustrated books and greeting cards, based on his considerable first-hand knowledge of Celtic ornamentation. One of his techniques was to draw the outline of the letter forms in pencil and then fill in the shapes with watercolour.

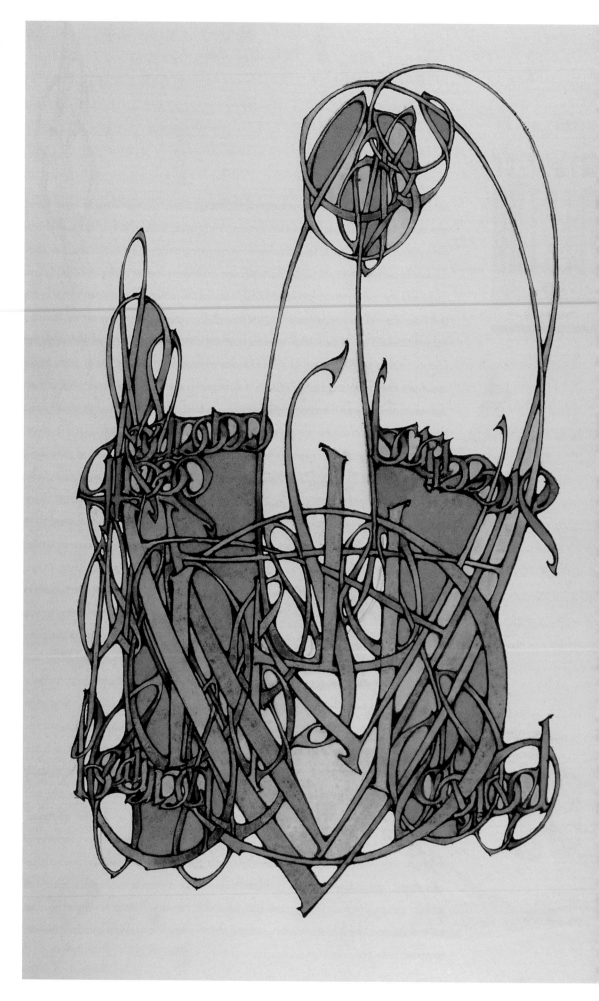

about 1910 the new ideas emerging from art and architecture began to have an inevitable effect on type and design. Just as architecture challenged the idea that buildings should refer to historical sources, type designers also experimented with new forms.

important here were the Italian Futurists who saw new type design as a way to "redouble the force of expressive words".

Kurt Schwitters was a leading force behind another art movement – Dada. Using type, he put together a series of famous collages employing the principle of random choice. In doing so Schwitters placed type within a fine art context and opened up the possibility that type was not only concerned with function and legibility.

DATE: 1920

DESIGNER: Kurt Schwitters (1887–1948)

Million Mark Note

DATE: 1923

DESIGNER: Herbert Bayer
(1900–85)

The Bauhaus has become the most famous design school of the twentieth century. It was always a small school and during its fourteen-year life only trained 1,250 students. It has, however, come to represent the century's new Modernist approach to design and industry. In 1923 one of its successes was to win a commission from the State bank of Thuringia to design a series of emergency banknotes. The production of banknotes was an expanding industry in Germany's Weimar Republic at this time, due to an ever-increasing inflation rate.

Herbert Bayer, then a young student, was asked to design no in denominations of one million, two million and two billion. By time they were issued on September 1, 1923, the Germ economy was in a state of collapse and even higher denominatic were required. Bayer's designs reflect the ideology of hardl Modern Movement graphics – direct and simple typography, decoration, and strong horizontals and verticals. For bankno they are highly individual, with an experimental approach ma possible by the unique economic circumstances of their era.

ward Johnston is responsible for one of the most famous
rporate identity programmes in the world, for London's Underground
stem. Based on a font he had designed in 1916 for Frank Pick,
ndon Transport's design manager, it was also Britain's first
odernist typeface using clean, geometric forms that proved easy to
ad and immensely popular with the public. Arguably it was the first
ns serif face of the twentieth century and was deeply influential on

British graphic design in general and in particular on Johnston's pupil, the famous sculptor and typeface designer Eric Gill (1882–1940). London's Underground system expanded rapidly after World War One and provided the British public with their first, sometimes only, opportunity to see modern architecture and design. In the 1980s the type was redrawn by Banks and Miles to meet the more complex applications of the 1990s.

DATE: 1916

DESIGNER: Edward Johnston (1872–1944)

Penguin Book Covers

DATE: 1946–49

DESIGNER: Edward Young/Jan Tschichold (1902–74)

Jan Tschichold was born in Leipzig in Germany but emigrated to Switzerland in 1933 and became a Swiss citizen in 1942. He became one of the twentieth-century's most renowned typographers and his achievement was to lead the new postwar developments in typography while remaining firmly committed to traditional Modernist principles. In 1923 Tschichold saw an exhibition of work from the Weimar Bauhaus and was converted to the principles of the Modern Movement.

The Penguin book covers, including the Penguin Logo, were originally designed in the 1930s by Penguin's Production manager, Edward Young. In 1946 Tschichold was employed by Sir Allen Lane,

chairman of Penguin Books. Although he only worked for th[e] publisher for three years, Tschichold introduced new standards [in] text layout and design that influenced the whole of British postw[ar] graphic design. His achievement was to apply the theories [of] Modernism to the requirements of book production, with th[e] establishment of the "Penguin Composition Rules".

Tschichold was also a dedicated historian and writer with ov[er] twenty books to his credit on subjects ranging from Chines[e] calligraphy to polemics on design. In the 1960s he worked as [a] freelance consultant to numerous Swiss and German publishers. [In] 1968 Tschichold retired to Locarno, where he died six years later.

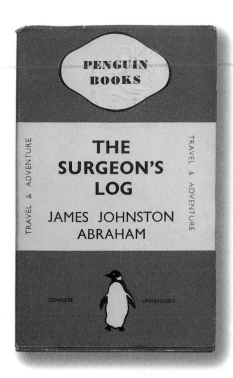
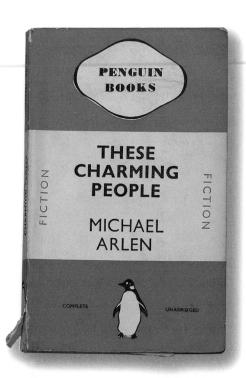
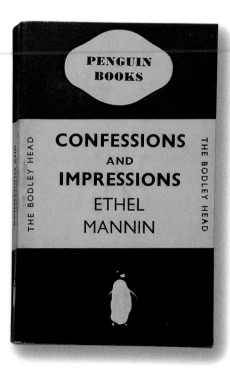

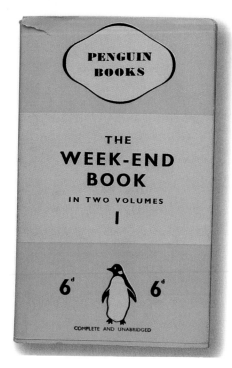
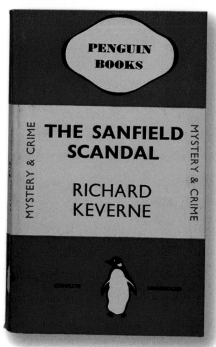

DATE: 1954–55

DESIGNER: Adrian Frutiger
(born 1928)

Univers Medium

ABCDEFGHIJKLMNOPQRSTUV
WXYZ 1234567890
abcdefghijklmnopqrstuvwxyz
&:;!?"%£)

Univers Medium Italic

ABCDEFGHIJKLMNOPQRSTUV
WXYZ 1234567890
abcdefghijklmnopqrstuvwxyz
&:;!?"%£)

Univers Bold

ABCDEFGHIJKLMNOPQRSTU
VWXYZ 1234567890
abcdefghijklmnopqrstuvwxyz
&:;!?"%£)

Univers Bold Italic

ABCDEFGHIJKLMNOPQRSTU
VWXYZ 1234567890
abcdefghijklmnopqrstuvwxyz
&:;!?"%£)

After the chaos of the war it is hardly surprising that many European type designers looked to order and unity as a vision of the way forward. Their intellectual response was to look back to the Bauhaus and take a rational approach to the problem of developing typography for the new era. Nowhere was this new spirit more clearly expressed than in the development of the International, or Swiss Style, which was pioneered at the Zurich School of Applied Art, the Kunstgewerbeschule. The designers there believed that they were setting universal and unchanging typographic standards.

Their aim was to make typography as objective as possible, believing that the design and typography should be "neutral", so that the information contained in the text would not be clouded by the form the text took. As the Swiss style, with its insistence on the use of sans serif faces, became more influential, a whole series of new fonts reflecting this influence were created. One of the most important of these was Univers, designed by Adrian Frutiger who, as a young man, was appointed artistic director of one of Europe's most famous type companies, Deberny. Created as a "universal" typeface, it was drawn in twenty-one variations – combinations of italicized, condensed and bold versions, as well as a range of weights – so that the one face could be used for any application.

Mother and Child

DATE: 1966

DESIGNER: Herb Lubalin
(1918–81)

In the postwar years, New York City became the world's cultural capital and one of the city's achievement's was the emergence of a distinctly American school of typography. It was not until the 1950s that a new group of graphic designers including Milton Glaser and Saul Bass established an original American approach. Arguably the most talented type designer of his generation was Herb Lubalin.

If European typography was theoretical and structured then American typography was intuitive and informal, with a more open, direct presentation. Herb Lubalin's decorative and hand-drawn lettering appeared in marked contrast to the formal mechanical Swiss and German Schools of typography and reflected the unique economic affluence and cultural confidence of 1950s America.

Born in New York City of immigrant Russian and German parents Lubalin studied typography at the Cooper Union School of

Architecture. He led the way in manipulating typography to expre
an idea; letter forms became objects and images, and his figurat
typography allowed visual properties a new freedom and importanc
One of his most famous inventions was a new genre called t
"typogram", a kind of brief visual poem.

Perhaps the best-known example of this expressive typograp
is a masthead, designed in 1966, for a magazine called *Mother a
Child* in which the ampersand evokes the image of the wor
complete with foetus. These experiments, using what Luba
called "the typographic image", were widely imitated in advertisin
Designers realized the possibilities of using typography to create
"word picture" that allowed them a new creative potential. It w
Lubalin's achievement to pack an idea into a single, convinci
piece of typography.

...ss is an American graphic designer best known for his innovative ...rk for the film makers Otto Preminger and Alfred Hitchcock. A ...tive New Yorker, Saul Bass studied graphic design at night ...hool in Brooklyn College between 1944–45, while practising as a ...elance graphic designer. In 1946 he moved to Los Angeles and ...unded Saul Bass and Associates. Bass designed more than sixty ...aphic symbols for films and more than forty motion picture title ...quences. He is particularly well known for his work with the ...rector Otto Preminger, for whom he designed the symbols and ...pening titles for *The Man with the Golden Arm* (1955), *Bonjour ...stesse* (1956) and *Anatomy of a Murder* (1959) and for his ...orking relationship with Alfred Hitchcock, designing the opening

credits and, some suggest, directing the shower sequence, from *Psycho* (1960).

From Hollywood's earliest days until the mid-1950s, credits to mainstream American movies had been set in virtually uniform templates and superimposed over an unchanging static image or the film's introductory scene. Bass used animation and, later, live action to create graphically considered title sequences that attracted the attention of audiences and critics and were soon widely imitated.

Bass designed relatively few film credit sequences after the early 1970s, although he created the opening titles for the remake of *Cape Fear* (1991) at the request of the film's director, Martin Scorsese.

DATE: 1959

DESIGNER: Saul Bass (1920–96)

IBM Logo

DATE: 1956

DESIGNER: Paul Rand (1914–96)

Paul Rand was America's most respected graphic designer. Born in New York City, he began his career as assistant designer in George Switzer's studio, and became art director of *Esquire* and *Apparel Arts* magazines from 1937 to 1941. During the 1940s and early 1950s he was creative director at William H. Weintraub advertising agency, and from 1955 went freelance, working as a consultant to companies such as Cummins Engine Company, Westinghouse Electric Corporation and IBM.

One of Rand's achievements was to secure the influence of modernist art movements such as Cubism, Constructivism, De Stijl and the Bauhaus to overthrow traditional American graphic design – with its symmetrical, isolated elements and narrative illustrations. He also began to work with the visual space as a whole, integrating copy, art and typography. Rand understood the expressive potential of colour, texture and collage and used these to develop his style. His work for IBM is seen as seminal in the development of corporate graphic identity, notably his use of abstract and pictographic symbols, which he saw as a common language linking artistic expression and its audience.

Galt was an established British furniture company that moved into children's toys in 1961. At the time, they invited Ken Garland to create their graphic identity and the result remains one of the most successful and distinctive corporate identity schemes of the 1960s.

Garland was typical of the generation of designers who allied themselves to Modernism. To his generation of designers the International Style, with its emphasis on the minimalism of clean lines and rational systems, seemed much more relevant to planning a Britain of the future than the gentle humour, whimsy and nostalgia that had informed much 1950s graphic work. Garland combined a knowledge of technology and basic practice with an ability to deal with ideas and communicate information. An early publication, *The 1966 Graphics Handbook,* was typical of Garland and the British School. It focused on the practicalities of being a professional graphic designer. Solid and practical, it dealt with type, letter-spacing, print technology and so forth, but also emphasized less obvious communication skills such as the importance of knowing how to answer the telephone and take notes!

DATE: 1963–64

DESIGNER: Ken Garland (born 1929)

Biba

DATE: 1960s

DESIGNER: John McConnell
(born 1939)

John McConnell was responsible for the design of the famous Biba logo. Biba as a concept marked a change in direction for the brightly coloured geometry of Pop design. McConnell's use of Art Nouveau and, in particular, Celtic imagery reflected a new interest in the rich decorative tradition of type design. Biba also introduced a range of products alongside its famous clothes. Barbara Hulanicki, Biba's founder, virtually invented the idea that it was possible to recreate a way of living through shopping, inspiring the idea of the design lifestyle. It was the first time a distinctive designer logo appeared on all kinds of products from perfume and make-up to baked beans and soap powder. As a styling concept it was ahead of its time and one became part of the mainstream in the 1980s. McConnell went on, 1979, to join Pentagram, where his talent for effective design solutions found an outlet in work for publishers Faber and Faber.

rhaps the nearest that Britain came to accepting the International
yle was in its road sign system, designed in 1964 by Jock Kinneir
d Margaret Calvert. The Government had commissioned the
orboys Report to report on overall road signage, which they
nted to bring in line with the Continental conventions established
the 1930s. With the advent of the motorway age the rationalization
signage systems for both motorways and other roads became a
ority and the Ministry of Transport commissioned a team including
ck Kinneir, who had previously worked in the 1950s on the signage
stem for Gatwick Airport. Kinneir and Calvert adapted a standard
be from the Bertold foundry but introduced some quirky and very

British elements, such as the stroke on the lower case "l", taken from
Edward Johnston's London Underground type of 1916, and the
design of the lower case "a", borrowed from an Eric Gill typeface.
When the designs were published many people wanted more
conventional roman letters for the capitals rather than a sans serif
upper and lower case. With its reliance on sans serif type, a
hierarchical structure for ordering information and its colour coding,
the motorway signs follow many of the principles of Modernism. At
the same time the signage avoids the almost expressionless clarity
of true Swiss Style and its inherent Britishness is so pervasive that it
has been called the corporate identity of Britain.

DATE: 1964

DESIGNERS: Jock Kinneir
(1917–74) and Margaret Calvert
(born c.1935)

Museum Poster

DATE: 1982

DESIGNER: Wolfgang Weingart
(born 1941)

In the 1970s, the first serious experiments using the new Postmodernist aesthetic for type came from surprising sources. One of these was the work of Wolfgang Weingart in Basel, then the centre of formal Swiss Style type design. His work sought to subvert the formalism of International Style and in doing so breathed new life into new type design. Weingart's approach was expressive, intuitive and experimental. Typical of his work is this poster for Basel's Gewerbe Museum in which he played around with word and letter spacing, contrasted weights and the layering of images. These devices were widely imitated and were to become the clichés of Postmodernist graphics in the 1980s.

Weingart still teaches at the Kunstgewerbeschule in Basel where he trained as a student. It has been his influence as a teacher, rather than as a practitioner, that has been paramount. Particularly influential was his period as a visiting professor at the Cranbrook Academy, near Detroit, where he inspired a whole generation of graphic designers to experiment with a new approach to type design. One of Weingart's best-known students is the West Coast designer April Greiman and, via her, Weingart's influence has filtered through to a new wave of Californian design.

Kaleidoscope

DATE: 1960s

DESIGNER: Rick Griffin (1944–91)

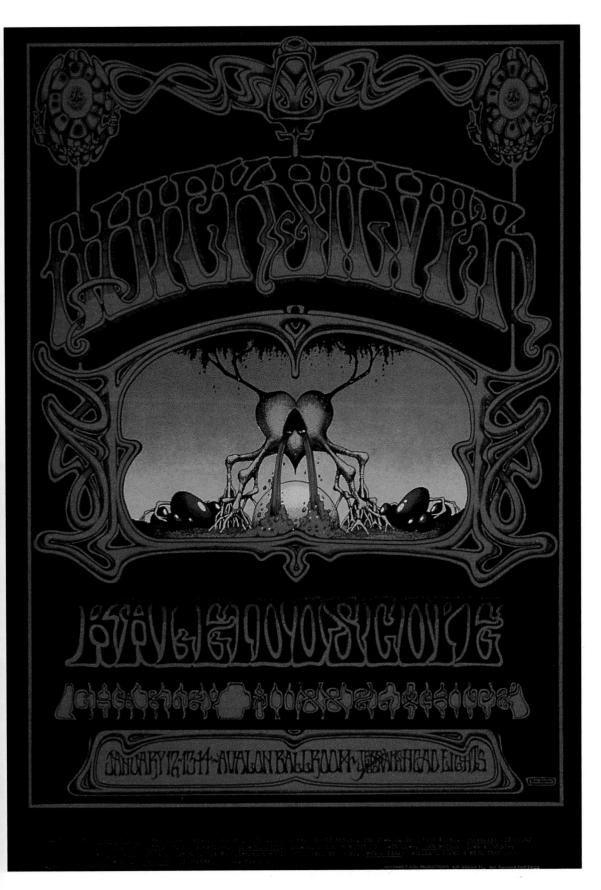

As a teenager Rick Griffin's roots were in 1950s California surfer culture, with its own unique music and clothes. Griffin went on to study for a short time at the CalArts school in Los Angeles. However he took an immediate dislike to simple modern type and good taste and took off, moving in 1965 to San Francisco where he designed posters for rock 'n' roll bands at the city's legendary Fillmore Auditorium and the Avalon Ballroom.

Griffin was an enthusiastic participant in the new drug culture and had taken part in the writer Ken Kesey's experimental counter culture gatherings. The influence of these experiences is reflected in one of the hallmarks of his style; the use of weird imagery, snakes, skulls, insects, bizarre science fiction creatures and Hell's Angels motifs. The effect of LSD on Griffin's work was in his use of luminous and intense colours that were balanced but chromatically opposite. In the 1960s Griffin reclaimed colour as a valid means of graphic expression. The new pop poster became the perfect expression of the new drug culture.

Griffin's work also epitomized the psychedelic rejection of legible typography. The copy on his posters took legibility to the limit, working on the premise that if the image was exciting enough people would not only take the trouble to decipher the information but also enjoy the process of decoding.

Berlin Underground Signage

DATE: 1990

DESIGNER: Erik Spiekermann
(born 1947)/MetaDesign

The tradition of Modernism in type design did not disappear in the 1980s but ran alongside the new experiments with technology. The rational work for the Berlin underground system by Erik Spiekermann is an example of this continuing tradition. After the fall of the Berlin Wall public transport in the city needed new passenger information and Meta was asked to look at the redesign of the corporate symbol and logotype to signage and maps. The work was so successful that BVG asked MetaDesign to undertake a complete corporate design programme. They are currently working on the design of fully interactive information kiosks to help the traveller.

Erik Spiekermann trained as an art historian at Berlin's Free University in West Germany in the late 1960s, where he established a small press. During the 1970s he worked in England, but in 1983 he returned to Berlin and set up his own studio, MetaDesign. MetaDesign attracted some of Europe's most talented young designers, including Jan van Toorn and Max Kisman, and became something of a catalyst for new ideas. Spiekermann well known as a writer on type and typography; his best known book, *Rhyme & Reason: A Typographical Novel*, is a handbook f typographic designers. MetaDesign specializes in corpora identity for clients such as H.Berthold AG, the Deutsch Bundespost, Apple Computers and in 1991 a timetable for th Berlin Transport Authority. Spiekermann's approach to typ design combines a respect for history and tradition with commitment to new technology.

In 1988 Spiekermann, with his wife Joan, set up a compar called the Fontshop to market typefaces. The company ha become a key outlet for both radical work and more commerci typefaces including Spiekermann's Meta, now one of the mo popular electronic fonts, widely used for signing systems and f magazine design.

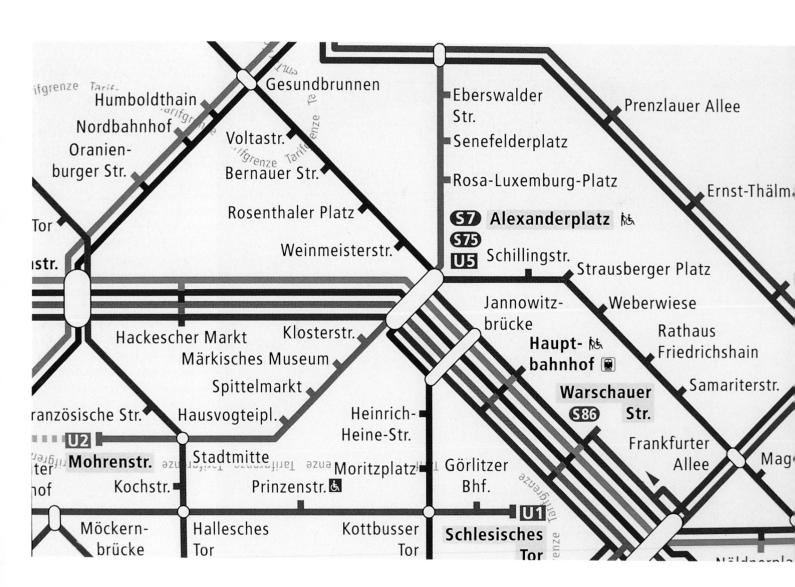

Cranbrook School of Art Poster

DATE: 1985

DESIGNER: Katherine McCoy
(born 1945)

CLIENT: Cranbrook School of Art,
Michigan, USA

Katherine McCoy is not only a designer; she has also come to represent a new attitude to typography and graphic design, expressed in the work of the staff and students at a small American design school called the Cranbrook Academy of Art in Michigan. Cranbrook has established itself as one of the world's most influential design schools, attempting in the sphere of graphics to introduce an intellectual rigour and environment of experimentation to the discipline.

In 1971, Katherine and Michael McCoy, a husband and wife team, were invited to take over the department. They set up a course with an emphasis on theory and analysis and which concentrated "on the purely syntactic aspect of typography on structure and form – with semantic exploration and analysis." During the 1970s the theoretical basis of Postmodernism began to interact with graphic design. These research ideas and the range of critical writing within Postmodernism offered a rationale for a new language of form within graphic design. Semiotics, for example, and the work of Claude Levi-Strauss provided a theoretical base for graphic design. At Cranbrook these theories encouraged an approach to type which produced layers of imagery and text, an approach to the subject disseminated by leading graduates of Cranbrook who included April Greiman and Jeffrey Keedy.

Emigré Magazine

DATE: 1986

DESIGNER: Zuzana Licko (born 1961) and Rudy VanderLans (born 1955)

Zuzana Licko is a type designer whose work has pioneered the use of typefaces designed on, and for, the Apple Macintosh. Born in Bratislava in Slovakia, her family emigrated to America in 1968. While at college she met the Dutch designer Rudy VanderLans, whom she married in 1983. In 1986, she set up the design consultancy Emigré with VanderLans and together they designed and produced the cult magazine of the same name, a journal for experimental graphic design. They bought their first Apple Mac in order to produce their arts magazine but soon realized that they could use the Mac to create typefaces. These faces started as an attempt to overcome the ugly bitmapping which occurred when traditional faces were transposed onto the then low-resolution machine. As the machine became more sophisticated, so did their typeface design, and, realizing that they could easily copy and sell their designs, they began to publish their typefaces as well as the *Emigré* magazine. In 1986 Licko and VanderLans set up Emigré Fonts, to market digital typefaces designed for low-resolution systems, including Emigré, Emperor and Universal.

The Face

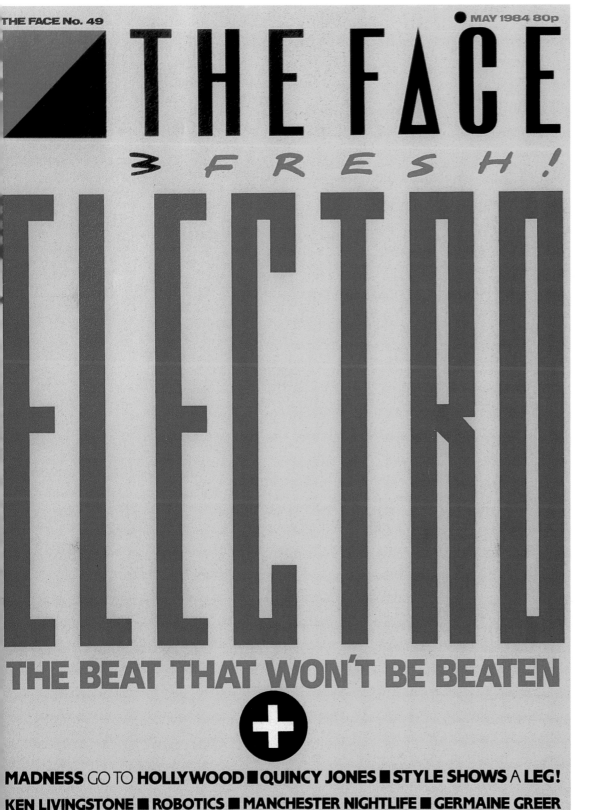

Neville Brody is Britain's best-known designer and his work, in particular his Brody font, defined the graphic style of the 1980s, not only in this country but internationally. Brody was born in Southgate, North London and in 1976 went to study graphic design at the London College of Printing (LCP). The LCP then enjoyed a reputation as an institution dedicated to a disciplined, vocational training based on the prevailing Swiss Modernist orthodoxy of the 1970s. It was not an educational culture that Brody enjoyed, teaching – in his words – "the traditional type rule book by rote". By 1979, the year he graduated, the Punk revolution was in full swing and Brody gravitated towards the clubs and magazine scene of London.

In the early 1980s, if you wanted to know what was happening in terms of new style trends you simply read two magazines, *i-D*, designed by Terry Jones, and from 1981 *The Face*, which was originally designed by Brody. These two magazines were read by enthusiasts from Tokyo to New York and beyond. From the first early designs for *The Face*, Brody attracted a cult following. His ideas of page layout and type design seemed fresh, radical and innovative. He developed certain distinctive trademarks, using, for example, symbols and logo-type almost as road signs to guide the reader through the pages. Brody created a vocabulary for magazine design of the period using handwriting marks and type that ran sideways. This cover of *The Face* is the only issue that used only type and no cover photograph.

Uck N Pretty Typeface

DATE: 1992

DESIGNER: Rick Valicenti (born 1958)

Uck N Pretty is a decorative typeface designed for issue 4 of *Fuse* magazine in 1992 by Rick Valicenti. Valicenti has been described as a Deconstructionist. Educated at Bowling Green State University, New York, he graduated in painting in 1973 and then took a Masters course in photography at the University of Iowa in 1975. In 1988 he launched his company Thirst, or 3st, in Chicago, a group he describes as devoted to the creation of Art With Function. In the 1990s, Thirst has enjoyed a high profile in US graphic design.

Valicenti works with Ark Rattin, who graduated with a degree in visual communications from Northern Illinois University in 1988 and a Masters in photography in 1990. Their approach, using witty word constructions and layering text and imagery, has more humour and irony than that of most of their contemporaries. Clients include the Japanese cosmetic company Shiseido, the Museum of Science and Industry, Chicago, and the Lyric Opera, Chicago.

DATE: 1995

DESIGNER: Designers Republic, Sheffield, England

Designers Republic is a British graphic design practice based in the northern town of Sheffield and specializing in work for the music industry. It was established in 1986 by Ian Anderson (born 1961), who had had no formal training in graphic design, graduating in philosophy from Sheffield University in 1982. Anderson had worked in the music industry as a club promoter and DJ, and as a band manager, so the shift into designing album covers seemed a natural progression. The original team included Nick Philips, Helen Betnay, Dave Smith, Nick Bax, John Crossland and Bette Anderson and now consists of Michael Place (born 1967), Roger Coe (born 1969) and Vanessa Swetman (born 1965). All published work from the studio is, however, simply signed Designers Republic. Clients include Pop Will Eat Itself, Age Of Chance, Cabaret Voltaire, Guerrilla Records and Chakk. Their anarchic approach to practice and to imagery, which this offset lithograph illustrates, is reflected in their press release, which suggests the company's positioning: "Auto Martyrs on the Wheels of Steel City Say it Loud" or "Sanyo – Go! Dynamo Designers Republic – The Clash of the Bulletproof Icon-titans. The Designers Republic: a new and used taste of paradise."

Their work has been exhibited at the Boymans van Beuningen Museum in Rotterdam and the Victoria and Albert Museum in London. In spring 1993 the Mappin Art Gallery in Sheffield mounted a retrospective of their work called "Designers Republic: New and Used".

Sport 90 Exhibition Poster

DATE: 1990

DESIGNER: Malcolm Garrett
(born 1956)

In the 1980s Malcolm Garrett's name was increasingly linked with Peter Saville and Neville Brody as one of the three British designers who had done most to introduce new directions in graphics. An early computer enthusiast, Garrett became increasingly excited by challenges offered by interactive media and electronic publishing. Sport 90 was a turning point. To complete this exhibition project, which included catalogue, posters, captions and an interactive guide, Garrett introduced himself to new digital software: QuarkXpress for page layout, Adobe Illustrator to draw lettering and Apple's HyperCard to build the interactive exhibition guide. The poster's number type suggests a running track. The aim was to combine sport's recreational and more competitive, technological image.

Born in Northwich, Cheshire, Garrett studied typography and psychology at Reading University and graphic design at Manchester Polytechnic. He then formed the design group Assorted Images and was joined in 1983 by his partner Kasper de Graaf. In 1977 he worked on packaging and promotion for the Manchester Punk band Buzzcocks. Garrett's work includes graphic identity, exhibition and television design, and design for literature of all kinds, as well as respected music industry work for well-known artists. In 1997 he was appointed professor by the London Institute.

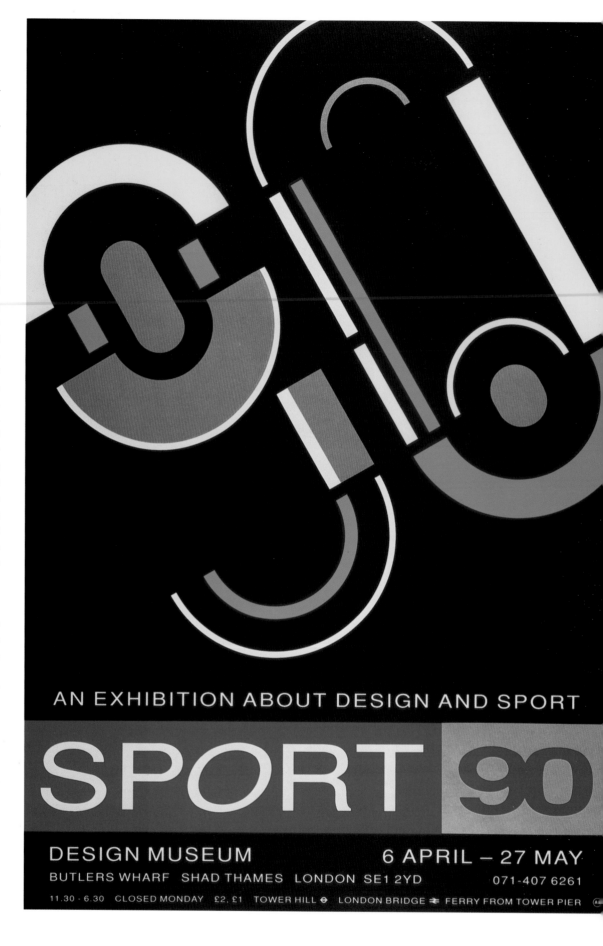

The American David Carson has become one of California's best-known graphic designers. His use of type and imagery and his work for *Ray Gun* magazine, which established his reputation, became highly influential in the 1990s. Carson is a self-taught graphic designer who originally studied sociology at university. Part of the Californian new wave, his work is based on magazine design, starting with *Beach Culture*, which has won over 100 awards worldwide for its innovative design. The American magazine *i-D* selected Carson as one of the US's most innovative designers and he has maintained this profile with his more recent work for *Ray Gun*. This magazine for the visual arts rapidly achieved cult status for young graphic designers all over the world.

Carson no longer designs the magazine and has established his own design studio. His clients include Nike, Pepsi, whose 1994 campaign used a Carson type design, MTV, David Byrne, Kentucky Fried Chicken and Sony. Carson also works with Tony Kaye Films as a commercial and video director. He lectures worldwide on typography.

DATE: 1990s

DESIGNER: David Carson (born 1958)

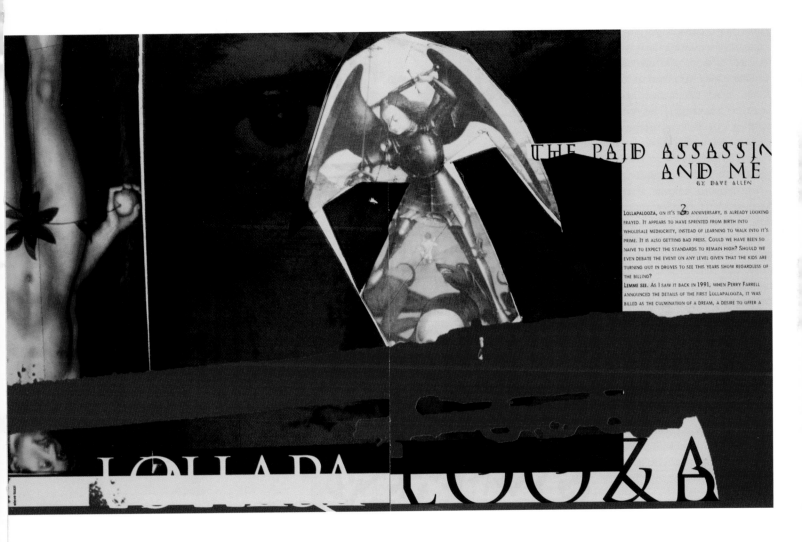

Radio Scotland Television Advert

DATE: 1993

DESIGNER: Tomato, United Kingdom

Tomato, founded in February 1991, are recognized as the innovators in their field. The group of ten designers form a loose but highly cooperative affiliation whose professed aim is to "blur" and transgress boundaries of response and method. Members have included John Warwicker (born 1955), Simon Taylor (born 1965), Dylan Kendle (born 1971), Dirk van Dooren (born 1959), Graham Wood (born 1965), Jason Kedgley (born 1969), Greg Rood, Karl Hyde, Steve Baker and Richard Smith. Tomato's iconoclastic approach polarizes opinion, yet continues to gain the respect and commercial commitment of leading clients such a Pepsi, MTV and Nike. Their insistence on extending their range references beyond those normally employed in typograph design means that their conceptual language is one that is n open to easy absorption by competitors.

For this project Tomato had to attract listeners to Radio Scotlan through a television advertisement. They ingeniously combine spoken words – snatches of the programmes – with moving typ as subtitles.

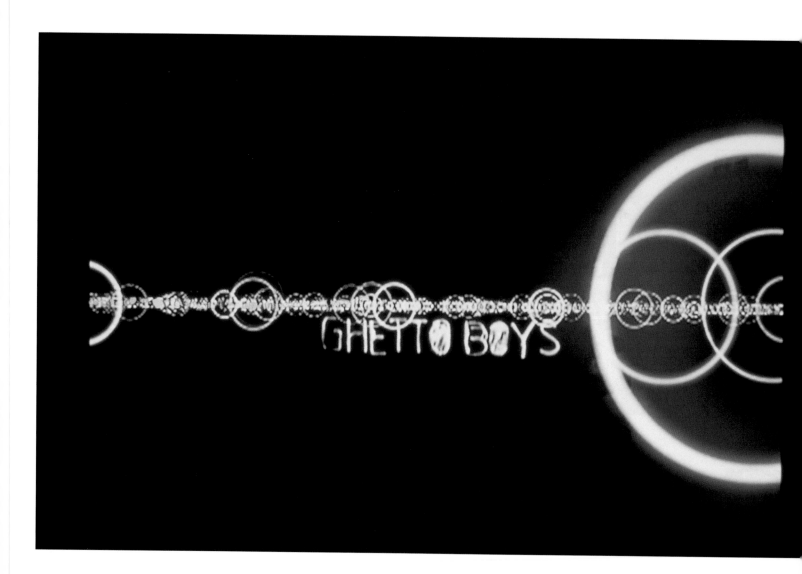

DATE: 1990s

CLIENT: Saatchi and Saatchi

**DESIGN AND
PRODUCTION:** AMX Studios

The Saatchi and Saatchi Award for Innovation in Communication website was launched in autumn 1997. A team made up from members of new media design consultancy AMX, which was headed by Malcom Garrett, and the senior creatives from the Saatchi and Saatchi London office worked to create a site which was both technically innovative and creatively stimulating, yet sacrificed nothing to global accessibility.

At the heart of the navigation system for the site was the image of a brain, representing as it does the origin of all human creative thought. By "scanning" the brain, visitors could access information about the award and how to enter it, or could read about the judges, who included the writer William Gibson, performance artist Laurie

Anderson, scientist James Burke and astronaut Buzz Aldrin.

Perhaps the most inspiring part of the site, however, was the section that aimed to excite the visitor with online demonstrations of a number of recent inventions, which themselves could have been contenders for the award had the scheme been running previously. Making judicious use of technology such as Real Video, Real Audio and Shockwave Flash, inventions such as the Micromap, the wind-up radio, and vision enhancing glasses were brought to life in a manner that was visually sympathetic to each invention. Visitors could also read or listen to interviews with the inventors where they explained how they developed their prototypes and elaborated on the philosophy of thinking behind them.

Sun Maid Raisins

DATE: this example 1990s

The Sun Maid brand of Californian raisins uses an obvious yet appealing visual pun, linking the appeal of a natural sun-made product with the eponymous and suitably wholesome sun maid. This traditional illustration style has remained popular throughout the twentieth century and is firmly linked in the mind of the consumer to the values of tradition and quality. The continued success of the brand can also be attributed to the adaptation of the packaging to changing consumer lifestyles. This can be see in the mini-packets introduced for children's lunchboxes and the adaptation of Marvin Gaye's hit song "I Heard It Through th Grapevine", complete with cartoon dancing raisins to tap in the juvenile market. Its distinctive packaging is difficult to cop and has also allowed it to compete well with the rise supermarket own-brand labels.

There is some packaging that has become so closely identified with a product that it has come to represent the food itself. Colman's Mustard is one such example. The Norwich firm of J. and J. Colman was founded in 1823. The use of mustard yellow, coupled with the distinctive bull's head trademark on the mustard's packaging, ensured that the brand became an immediate success.

Colman's understood a fundamental principle of pack design – the vital role that colour always plays in customer identification of the product. Using the vivid yellow meant that Colman's customers recognized the product before they even registered the bull's head design. The consistent use of the latter has meant that Colman's has maintained its place in the market over the years.

DATE: this example c.1905

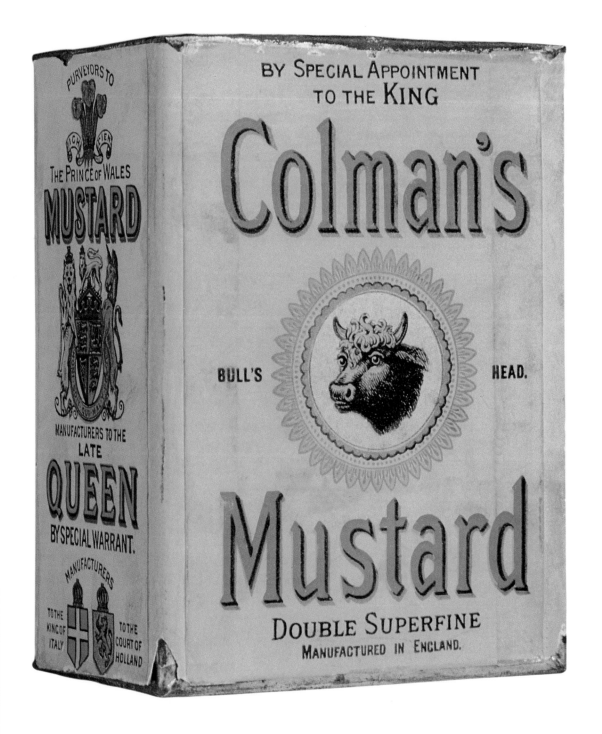

Ajax Scouring Powder

DATE: this example 1970

The design of the Ajax tube originated in the nineteenth century when several food manufacturers began experimenting with the idea of airtight tins, particularly for perishable products such as biscuits and tobacco. When this technical problem was solved not only could manufacturers increase sales in the domestic market, but expand their business overseas. Some early tins were cylindrical and opened with a revolving lid, which had an in-built cutter designed to pierce the airtight inner foil. In the postwar period the Ajax tube, effective in keeping the contents dry, represented the epitome of modern packaging technology and efficiency to the consumer.

Although the scouring powder itself has now been replaced in the home with creams and cleaning sprays, the spirally wound cardboard tube lives on. Its combination of rigidity, low weight and reduced shelfspace makes it particularly effective for the packaging of snacks.

o effort, no waste, no rags, no powder". It was with this snappy gan that the Brillo Manufacturing Company of New York roduced its new scouring pad in 1913. Brillo was intended as a aning agent for a complete range of difficult household jobs m pans to stove tops. The product used a steel wool pad

containing soap, which produced a lather and had a vigorous scouring effect. Originally Brillo was marketed in a green-coloured pack; it was changed to red in the 1950s. Along with the Campbells soup can, Brillo's transit shipping carton was reproduced by Andy Warhol as a famous icon of Pop Art in the 1960s.

DATE: this example 1950s

Campbell's Soup Can

DATE: this example 1930s

Joseph Campbell first began to can foods in 1869, in his factory in New Jersey. In 1898, he launched his canned soups with their characteristic red and white label. Campbell's were not the first company to use coloured labels on canned products; by the end of the nineteenth century they were used extensively in the USA. However, the design of the Campbell's can has endured, the soups were instantly popular and are still dominant in the American canned-soup market today. In fact they proved such an ubiquitous American product that in the 1960s Andy Warhol used the cans as a theme for a series of famous Pop Art paintings. Through his use of the product, packaging gained an important place in the history of twentieth-century art.

DATE: this example 1937

amed after the infamous eighteenth-century gentlemen's drinking lub, the Kit Kat chocolate wafer was originally produced by the uaker Rowntree family company in 1935, having initially been nown as Chocolate Crisp. Rowntrees had been established in the 880s and produced crystallized gums and boxed chocolates. The ame Kit Kat, although it had historical connotations, also evoked the Jazz Age. It has since become the most popular chocolate bar in the United Kingdom and is exported all over the world.

The success of Kit Kat was inextricably linked to the innovation of its packaging – the chocolate wrapped in foil with a separate paper wrapper cover – and the fact that this distinctive wrapping remained unchanged for more than sixty years.

Egg Box

DATE: this example 1997

The pressed paper-board egg box is one of the most familiar generic forms of packaging of the twentieth century. It provided a simple but effective solution to marketing a fragile food that could then be stored compactly in the home larder or fridge. Although plastic versions are now widely available, they do not provide the same quality of protection for the eggs, as they still need some extra protection from damage in the form of bubble wrap. The success of the cardboard version is proven by the fact that a successor to this low-tech product has not been found.

Milk Bottle

DATE: this example 1950s

Some British households still enjoy one of the world's most successful packaging recycling schemes – the doorstep delivery made possible by the milkman's round. First thing in the morning, milk is delivered in traditional glass bottles and the empty bottles are simply picked up, washed and reused. Originally the bottles were sealed with card, but these were replaced by aluminium tops during the 1930s. The bottle itself has evolved from a tall-necked vessel, shown here, to today's more compact and stocky bottle. Over the years the weight of the bottle has been steadily decreased without loss of strength, making a substantial saving in materials and energy.

Because the bottles are recycled and reused, the glass used to construct them must be capable of withstanding repeated use. The glass milk bottle is more than just packaging – it is linked to a valuable consumer service. Unfortunately the future of the traditional milk bottle is under threat, with increased use of supermarket plastic bottles and Tetra Paks.

Toilet Duck

DATE: this example 1985

Increasingly, manufacturers seek to differentiate their brands by commissioning unique outer package shapes that can be legally protected in the same way as brand names or logos. Plastic, in particular, lends itself to this aspect of the designer's task. Containers made from plastics are extremely light and can be moulded into any number of shapes, sizes and colours. This versatility has led to many innovative forms of packaging. One famous example is the angled toilet jet made famous by Toilet Duck. Manufactured by Johnson Wax, the bottle is shaped to fit the hand and the angle of the neck is moulded for ease of use. More recently, designers have devised a number of different finishes for plastics, to counter the challenge from the glass manufacturers that plastics packs can never project a high-quality image.

Jif Lemon

DATE: this example 1954

DESIGNER: W.A.G. Pugh

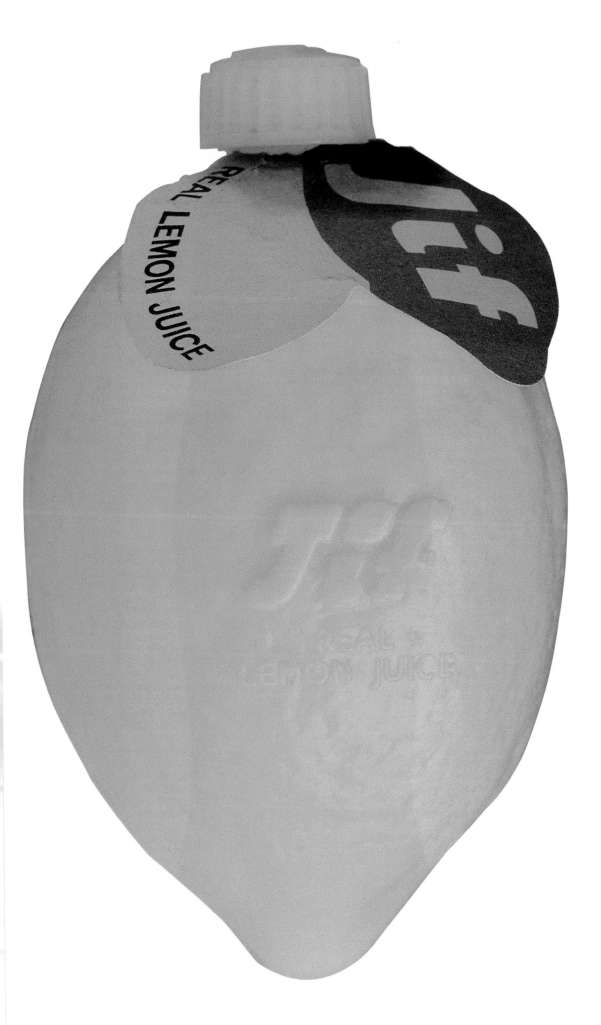

For many people, the Jif lemon is the definitive pack design: functional, easy to use and highly distinctive. In the United Kingdom no Shrovetide was complete without the distinctive "Jif" lemon to help complement the annual pancake and golden syrup treat. The lemon was designed by W.A.G. Pugh and launched by Colman's in 1956. The obvious shape and its "squeezability" ensured that the Jif lemon was a huge success. It was one of the earliest food applications for blow-moulded polythene, replacing glass bottles for lemon juice.

By the 1950s plastic packaging offered new possibilities for shape and innovation, such as the toothpaste tube. A particular favourite with the consumer is the squeezable plastic bottle, which is used for a wide variety of products. The Jif lemon design has remained virtually unchanged for over fifty years.

Budweiser Beer Bottle

DATE: this example 1990s

The biggest beer brand in the world owed its success in America to the early adoption of refrigeration. This allowed Budweiser to be sold far from the brewery site and establish itself as a national American brand. Budweiser itself was launched in 1876, named after the town of Budweis, in Bohemia, from which the brewery's founding Anheuser and Busch families originated. The red, white and blue label evolved throughout the twentieth century, althoug the elaborate Victorian style remains.

The "long-neck" bottle shown was originally used in th local Texas market but with the success of similarly shape Mexican import brands, the "long-neck" was increasingly use in other markets.

Lucky Strike Cigarette Pack

e majority of pack designs are not attributable to a single ividual. Lucky Strike cigarettes is one exception. Raymond ewy is an example of a famous designer working in the field of ck design. The brand was established in 1917 by the American bacco Company, founded by James Buchanan Duke. The red ll's-eye motif originated on the packaging of Lucky Strike

Tobacco, which was already an established brand. In 1942 Loewy was commissioned to change the pack, his brief being to increase sales. He did this by introducing a white background (it was previously green). This strengthened and defined the pack's distinctive logo. The word "cigarettes" was placed in an Art Deco-style typeface, running across the bottom.

DATE: this example 1942

DESIGNER: Raymond Loewy (1893–1986)

Planters
Peanut
Packaging

DATE: this example 1990s

Because they are so light and flexible, foils are an essential material in the modern packaging of food. Aluminium foils have been used as packaging since the 1960s, when sachets of powdered soup and coffee were first produced. In the 1980s the development of high quality printing effects on aluminium foil introduced new designs onto the supermarket shelves. These designs lent added value to several luxury snack items which appeared on the market as part of the increasing diversification of foods available. Planter's Peanuts were not marketed as any ordinary peanuts – they used special roasting techniques and seasonings to increase their flavour and consequently their price. Although aluminium was initially used to manufacture these packs, most metallic laminates now use a foil effect.

DATE: this example 1990s

The Tetra Pak was developed by a Swedish firm in the 1950s. Originally used to package milk, the revolutionary pack was constructed from a paper tube, which was pinched together at regular intervals to create a pyramid-shaped container. The user could then simply cut a corner off the package to pour the liquid.

During the 1950s and 1960s use of the Tetra Pak grew, eventually evolving into a more traditional rectangular shape. Through the 1970s, '80s and '90s it became a hugely popular vessel for milk, providing a serious challenge to the traditional glass milk bottle, and other liquids such as the fruit juice shown here. Tetra Paks are also used for liquid foods such as sauces and soups, and as refillable containers for products such as fabric conditioner for washing machines.

The Tropicana package utilizes the Tetra Pak to promote the contents by depicting their natural ingredients whole and in vibrant colours. Here the packaging offers a fresh, healthy and colourful image of a refreshing drink.

FedEx Mailing Packages

DATE: this example 1995

DESIGNER: Lindon Gray Leader (born 1949)

Federal Express is America's best-known courier company, dispatching mail order purchases and important documents all over the world. In Europe and the USA, where mail order is well established in all retail sectors, packaging for Federal Express is largely concerned with pro-tective boxes, envelopes and resealable plastic sacks. Their packaging has to project the image of efficiency, security and speed to the customer. The use of a distinctive logo is the key to success.

In 1994 Federal Express commissioned the San Francisco-base consultancy Landor Associates to redesign their packs. Lindon Gr Leader's new look for Federal Express's public image canonized phrase from everyday speech: he cut the company's name down FedEx, capitalizing on the international slang that had, through popul use, begun to replace the company's proper name. In contrast w the dramatically shaped and angled letters the company had use since the 1970s, the new logotype employs upright roman letters.

ounded in 1955 in the US, McDonald's is the international chain of st food hamburger restaurants. Their product is available in most odern cities – twenty-six million people eat in McDonald's every ay. McDonald's have manufactured food as an industrialized oduct. Their aim is standardization and quality, and the packaging integral to their success. The French fries pack is a typical example of the company approach. The cardboard scoop container is designed to appear overloaded but in fact it holds an exact quantity of fries. This prevents the server wasting or spilling any of the product, which would affect quantity control and profits. The bright red and yellow corporate colours reinforce McDonald's branding and add value to what would otherwise be a commodity product.

DATE: this example 1990s

Contraceptive Pill

DATE: this example 1960s

In the 1960s the first contraceptive pills appeared, but on prescription rather than on the open market. "The Pill" offered the first reliable method by which women could control their own fertility. In this context the contraceptive pill represented much more than a pharmaceutical advance – it triggered a social and economic revolution. Manufacturers designed their packs as accurate dispensers, not just containers, with pills to be taken in sequence using the new technology of blister packs. The technological aspect is softened, however, by the almost personal diary-like abbreviations. The cardboard pack shows further deference to the female market, using pink as a colour felt to appeal to women and to make the Pill more user-friendly.

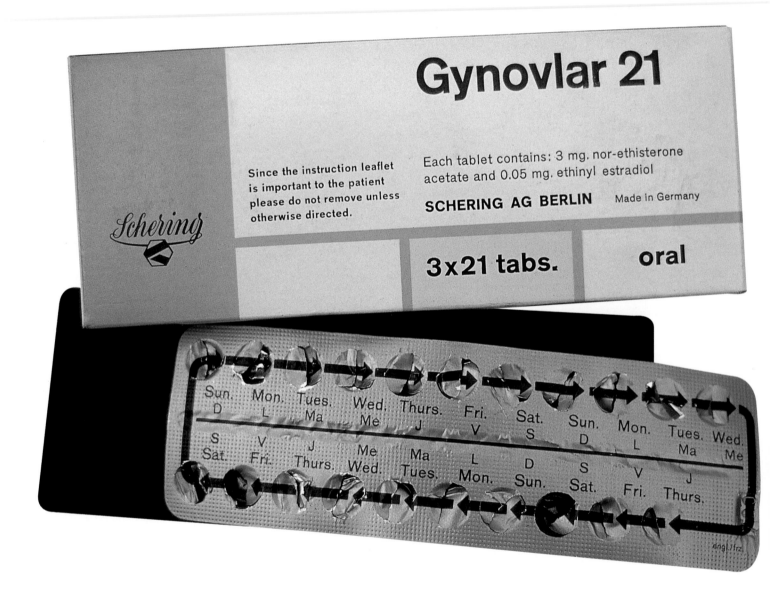

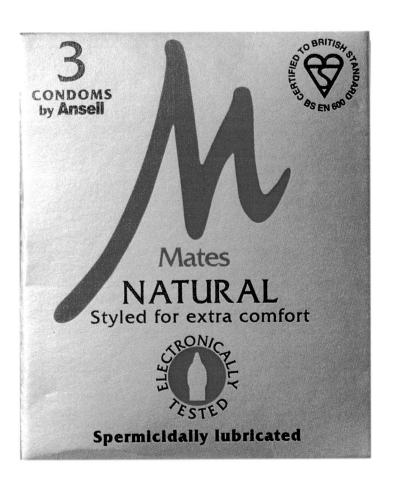

DATE: this example 1990s

Until the 1980s condoms were a contraceptive device you bought over the chemist's counter, at the barber shop or from a slot machine in the lavatory. This product placement made its purchase if not difficult, then certainly restrictive.

Ansell's Mates were one result of a general move to open up the accessibility of condoms in the light of international concern about Aids. The name and typeface move the product category away from that implied by serious medical names and seek to make Mates a kind of accessory for the young club-goer. This was one product emanating from Richard Branson's Virgin Group that did not carry the Virgin name.

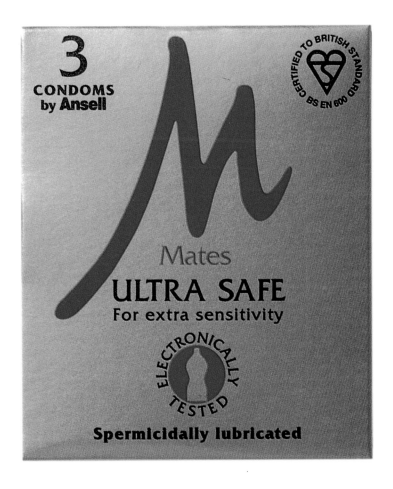

Ty Nant Water Bottle

DATE: this example 1989

In 1988 a new technique for colouring glass was introduced by a division of UK company British Foods under licence from an Australian research company, and in 1989 the stylish blue Ty Nant bottle appeared. Ty Nant was the first modern packaged brand to use a distinctive colour of glass to add value and distinction in the highly competitive table water market. The company is one of the few manufacturers in the world that have successfully trademarked a colour–shape combination. The rich blue colour is similar to that of the "Bristol" blue glass introduced in the seventeenth century. Intended as a designer accessory, to be placed alongside the wine bottle in homes and restaurants, the Ty Nant bottle, with its extremely sensuous shape based on burgundy and champagne bottles, looked expensive and exclusive.

The distinctive style and strength of colour enables the consumer to immediately identify a product that would otherwise be inseparable from its contemporaries. In 1989 the bottle won the British Glass Award for Design Excellence. It has been marketed internationally and has proved very popular in the Arab States as well as Italy and Japan.

Sapporo Beer Can

DATE: this example 1988

Sapporo was launched in 1876, and is the oldest surviving Japanese beer on the market. The Sapporo beer can was launched in the UK in 1988 and quickly became the choice of the design-conscious consumer. The can was distinctive in three ways. First, it reflected the minimalist aesthetics of Japanese culture to great effect with its use of black graphics and a tiny red star printed directly onto the natural silver coloured can. Second, the can had a waisted shape, a development that moved it away from a simple functional container towards a shape that evoked a more elegant drinking vessel. Finally, to complete the vessel effect, the can was given a specially constructed lid which could be entirely removed to allow the drinker to use it as if it were a glass.

Body Shop Cosmetics

DATE: this example 1990s

"No glossy advertising, no wild promises, no products tested on animals, only minimal packaging and products which have minimal impact on the environment." This quote, taken from the Body Shop's official website, perfectly encapsulates the philosophy of the company. The Body Shop was founded in 1976 by Anita Roddick. Originally just one small retail outlet in Brighton, it is now an internationally successful company.

With environmental concerns now at the forefront of public concern, emphasis has been placed on excessive consumption, which relates directly to packaging and its possible waste of natural resources. The Body Shop, with its green image, has tapped in to the public conscience, with its minimal packaging – no excess packaging is used – and policy of recycling and refilling. The distinctive labels are generally green and white, colours that themselves evoke the company's ecological and environmental standpoint.

Daz Detergent Pouch

DATE: this example 1990s

Some of the more important changes in packaging include the introduction of refill systems, and with concerns about the wastage of natural resources high on political and social agendas these developments have the important effect of reducing the amount of materials used. Refill is nothing new in itself. In the United Kingdom many still enjoy the survival of doorstep delivery of milk and in France some wines are sold in refillable bottles. A new idea is the availability of refilling at home. This can be seen in the reduction of packaging sizes for detergents such as Daz, allowing them to be used in concentrated form. In addition shops now sell these products in two different packages: a strong metal or cardboard box and in lightweight pouches, which typically save seventy per cent of the material. Customers first buy the stronger containers, then the pouches as refills. The packaging of liquid detergent in thin pouches that can easily be taken home is now a popular trend. Although detergent is the best example such packaging has also been introduced for shampoo, while Germany has seen experiments in pouch packaging for food products such as jam.

Riverford Organic Vegetable Box

DATE: 1999 (box); 2004 (illustrations)

DESIGNER: illustrations by Julie Depledge

Growing consumer awareness of the benefits of eating organically grown food has led to the growth of local organic vegetable box delivery schemes which allow the customer to retain a direct relationship with the grower. Riverford Organic Vegetables is a British business founded by Guy Watson who converted three acres of farmland to organic status in 1987 and began by delivering vegetables to local farm shops and then to customers' homes.

The business has expanded through franchising, maintaining its local delivery ideal but operating on a national level. Vegetables are delivered to the client's front door in reuseable cardboard boxes. The design brief for the original box was to provide a collapsible, returnable and recyclable box which met the hygiene requirements of the food industry. It also needed to be impervious to moisture from the vegetables and able to withstand shipping through the transport system to the end customer.

The boxes are printed in the flat and converted through a box gluer/folder, in the same way as the corrugated fruit boxes widely used in the industry. The Riverford boxes, however, use solid board that is fully recoverable and recyclable once the box is unfit for further use. The vegetables are not over-packaged with unnecessary layers of packaging.

The illustrations on the boxes are by Julie Depledge of DeMo Communication, a local design practice based near Riverford in Devon. The design of the Riverford brand identity is consistent throughout its packaging and website and emphasizes its connection with the countryside. It retains a simplicity that is coherent with the brand, which has expanded to include farm shops and dairy and meat box deliveries in addition to the vegetable box.

I'm Not a Plastic Bag

throughout the first years of this century, public awareness of environmental concerns such as organic farming, recycling and fair trade was increasing. Debate about issues such as minimising one's carbon footprint and the damaging effects of plastic bags on the environment were part of this new awareness. The "I'm Not a Plastic Bag" campaign came from a global social change movement called "We Are What We Do We" which has the philosophy that "lots of small actions x lots of people = big change." The organisation worked with Tim Ashton, creative director of Antidote to publish a best-selling book, *Change the World for a Fiver*. It was Ashton's idea to create a piece of merchandise inspired by the book's first recommended direct action to readers: decline plastic bags whenever possible. He wrote the copy line, designed the typography and persuaded Anya Hindmarch to design and source a simple alternative to the plastic shopping bag that could sell for just £5.

It proved to be a phenomenal success: 30,000 bags were made available in the UK, North America and the Far East. In the UK the bags sold out in 90 minutes. In Japan two stores refused to stock the bag after twenty people were hospitalized due to a stampede when their doors opened. As Hindmarch's own-brand bags usually sell for several hundred pounds and the bag was available in limited numbers, queues were seen outside all outlets from the early hours of the morning, emphasizing the great contradiction between the issues the project was trying to raise and the consumerism with which our society is saturated.

DATE: 2007

DESIGNER: Anya Hindmarch (born 1963)

MATERIAL: Cotton

Salon des Cent Exhibition Poster

DATE: 1896

DESIGNER: Alphonse Mucha
(1860–1939)

Europe at the turn of the century saw the birth of Art Nouveau. Mucha was the first master of erotic advertising. His skill as an artist attracted many leading companies who paid him royally to design posters advertising products as diverse as champagne and bicycles. In most of his posters the products advertised are upstaged by Mucha's mysterious and beautiful women, scantily clad in veils. Art Nouveau was an inevitable reaction against the repressive attitude to sexuality that typified life in the nineteenth century. In the world of art and design these defining concerns surfaced not only in the posters of Alphonse Mucha but those of Toulouse Lautrec and Aubrey Beardsley. They produced unique artistic forms that contained exaggerated forms and naturalistic shapes that almost invariably focused on the female body and cast the woman in the role of the femme fatale.

DATE: 1910

DESIGNER: Peter Behrens
(1868–1941)

Although Peter Behrens began his career working influenced by the new *Jugendstil* movement, a restrained form of Art Nouveau, he is important in the history of advertising because he was one of the first poster designers to articulate a visual language for the new spirit of the twentieth century. When in 1907 he was invited by Emil Rathennau, director of the *Allgemeine Elektricitäts-Gesellschaft* (AEG), to become its artistic director he developed the first concept of company corporate identity. AEG occupied a considerable power in German industry and its output covered generators, electrical cable, light bulbs and electrical appliances not only for the domestic but the world market. From 1907 until 1914 Behrens was responsible for all aspects of the company's output from architecture to posters and products and he used his position to establish AEG as a model for the new German design. His influence was manifold. In 1907 he was a founder member of the Deutsche Werkbund, he designed typefaces and was responsible for one of Germany's earliest Modernist building the AEG's steel, glass and concrete turbine factory of 1909. In his position as art director he employed some of Europe's brightest young talents, including Le Corbusier, Mies van der Rohe and Walter Gropius.

Nord Express

DATE: 1927

DESIGNER: A.M. Cassandre
(1901–68)

A.M. Cassandre is one of the best-known poster artists and type designers of the twentieth century. From the late 1920s to the early 1930s he produced a series of memorable advertisements whose influence continues to this day. Cassandre's achievement was to bring the creative experiments of avant-garde movements such as Cubism into the mainstream world of advertising. His technique employed a brilliant use of colour, powerful geometric forms and a brilliant integration of the company name with the image. Posters advertising trains like the classic Etoile du Nord and ships like the Normandie have now become some of the best-known advertisements in the world. The advertising agency that produced this work, and of which Cassandre was a founding partner, was the Alliance Graphique in Paris. They produced some of the most memorable poster images of the century and established a French style that evoked stylish, urban Parisian life. At the same time Cassandre also designed typefaces for the old-established Paris-based type supplier Deberny and Peignot. Cassandre typefaces balanced Modernism with a fresh approach to letterforms and this was to become a deeply influential tradition. He restricted letterforms on his posters to capitals, believing that they enhanced the effect of the poster and allowed the type to be used on a large scale without affecting legibility.

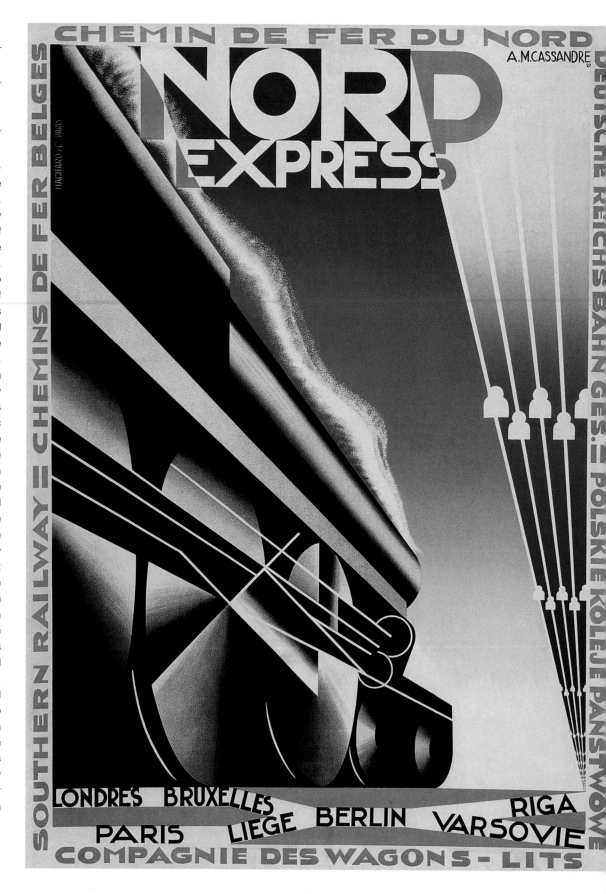

LONDON TRANSPORT-

London Transport Poster

DATE: 1932

DESIGNER: Man Ray (1870–1976)

CLIENT: London Transport, London, England

Man Ray studied art in New York and participated in the city's famous Armoury Show of 1913, which introduced to America to the new spirit of European Modernism. Shortly after this date he became the friend and collaborator of the artist Marcel Duchamp and worked across many different media. Perhaps Man Ray's most original contribution was to photography, with his invention of images made directly onto film, which he called Rayographs. In the 1930s his work as a commercial photographer for a number of important fashion magazines disseminated his unique style to a wider audience and in 1939 he was invited to design a poster for London Transport. Man Ray actually produced two posters, one with the text, LT, the other with the copy "Keeps London Going", which were intended to be seen as a pair. Here the famous London Transport logo is transformed into a 3-D planet, which orbits around Saturn. London Transport therefore enters the firmament of the stars with its connections of speed, distance and the future. In this way Man Ray introduced to the British public the ideas of the Surrealist movement. The Surrealists experimented with ways of delving into hidden desires and memories through chance operations and automatic writing. The Man Ray poster is an example of the way the fine art imagery of Surrealism in the 1930s filtered through to the world of advertising and graphic design.

London
Transport
Poster

DATE: 1949

DESIGNER: Edward McKnight Kauffer (1890–1954)

CLIENT: London Transport, London, England)

Born and trained as a painter in America, McKnight Kauffer became a leading figure in British advertising when he moved to London at the age of twenty-five, although he continued to paint for the rest of his life. From 1913, as a young man, he had seen at first hand the work of the leading avant-garde movements including Vorticism, Futurism and Cubism. His talent was to simplify the elements he recognized in this new art to produce a original advertising style that was effective, popular and successful. His first job was designing posters for London Transport whose publicity manager, the legendary Frank Pick, was scouting for young talent to create a modern image for what was to become the world's most extensive city transport system. For over twenty years, until the outbreak of World War Two, when he emigrated to America with his wife, the well-known Modernist designer of carpets and textiles, Marion Dorn, McKnight Kauffer was considered to be London Transport's leading poster designer and completed over one hundred advertisements.

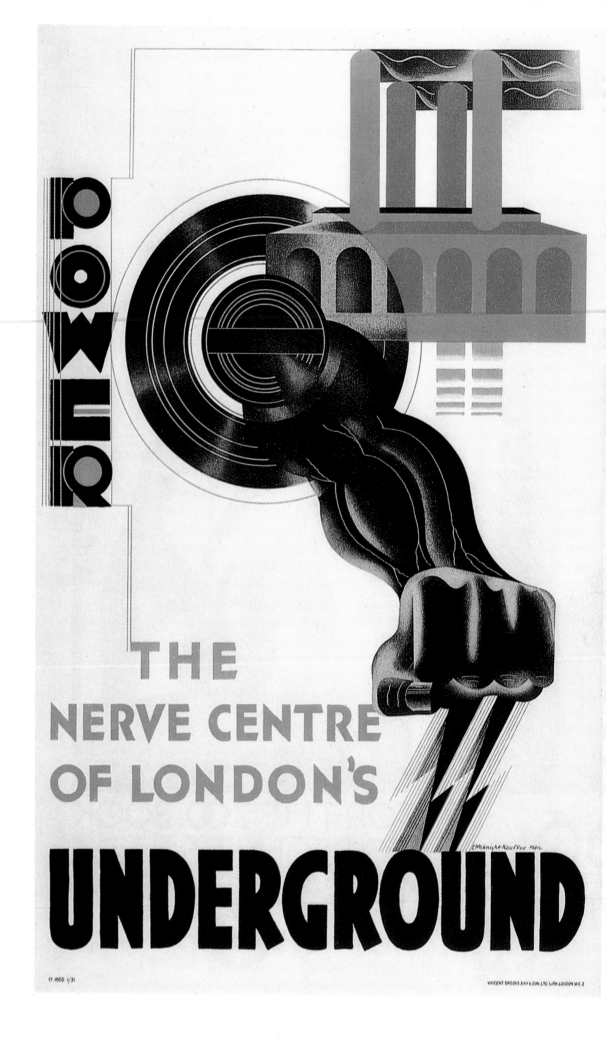

hell Mex Limited was the name under which the international hell Group ran its British marketing operation and in 1932 they ppointed a new Publicity Director, J.L. Beddington. His insight rned the British Shell advertisements of the 1930s into one of ie classic campaigns of the twentieth century. Shell used the dvertisements on the sides of their lorries and in the press. hey were intended to appear in series, and to change every few reeks with the aim of striking a blow against the use of ugly oardings that many felt were becoming a blight in the ountryside. It was Beddington who decided to use a range of eading Modernist painters to provide strikingly original images or their product and the posters became works of art in their

right. The idea of using leading artists to create advertising images was not new, there is a long tradition of such examples going back to the famous "Bubbles" painting by John Millais for Pears Soap. What made the Shell campaign so interesting, however, was that it was a clearly directed series that attracted attention for the product via its association with the new, and then daring, art of painters including McKnight Kauffer, Barnett Freedman and Graham Sutherland, who created this poster depicting the Great Globe at Swanage. The original paintings and artwork were hung throughout Shell Mex House and gathered together for special exhibitions including one at the London's National Gallery.

DATE: 1932

DESIGNER: Graham Sutherland (1903–80)

CLIENT: Shell Mex Limited, London, England

War Poster

DATE: 1940

CLIENT: HMSO, England

PRINTER: J. Weiner Ltd,
London, England

In 1939 World War Two brought the careers of most designers to a close. The majority were called up for active duty, but the war effort did require certain design specialists and nowhere was this more urgently needed than in the field of propaganda. The British Ministry of Information needed the talents of graphic designers to spread public information, to increase morale and to use every weapon they could in the fight against the Nazis. A team of the best designers was therefore recruited to work for the Ministry, and subject to strict censorship, were allowed to develop the most effective design solutions to produce wartime propaganda. For many this meant going back to the most influential themes of the 1930s, including the impact of Surrealism, the introduction of photomontage and the bold use of type to create the strong visual images needed to bring home vital messages for the war effort.

The message in this poster was simple: save resources and grow your own food. "Dig For Victory" employed these avant-garde experiments to great effect, the bright orange colour, the scale and the bold use of large type enhance the dramatic image of the digging foot and spade.

DATE: 1934

DESIGNER: Piet Zwart (1885–1977)

During the twentieth century The Netherlands has always enjoyed a rich tradition of innovation in graphic and type design. From the 1920s Piet Zwart was the designer whose work helped to establish a particularly creative and fresh flavour to Dutch Modernist advertising. After World War One, Zwart became closely involved with the radical Dutch De Stijl movement working for one of its leading architects, Jan Wils. Through him Zwart met an important client, N.V. Nederlandsche Kabelfabriek, for whom he began designing posters. Zwart overturned the conventions of advertising by introducing the techniques of photomontage and random lettering.

This work owes a debt to the experiments of Russian Constructivists whose work was published in the *De Stijl* magazine of the time. Although Zwart used the De Stijl preference for primary colours in his work his approach was freer and more exuberant than the formalist tradition of Dutch graphic design. He introduced the ideas of the Dada group and their exploitation of elements of humour and irony. The appeal and originality of Zwart's work attracted the attention of the Dutch Post Office (PTT) and from 1929 he began a long collaboration with them, working on the design of stamps and other material.

Air France

DATE: c.1965

DESIGNER: Roger Excoffon (1910–83)

Roger Excoffon is not well known outside his own country, but his work, more than any other graphic designer's, came to define a sense of postwar French style shown here in this powerful poster for Air France. Best known as the designer of freeform typefaces in the 1950s, in the 1960s he moved away from the flamboyance of his earlier work with the design for the typeface Antique Olive, now called Nord. It was a move he acknowledged as a commercial decision, prompted by the demand from French printers for a clean 1960s feel, in line with the success of the Helvetica and Univers sans serif faces.

Antique Olive started life in the late 1950s as a prototype upper case face for the Air France logo. With his assistant Gerard Blanchard, Excoffon embarked on a serious research programme reading all the literature and research they could find on legibility and the psychology and impact of reading. They came to the conclusion that the upper half of the letters are the most important in word recognition and Excoffon therefore emphasized that aspect of the new face's character. Antique Olive was hugely popular and is largely credited with revitalizing the sans serif letter forms. Key advertising projects included work for Bally shoes, French Railways and Christian Dior perfume. Typical hallmarks of the Excoffon style included the use of off-register or double printing, and interesting use of colour.

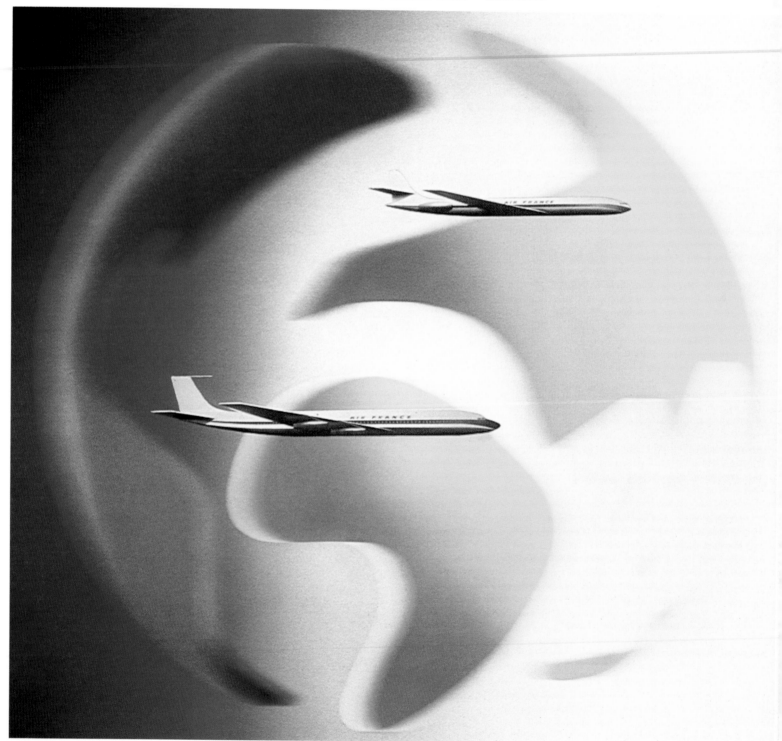

Olivetti

DATE: 1949

DESIGNER: Giovanni Pintori
(born 1912)

Olivetti have played a key role in the development of twentieth-century Italian design. This family firm applied key lessons learnt from America about production methods and marketing techniques and more importantly, the need for good design. Adriano Olivetti, the company founder's son employed Pintori along with another leading Italian designer, Marcello Nizzoli, the former given responsibility for advertising and graphics, the latter for industrial design. In the postwar period Olivetti's ambitions were to place the company at the leading edge of new technology and Pintori's brief was to reinforce this message via its advertisements. In 1947 he was responsible for the redesign of the company's logo and went onto develop a series of major advertising campaigns of which this poster was one of the most significant. In the 1940s Olivetti was justifiably proud of its technological achievement in the field of calculating machines most notably Nizzoli's Divisumma 14 adding machine. It was the spirit of such machines that Pintori's type design evoked with his use of chaotic, randomly sized and spaced numbers in bright colours. This image owes a debt to the Italian tradition of Futurist graphics but here given a contemporary modern feel with Pintori's Olivetti logo placed prominently in the centre.

Benson and Hedges

DATE: 1978

DESIGNER: CDP, London, England

In the late 1970s the Hayward Gallery in London put on an important exhibition exploring Surrealism. The exhibition revived interest in the language of Surrealism and the way in which imagery could delve into hidden desires and memories through chance operations, automatic writing and collaborative drawings. The Surrealists believed that the removal of objects from their context and the juxtaposition of unassociated objects would produce a momentary shock in the viewer that would facilitate the release of subconscious thoughts. The potential to exploit these elements for advertising was recognized early on and during the 1930s these images filtered through to the wider world of film design, fashion and furniture as well as advertising and graphic design. Benson and Hedges were one of the first companies to exploit Surrealism for another agenda. In the 1970s the message that smoking kills began to reach a wider audience and governments began to restrict the kind of advertising manufacturers had used to promote their product in the past. No longer could smoking be shown as attractive to young people, as enjoyable and safe. Surrealism provided a visual medium to sell cigarettes which still continues to this day in campaigns for the Silk Cut and Marlboro brands. By using the Surrealist device of the unexpected, the consumer is drawn to the package and identity of the product but no claims are made, merely the association of the pack with wit, creativity and humour which the consumer has to learn to identify.

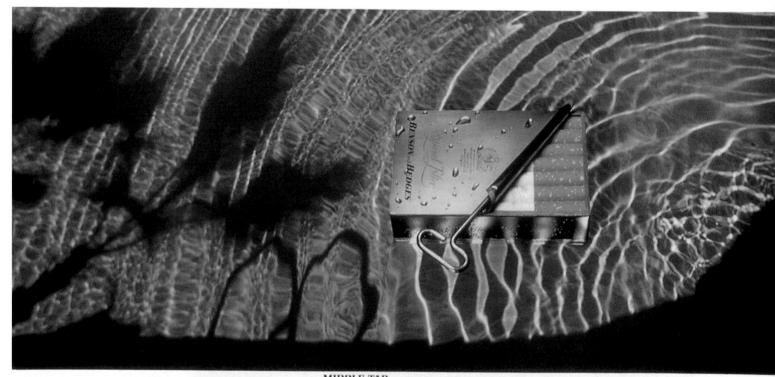

MIDDLE TAR As defined by H.M. Government
H.M. Government Health Departments' WARNING: CIGARETTES CAN SERIOUSLY DAMAGE YOUR HEALTH

Birth Control

DATE: 1970

DESIGNER: Saatchi and Saatchi, London, England

CLIENT: Health Education Council, England

This public health campaign also defined the trademarks of the new British advertising industry of the 1960s and 1970s. British agencies were now known for their use of humour, bold imagery and strong copy, taking on New York as the centre for creative advertising. For the generation born in the 1950s this poster promoting the use of contraception to prevent unwanted pregnancies remains an enduring image. The simple idea of faking an image of a male pregnancy made a simple and direct point that the responsibilities of a sexual relationship involved two people. By suggesting that men could get pregnant the campaign challenged the then widely held belief that unwanted babies were the problem and responsibility of the woman alone. In 1970 by emphasizing this obvious point the campaign touched upon the newly emerging ideas of the women's movement but gained widespread sympathy with its use of humour and Surrealist imagery.

Would you be more careful if it was you that got pregnant?

Anyone married or single can get advice on contraception from the Family Planning Association
Margaret Pyke House, 27-35 Mortimer Street, London W1 N 8BQ. Tel. 01-636 9135.

The Health Education Council

Launderette

DATE: 1985

DESIGNER: Bartle Bogle
Hegarty, London, England

CLIENT: Levi Strauss, USA

In the 1980s the world-famous Levi's Jeans company faced a financial crisis. Levi's had diversified into the wider clothing market, producing suits and accessories, but in doing so had lost its unique product focus. In the decade of the designer 1980s it looked to target its classic original denim jeans, the Levi's 501, and it needed a powerful advertising campaign to put across the message. When John Hegarty of Bartle Bogle Hegarty, one of London's best-known advertising agencies, created this sexy nostalgic theme an advertising legend was born.

Using a brilliant mix of the allure of the model Nick Kamen references to 1950s youth culture and a touch of humour, th campaign was an instant success. Sales of Levi's 501s soare and the jeans became one of the most important fashio accessories of the decade. Bartle, Bogle and Hegarty followe this first advertisement with a series of eye-catching ads usually based on a classic films and movie genres, which no only established a standard for Levi's but for the rest of th advertising industry.

These black and white advertisements created a sensation when they first appeared in 1991. The blatant sensual sell of these images was not unique, but the combination of product and association was. Ice cream was traditionally a seasonal market dominated in Britain by companies such as Walls and Lyons Maid. Campaigns were usually targeted at housewives and children or, exceptionally, a product aimed for the dinner party. Here the American company Häagen-Dazs targeted young affluent couples, using ice cream as a luxury up-market experience. The vogue for black and white erotic imagery originally came from the work of pioneer New York photographers including Herb Ritts and Robert Mapplethorpe and here, in an image taken by Jean Loup Sieff the same explicit sensual allure is used to sell a product previously marketed as an ordinary commodity for the family.

DATE: 1991

DESIGNER: Bartle Bogle Hegarty, London, England

CLIENT: Häagen-Dazs, USA

Wolford Tights

DATE: 1994

DESIGNER: Helmut Newton
(born 1920)

In the 1970s Newton dominated the world of fashion photography with his images for French *Vogue* magazine, which were more often to do with the naked woman than the clothes they wore. He played up to decades of fashionable obsessions with themes of cross gender and chic gay and transvestite culture seen in the imagery of pop via David Bowie and Roxy Music. Newton's style became enormously influential and set the scene in the 1980s for the work of equally controversial photographs from Bruce Weber and Herb Ritts.

Helmut Newton was commissioned to take a series of startling black and white photographs to market Wolford tights. In his commission for Wolford, Newton used blatant sado-masochistic imagery, here in the use of leather ankle straps, black gloves, metal handcuffs and the leather riding crop. Wolford is a well-known hosiery company which produces top of the range tights and stockings much favoured by the fashion industry. In the 1980s it pioneered dense black tights using Lycra. Their products are expensive quality items aimed at a sophisticated market which Wolford felt could appreciate such controversial imagery.

What makes these images so extraordinary is the way the campaign played on references to lesbianism and sexual violence and combined them in such a blatant way to sell tights to women. Although tights and stockings both have a deeply fetishistic appeal, nonetheless this is a fascinating reflection of cultural values in the 1990s.

Tiger Savage is exceptional in the advertising world as a successful female art director. Her distinctive approach was expressed in a series of press advertisements and posters for Nike, a campaign that won several awards for its fresh and arresting use of images. The market for trainers is a huge and intensely competitive one which relies on advertising to create the right image. Savage felt that press advertisements and posters needed to be concise and to-the-point and that type and copy can often obscure the important selling message. If the image is strong enough, she argued, why detract from it?

The Nike campaign in the United Kingdom proved to be something of an advertising milestone, as it was the first campaign to use advertisements with no copy. Instead it built its reputation on the dynamic interplay between image and headline. The first advertisement featured tennis champion Pete Sampras serving not a tennis ball but a grenade. This was followed soon after by a road symbol placed over a group of marathon runners. Tiger Savage's ability to achieve a strong, personal visual style for this client won her the award for best newcomer from the Creative Circle in 1984.

DATE: 1996

DESIGNERS: Simons, Palmer Denton, Clemmow and Johnston, London, England

CLIENT: Nike

National Gallery Grand Tour

DATE: 2007

DESIGNER: The Partners

In 2007 a very interesting collaborative project called The Grand Tour brought together three high profile organizations. The UK's National Gallery, founded in 1823, is one of the world's best known collections of paintings. Hewlett Packard (HP) is a leading global IT company best known for computing and printing and The Partners is an award winning UK brand and design consultancy with an international portfolio of high profile clients. The project was an innovative installation of 30 full-size recreations of old masterpieces from the National Gallery's collection, ranging from Caravaggio to Constable, which were placed in unexpected locations across a range of London's diverse city streets. The idea was to enable wider access and enjoyment of paintings and to encourage people to come and see for themselves the originals which were only a few minutes walk away and free to all visitors. The curatorial concept for the project was a twelve-week mini-tour with its own website; each of the chosen paintings had a replica frame and a formal museum caption exactly as displayed in the gallery, which also included a telephone number to access a recorded audio guide about the painting and the artist. HP demonstrated leading-edge printing capabilities for amazingly accurate reproductions. The project was an advertisement for the National Gallery to raise its profile and visitor numbers but its success was in bringing art to a local community and building new audiences.

Stefan Sagmeister is the illustrator and designer of this iconic poster celebrating the national biennial conference of the American Institute of Graphic Arts (AIGA), which was founded in 1914 to support ideas around design research practice. AIGA is one of the world's oldest and largest professional design bodies and a poster for such a discerning community was a challenge that Sagmeister was more than interested in taking on. AIGA posters are part of a wide portfolio of commercial clients and this headless chicken running across the landscape is for the 1997 New Orleans conference. Known for sensational, even slightly sinister imagery, the poster led to one of Sagmeister's most famous performance pieces, AIGA Detroit. For this work text was originally marked out with a knife onto his torso by an assistant and then photographed for a piece now in the permanent collection of MOMA. Using his own body in this way, to create the type, is typical of his original creative vision. Sagmeister's conceptual approach connects his works with those of contemporary art, even Punk culture but they are, as here for AIGA, convincing and relevant design solutions for the client brief. Sagmeister was born in Austria and originally studied engineering but decided to switch to graphic design, making his name with a series of theatre posters which owed a debt to the British Punk graphic revolution of the late 1970s. A Fulbright scholarship took him to New York where he remains one of the US's most original creative voices, with a reputation for delivering original visual solutions. One strong element in his work is designs for contemporary music, first with album then CD covers, which has won him four Grammy nominations. He enjoys a close working relationship with Lou Reed and David Byrne, musicians and writers who share his sense of otherness and surreal humour.

DATE: 1997

DESIGNER: Stefan Sagmeister

Candlestick Telephone GPO 150

DATE: 1924

MATERIAL: Bakelite

MANUFACTURER: General Post Office, London, England

The candlestick telephone was one of the most common designs in the early decades of the twentieth century and became the international standard table telephone. Although the version shown here is British, it was virtually indistinguishable from its American counterpart. One development that had a lasting impact on telephone design was the evolution of plastics. Telephone manufacturers looked for a material from which telephone components could be made easily and cheaply. In the 1920s improvement in chemical engineering and moulding techniques made Bakelite, from which the 150 is made. The major disadvantage of the candlestick was the fact that the mouthpiece was fixed onto the base, forcing the user either to crouch near to the telephone or hold both parts, one in each hand. Improvements in transmitter design, through electronic amplification, did not come until the late 1920s after research by engineers commissioned by the American Bell Company. Initially calls could only be made through the operator but the introduction of the dial, for which space was made on the base, enabled the caller to make connections automatically. The shape proved extremely popular and this standard table telephone lasted for many years. It is still marketed as a reproduction piece.

Ericofon

The Ericofon was conceived as a lightweight and compact version of the standard two-piece telephone. Its sculptural form was startlingly original, its shape incorporating the ear piece, speaker and dial into a single unit. This was made possible by the new technology of miniaturization. Over the course of the following fourteen years the Ericofon developed through new versions that saw successive improvements in its engineering and its form. The gradual evolution of the product was led by the Blomberg team of designers over a fifteen-year period. Its commercial success was established in 1954 when the Ericofon became available in a series of bright colours. Ericsson was the first company to manufacture telephones in Sweden and it remains the largest.

DATE: 1949

DESIGNERS: Hugo Blomberg (born 1897), Ralph Lysell (born 1907) and Gösta Thames (born 1916)

MATERIAL: plastic and rubber

MANUFACTURER: L. M. Ericsson, Sweden

Nokia 9000 Communicator

DATE: 1996

DESIGNER: Nokia in-house design team

MATERIAL: plastic

MANUFACTURER: Nokia Corporation, Finland

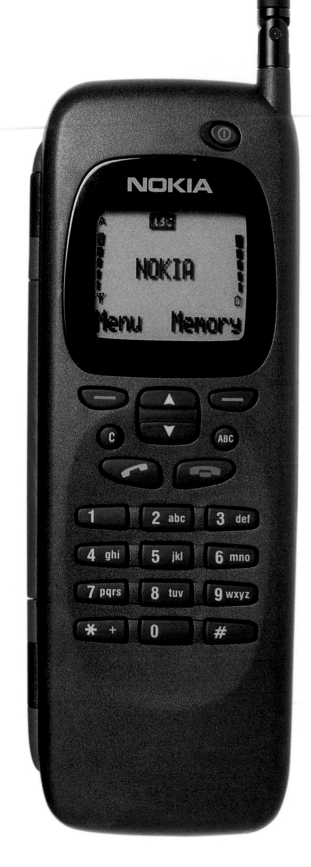

In the 1990s, the Finnish Nokia company developed a range of personal telephone communications, which represented an important step towards miniaturization. The Nokia 9000 Communicator allowed the user to carry around a whole series of facilities. It combined digital voice, data services and personal organizer functions into a pocket-sized and easy-to-use unit. The Communicator featured an impressive list of applications, including telephone, fax, e-mail, Internet browser, personal organizer, messaging terminal, calendar and calculator. It had an infra-red PC and printer connection and an eight-megabyte memory.

Proficia Internet Telephone Handset

DATE: 1997

DESIGNER: Geoff Hollington, Richard Arnott and Liz Ciokajlo

MATERIAL: injection-moulded ABS plastic

MANUFACTURER: Camelot Corporation, USA

Established in 1980, Hollington is a well-known British design consultancy with an international reputation for innovative products, ranging from furniture to pens and interactive design. Hollington was commissioned by a Dallas-based company, Camelot, specialists in Internet-related software, whose Digiphone Internet telephone package was a market-leader. To complement the Digiphone, Camelot wanted to develop a new class of telephone product. The Proficia was essentially a computer phone for making low-cost calls via the Internet; it was placed on the desktop along with the keyboard and mouse. The visual character of the handset has the quality of a small animal, with the back-wire resembling a tail; the ergonomic balance requires the handset to be stable and comfortable to use wherever it is placed.

Ekco AD 65 Radio

DATE: 1934

DESIGNER: Wells Coates
(1895–1958)

MATERIALS: moulded brown
phenolic Bakelite and chromium

MANUFACTURER: E.K. Cole
Ltd, UK

Wells Coates was a Canadian-trained architect who came to London in the early 1920s and became one of the pioneers of British Modernism. He designed important buildings in the new architectural style and it was inevitable that he would attract the attention of manufacturers like E.K.Cole, who wanted to modernize their industry. Wells' Wireless Receiving Set AD 65 was the result of a design competition held in 1932 by Eric K. Cole to produce the ideal plastic radio. Wells Coates' winning design was produced, with variations, from 1934 until 1946 and became a best-seller for the company. It was a radical departure from traditional forms and materials of radio cabinet construction. The AD 65 had a distinctive circular cabinet of moulded brown Bakelite made to fit a circular speaker. The shape was reiterated in the controls and arc of the channel display and gave the radio an entirely novel form that also reduced tooling costs. A less expensive and more popular "walnut look" version of the AD 65 was also available.

Philips 2514 Radio and Speaker

The Dutch company Philips was founded in 1891 to manufacture light bulbs and later diversified into the design and production of radio receivers, gramophone players and eventually televisions and other domestic goods. Philips was one of the first European companies to establish a design department – under the control of the architect Louis C. Kalff. Kalff was employed by Philips in 1925 and worked on the design of posters, exhibition stands and the interior of Philips showrooms. In 1929 his responsibilities were enlarged to include the aesthetic appearance of products. The design bureau employed technical draughtsmen and construction experts and the design of new products involved management,

sales and technical staff. Surviving company records from this period suggest that product design at Philips was a result of such collaboration, and not the work of a single individual. The design of the 2514 Radio symbolizes Philips's approach to design. It incorporated new materials such as the synthetic Bakelite, available in different colour combinations. It also incorporated a distinctive circular speaker, described by the company in terms of its artistic quality, intended to adorn the modern living room. Kalff was to have an enduring influence on the design philosophy at Philips and he remained the company's design director until 1960, completing a remarkable thirty-five years of continuous service.

DATE: 1926

DESIGNER: Louis C. Kalff (1897–1976)

MATERIAL: metal, rexine and Bakelite

MANUFACTURER: Philips Ltd, Eindhoven, The Netherlands

RR126 Stereo Hi-Fi

DATE: 1965–66

DESIGNER: Achille Castiglioni (born 1918) and Pier Castiglioni (1910–68)

MATERIAL: chrome, plastic and wood

MANUFACTURER: Brionvega, Milan, Italy

Originally radio manufacturers, Brionvega went on to produce televisions and hi-fi equipment. They employed a series of well-known Italian designers to transform their products. The Castiglionis' stereo was a radical concept in the hi-fi market that fitted with the dominant style of the mid-1960s; its bold forms and colours lending a dynamic image to the product. The RR126 Stereo is a free-standing mobile unit which has speakers that can be stacked on top to form a box, or folded out into a horizontal arrangement.

DATE: 1936

DESIGNER: Walter Maria Kersting (1889–1970)

MATERIAL: Bakelite

MANUFACTURER: Hagenuh, Kiel, Germany

Walter Maria Kersting designed, in a number of versions, the People's Radio (*Volksempfanger*), that was produced in enormous numbers in Nazi Germany. By 1939, it was estimated that twelve and a half million had been sold, thereby depositing in practically every German home a cheap, state-subsidized radio, an ideal medium through which to disseminate Nazi propaganda. The model number commemorated 30 January, 1933, the date when Hitler was made Chancellor of Germany. A political success for Hitler, the radio was powerful enough to receive home transmissions, but not the Allied broadcasts. The aesthetic was minimal and functional, a rectangular casing in dark brown, with simple dials and a large speaker: the only ornament being a Nazi swastika.

Phonosuper

DATE: 1956

DESIGNER: Hans Gugelot (1920–65) and Dieter Rams (born 1932)

MATERIAL: metal, wood and Perspex

MANUFACTURER: Braun, Frankfurt, Germany

This version of the Phonosuper transformed a product that had been manufactured since the 1930s. It also introduced the Perspex cover to hi-fi equipment. The original design featured a metal cover; this was replaced by Perspex in an effort to reduce vibration. The clean lines and strongly functional appearance wer in keeping with the Braun design philosophy; however, its over chaste and rather severe appearance earned it the nicknam "Snow White's Coffin".

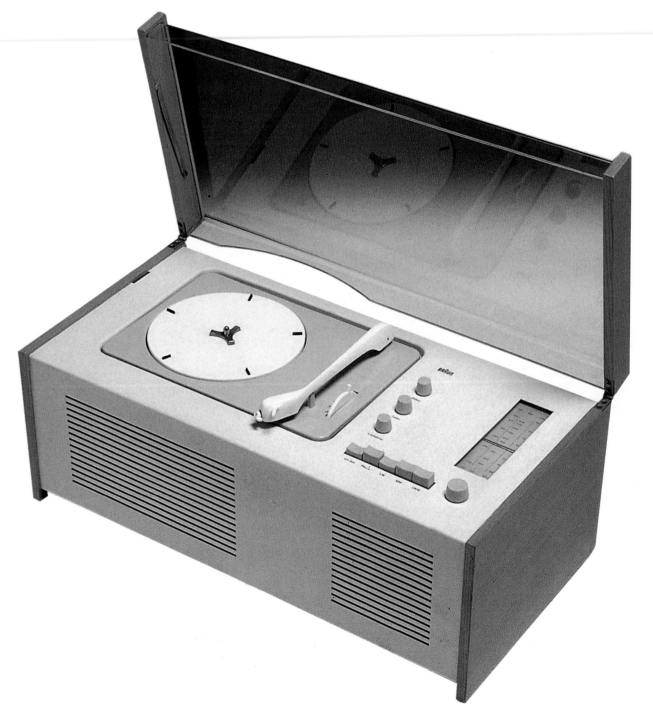

TS 502 Radio

Brionvega was established as a radio manufacturer in 1945 and began producing television sets in the early 1960s. The design team of Marco Zanuso and his Bavarian-born design partner Richard Sapper worked regularly with Brionvega, as did Mario Bellini and Achille Castiglioni, other stars in the Italian design firmament. When closed, the TS 502 forms an anonymous box that conceals its function. It is a natural partner to the ST/201 television set, also designed by Zanuso and Sapper for Brionvega.

DATE: 1964

DESIGNER: Marco Zanuso (born 1916) and Richard Sapper (born 1932)

MATERIAL: plastics and chromium

MANUFACTURER: Brionvega, Milan, Italy

Beogram 4000 Turntable

DATE: 1973

DESIGNER: Jakob Jensen
(born 1926)

MATERIAL: wood and
aluminium

MANUFACTURER: Bang
and Olufsen A/S, Copenhagen,
Denmark

In 1944 Bang and Olufsen launched the revolutionary Grand Prix 44 RG, a compact cabinet incorporating a record player and a radio. In 1968 the Danish designer, Jakob Jensen, was placed in charge of Bang and Olufsen's hi-fi design programme. His vision for the company was simplicity and elegance – timeless products notable for their logicality and technical precision. Jensen's anonymous and discreet styling for Bang and Olufsen has come to define the aesthetics of high-quality contemporary sound systems. Using state of the art technology with its precision components and electronic tangential arm, the Beogram was a rare example of a product from a European electronics company capable of holding its own in an industry dominated by the new Japanese companies. Bang and Olufsen continue to produce audio-visual equipment to high professional standards for the domestic market.

Totem Stereo

DATE: 1970

DESIGNER: Mario Bellini (born 1935)

MATERIAL: plastic

MANUFACTURER:
Brionvega, Milan, Italy

the 1960s miniaturization and more sophisticated technology suggested a new approach to sound system design – reduction to pure geometric form. One of Italy's most innovative rms, Brionvega, combined minimalism with fun and layfulness, stressing the sculptural potential of the object. It naintained a close relationship with avant-garde Italian designers in the 1960s and 1970s, and commissioned Totem from Mario Bellini whose inventive electronic equipment includes work for Olivetti. Totem was a directional design with speakers rotating out on a pivot to reveal the hidden record deck. When closed it formed a simple white cube that conceals its function.

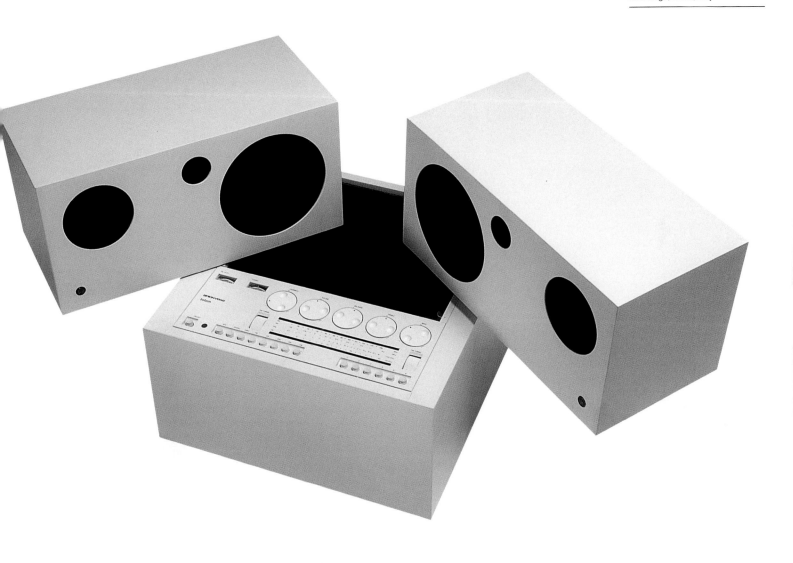

Sony Walkman

DATE: 1978

DESIGNER: Sony Design Centre

MATERIAL: plastic

MANUFACTURER: Sony, Tokyo, Japan

Sony chairman Akio Morita is said to have conceived this portable stereophonic cassette player whilst playing tennis, imagining a lightweight, easy-to-carry device for listening to music at any time. The Sony Walkman represents key changes in the 1970s and 1980s consumer markets. One of the first personalized products, both fashion accessory and functional object, the concept used existing technologies in an innovative and revolutionary way with new styling. With about fifty million sales, the Walkman was produced in many versions, such as the model shown here. It continued for some time to evolve in line with social and fashion trends and the need for individual customization.

Sony Playstation

Sony described the PlayStation as its most important product since the Walkman. The company wanted something offering the sales potential of the Walkman, and invested $500 million in development, using teams of designers from around the world. The product entered a market dominated by Sega and Nintendo.

Using 3D graphics, "real-time" on-screen action, and CD-quality sound, the PlayStation is powered by five processors computing half a billion instructions per second – over five hundred times more powerful than then-existing 16-bit consoles.

DATE: 1996

DESIGNER: Ken Kutaragi

MATERIAL: plastic

MANUFACTURER: Sony Computer Entertainment, Tokyo, Japan

Sony Portable TV 80 301

DATE: 1959

DESIGNER: Sony Design Centre

MATERIAL: plastic and metal

MANUFACTURER: Sony, Tokyo, Japan

The postwar US occupation of Japan and subsequent Marshall Plan and package had a tremendous influence on the country's reconstruction. New Japanese industries concentrated on capital-intensive goods such as radios, television sets and cars. One of the best-known companies to represent this economic recovery was the Sony Corporation. In the 1950s the newly founded company bought the manufacturing rights to a new American invention, the transistor, and in 1955 produced its first radio. This was followed in 1959 by the world's first solid-state television receiver, which had an 46-centimetre (18-inch) screen and weighed only 6 kilograms (13 pounds). The television set in train the association of Japanese products with the latest technological advances, particularly miniaturization, and this television went on to win the Gold Medal at the Triennale di Milano in 1960. Sony's product development has been guided by technological innovation, supreme quality control and sound business management. It played a major role in establishing the profile of the Japanese electronics industry that would dominate global markets and transform the Japanese economy. Unlike Western companies, Japanese companies have tended to use in-house, anonymous design teams for product development rather than outside designers. The Sony team is responsible for all aspects of the company's products and their corporate identity, expressed through packaging and promotion.

Brionvega Black ST/201

Brionvega is an Italian company with a long tradition of commissioning leading designers to give a distinctive form to its products. In the 1960s it was also one of the few international companies whose products stood out in contrast to the prevailing simple white aesthetics of the German Braun company and their Japanese imitators. The black 201 television set was designed by Marco Zanuso and Richard Sapper in 1969, continuing a partnership established in the early 1960s to develop a new generation of television sets and radios. More than any other object, this television represents the most uncompromising movement towards minimalism in 1960s Italian design. It defined the idea of the mysterious black box, emphasized by making the screen only visible when the television was switched on. The positioning of the controls on top of the set contributes to the sleek lines, making the 201 a novel form for a familiar appliance. It quickly became a cult object.

DATE: 1969

DESIGNER: Marco Zanuso (born 1916) and Richard Sapper (born 1932)

MATERIAL: plastic and glass

MANUFACTURER:
Brionvega, Milan, Italy

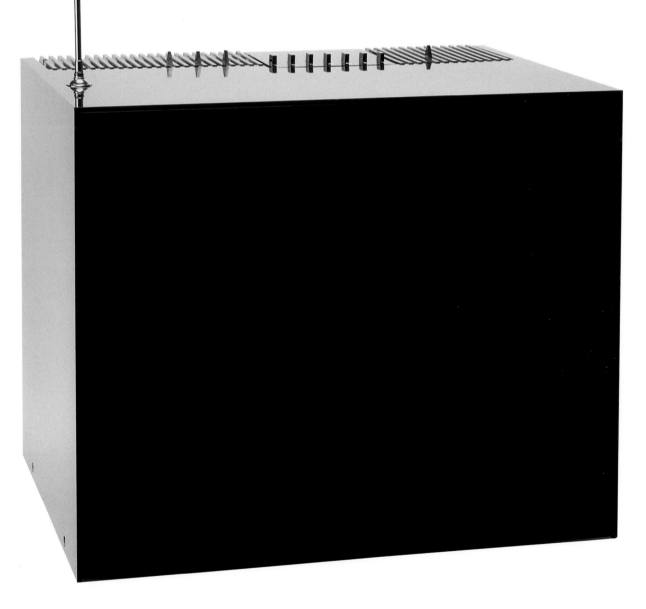

Sony Trinitron Television

DATE: 1968

DESIGNER: Sony Design Centre

MATERIAL: plastic, chrome and glass

MANUFACTURER: Sony, Tokyo, Japan

Sony's innovative approach to research and development has led to many ground-breaking products. The Trinitron television set was the result of research focused entirely on the creation of a brighter, clearer and less distorted picture. This revolutionary product employed a new and highly sophisticated picture production device. The Trinitron television set also used a much flatter screen that enhanced picture quality. The Trinitron was the starting point in the quest for high-resolution television images, which has culminated most recently in the inception of digital television.

Jim Nature

Now one of the world's best-known designers, Philippe Starck's output has been prolific. Not only has he produced important interiors, furniture and domestic products, he has also worked in the field of industrial products including this television, Jim Nature. Part of a more widespread move to challenge the dominance of the familiar Japanese techno box aesthetic, its sculptural case in some ways looks back to the spirit of 1960s Pop design, but significant here is Starck's use of multi-density wood or chipboard. This material raises the issues of ecologically sound materials in that the wood is essentially recycled. It also gives technology a more human and friendly face, a development that the consumer is beginning to find more appealing than the hard-edge black plastic used for most products in this field.

DATE: 1994

DESIGNER: Philippe Starck (born 1949)

MATERIAL: high-density wood and plastic

MANUFACTURER: Saba (Thomson), France

Kodak Brownie 127

DATE: 1959

DESIGNER: Kodak

MATERIAL: plastic

MANUFACTURER: Kodak, USA

The Kodak Company was founded in 1881 by George Eastman Kodak. His products pioneered the simplification of photography, as suggested by Kodak's advertising slogan: "You press the button, we do the rest". Kodak is the world's largest photographic organization. It has designed and manufactured hundreds of cameras this century. This postwar model has the rounded contours that were popular in by Walter Dorwin Teague's series of popular cameras designed in the 1930s, the best-known of which was the Bantam special of 1936. This made it appear old-fashioned even when it was new. Several million were nonetheless sold.

Leica

Small, quiet and discreet, in the 1930s the Leica camera produced a revolution. It was the first compact camera that could produce professional quality work and it quickly became the most popular photojournalistic camera in the world. Its origins go back to 1911 when Oskar Barnack joined the German engineering company Leitz. Barnack was trained as an engineer and an enthusiastic amateur photographer who started to work on prototypes for a small camera based on a simple idea: small negatives but big pictures. He produced prototypes of this camera and after World War One his boss Ernst Leitz decided to put it into production as the Leica. Their first camera was shown at the Leipzig Fair in 1925 followed by the Leica1 in 1930 which was a new compact size and offered interchangeable lenses. These technological advances ensured that the Leica became the serious camera for professional photography in the 1930s.

DATE: 1930

DESIGNER: Oskar Barnack (1879–1936)

MATERIAL: plastic and metal

MANUFACTURER: Leitz, Germany

Nikon F

DATE: 1959

DESIGNER: Nikon Design Team

MATERIAL: plastic and metal

MANUFACTURER: Nikon, Japan

Initially called Nippon Kogaku K.K., Nikon was the first Japanese company to challenge the supremacy of Leica for professional quality cameras. In 1950 two photographers from the American magazine *Life* used Nikon lenses under extreme weather conditions; the quality of these photographs won two important prizes and brought Nikon international recognition. In 1959, Nikon introduced the Nikon F, its first 35mm SLR lens camera, which featured an instant return reflex mirror, linked reflex mirror and shutter, interchangeable finders and screens.

The Nikon F was an immediate success, selling over a millio cameras. It became more than an admired piece of professiona equipment, as the Nikon F became bound up in the imagery an lifestyle of the Swinging Sixties. It was the Nikon that young British fashion photographers like David Bailey used to stalk th leggy mini-skirted models of the period. In this context the Niko was more than a camera: it was an accessory that helped t establish photographers as the new high-profile media stars the decade.

Olympus Trip 35

The Olympus Trip 35 was designed in 1968 and was in continuous production until 1988, selling over ten million units and making it one of the most successful cameras of the twentieth century. The camera was designed as a 35mm version of the Olympus range and combined high quality technical performance with a more affordable price. Aesthetically, the camera broke new ground, by wrapping the light meter cells ingeniously around the lens. It was simple and easy to use, compact in size so that it was easy to carry. Olympus continued its commitment to innovation. One of its later cameras, the 1993 Olympus Zoom, with distinctive sculptural contours, was the lightest 35mm camera on the market at that time.

DATE: 1968

DESIGNER: Olympus Design Team

MATERIAL: plastic and metal

MANUFACTURER:
Olympus, Tokyo, Japan

Canon CB10

DATE: 1982–83

DESIGNER: Luigi Colani
(born 1928)

MATERIAL: plastic

MANUFACTURER: Canon
Cameras, Tokyo, Japan

This early biomorphic design marked a shift towards a more organic-looking product. The CB10 formed part of a special project commissioned by Canon. The brief to the designer, the Italian–Swiss Colani, was to think, in an entirely free and unfettered manner, about the future of camera designs. Colani, well-known for his highly individualistic design style, was to create a series of cameras that would serve as "pointers" to the future. The result was indeed radical: a series of biomorphic shapes that looked more like deep-sea fish than cameras. The series still appears revolutionary today. It important to remember that at this time the black box ruled suprem – the marketing of such products was based largely on technic features and price. Colani introduced the radical idea that the simpl black rectangular shape was not the only way forward. Colani excessive aerodynamic forms may have been extreme but they wei a reaction against the functional aesthetic of the day and heralded a enormous shift in styling in the mass market for cameras.

Canon Ixus

DATE: 1996

DESIGNER: Canon Design Centre

MANUFACTURER: Canon
Cameras, Tokyo, Japan

The Canon Ixus was instantly hailed as a classic of design when it was launched in 1996. One of the smallest cameras on the market at the time, the Ixus was the size of a packet of playing cards: only 9 centimetres (3½ inches) wide and six centimetres (2½ inches) high. Much of its appeal came from the sleek, compact design of the metallic body. However, it was not just its appearance that placed the Ixus at the forefront of design, it also represented the latest advance in camera technology, as it was loaded with the Advanced Photo System. This was a new type of film that required no negatives and allowed the user to select any of three different formats when shooting or printing images.

Valentine Portable Typewriter

DATE: 1969

DESIGNER: Ettore Sottsass (born 1917) and Perry King (born 1938)

MATERIAL: plastic

MANUFACTURER: Olivetti, Italy

Inspired by American Pop Art, Ettore Sottsass wanted to humanize industrial design. The Valentine Portable Typewriter, which he designed with Perry King, was not the first portable; in the 1930s, the Swiss company Ernest Paillard had pioneered a model called the Hermes Baby. However, the Valentine signalled a new approach to office equipment, as it could so clearly be placed either in a domestic or office environment. Its brightly coloured plastic case, size and colour made it friendly, human and fun. The advertisements promoting the Valentine reinforced this image, often showing young couples reclining in fields alongside the typewriter or illustrated, as here, as giant works of Pop art.

Sottsass worked as a design consultant for Olivetti from 1957 and developed projects that range from typewriters to furniture and computers. Sottsass was concerned with ergonomics and new materials. A product that reflects the vitality of Olivetti and its informed approach to design, the Valentine proved a great commercial success.

the olivetti collection   1. Lettera 33   2 Lettera 31   3 Studio 45   4 Lettera 32   5 Valentine   6 A collector

Designed in 1963, IBM's golf ball typewriter revolutionized the 1960s office. For the first time a single machine offered interchangeable typefaces, carbon ribbon, electric drive, a small footprint and a weight of only 14 kilograms (31 pounds). Its success was due to a nickel-plated plastic type, positioned by a mechanism so that each stroke tilted and rotated to bring the required character to the front, before striking it against the ribbon and moving it on a space. Later variants gave an even greater quality of print. The International Business Machine Corporation (IBM) operated a clearly defined design policy in the 1950s under the direction of Eliot Noyes. With an eye on the work of Italian rivals Olivetti, in particular products designed by Nizzoli, the 72 represented not only a technical breakthrough but the expression of sophisticated sculptural form.

DATE: 1963

DESIGNER: Eliot Noyes (1910–77)

MATERIAL: plastic

MANUFACTURER: IBM, Armonk, New York State, USA

IBM Computer System 360

DATE: 1964

DESIGNER: Eliot Noyes
(1910–77)

MANUFACTURER: IBM,
Armonk, New York State, USA

Eliot Noyes became director of design for International Business Machines (IBM) in 1956. He transformed the direction of the company by insisting on an integrated approach to design strategy and corporate identity governed by a set of published standards. These design specifications covered all IBM products. Under Noyes, the company linked design to innovation and developed a number of revolutionary computer products. The System 360 is typical of Noyes' approach and epitomizes IBM design characteristics. It is functional, and yet softened in places by avoiding the stark form so often associated with computers. It was designed to be easily operated and the controls were developed in conjunction with IBM's Human Engineering division

Apple Macintosh

easy to use and housed in an off-white casing, the Apple Macintosh computer revolutionized the computer industry. Apple enjoyed a rather special corporate image – a reputation that it was a company managed by 1960s free-thinkers who believed that technology could empower the individual. Their choice of name evoked not big business but memories of the counter-culture and The Beatles' Apple Corps.

Based in California, Apple suggested the attitude of Haight Ashbury rather than Manhattan. In sharp contrast to their suit-wearing peers at IBM, Apple executives prided themselves on wearing jeans. Apple identified itself with the individual, not the corporate might of IBM. This profile was self-consciously exploited by Apple in their famous TV commercial for the Macintosh, directed by British film-maker Tony Scott and broadcast during the Super Bowl. Playing on images from Metropolis, the ad showed people staring at a ranting "Big Brother" image only to be liberated by an Olympic athlete who smashed the screen to reveal the copy: "On January 24th, Apple Computer will introduce the Macintosh and you'll see why 1984 won't be like 1984". The Classic shown here was one of the popular early models.

DATE: 1984

DESIGNER: Frogdesign/
Harmut Esslinger (born 1945)

MATERIAL: plastic housing

MANUFACTURER: Apple
Computers, Cupertino, USA

Apple iMac

DATE: 1996

DESIGNER: Apple Design Team and Jonathan Ive

MATERIAL: plastic

MANUFACTURER: Apple Computers, Cupertino, California, USA

In 1999, Apple took the world of product design by storm with the iMac, which is now generally recognized to be one of the most important products from the end of the last century. It redefined the way computers are perceived, coming in a range of fashionable colours and using a sexy aesthetic far removed from previous computer styling.

The design team was headed by Jonathan Ive, a British designer based in California. Ive is also a senior vice-president of the corporation, reinforcing the importance of the place of design within the company. The success of the iMac was overwhelming the reaction to it was all-pervasive from its sales figures to the number of websites dedicated to the product. Ive's objective was to try and create a computer that was functional and at the same time fun and easy to use. It fitted neatly into both the home and office environment, enriching the experience of the user. A detailed approach to every aspect of the product, from materials to the marketing, made the iMac a turning point in accessible design and technology.

The vC calculator, designed by Sebastian Bergne, redefined this basic object. With the miniaturization of electronics, designing a calculator had become more of a graphic exercise than the creation of a shell. vC re-established a clear identity for the calculator in a product area swamped with more and more complicated designs. In his design Bergne chose a slightly over-scaled form, as most calculators are too small to use comfortably and so miniaturization is no longer innovative or useful in itself. The mathematical functions that manufacturers include to fill up the grid of buttons have been dropped leaving space on the object and generating an asymmetric button layout. Here, the intention was to create a normal calculator that is highly useful for the everyday needs.

DATE: 1998

DESIGNER: Sebastian Bergne

MATERIAL: injection moulded polypropylene

MANUFACTURER:

Authentics, Artipresent, GmbH

Italy

BlackBerry Bold Smartphone 9000

DATE: 2008

DESIGNER: Mike Lazaridis

MANUFACTURER:

BlackBerry

The BlackBerry is a wireless handheld device developed in 1999 by Mike Lazaridis, founder of Canada's Research In Motion (RIM) based in Waterloo, Ontario. It has become one of the iconic objects of the twenty-first century and Lazaridis refers to the telephone message and fax era of the late twentieth century as the Dark Ages. His BlackBerry achieved huge commercial success (eight million users reported in 2007) with the corporate market because of its ability to send and receive e-mails in real time. The BlackBerry has a built-in keyboard, designed for thumbs-only typing ("thumbing") and system navigation controlled by a thumbwheel. RIM have also become market leaders in device battery life.

Instant communication meant the era of returning to home or office and switching on the computer to track e-mails was over. The BlackBerry offered the freedom to leave the office and remain connected to work life. However, it removed the boundaries between home and work to such an extent that a new term, "CrackBerry", was coined to describe patterns of addictive and dysfunctional usage of the device. There are reports of BlackBerry owners regularly using them in meetings at work and, with the addition of a light sensor that dims the screen, even in cinemas and the bedroom.

The success of the BlackBerry is down to its ability to do one thing – e-mails – really well.

Like their competitors, TomTom satellite navigation devices locate the user on the road using commercially available global positioning system (GPS) data. Using this device, the driver can receive spoken and visual directions to a destination; some models include indications of speed cameras on the road, services such as petrol stations and tourist sites.

Satellite navigation (sat-nav) software was originally the preserve of military communications. Over the last twenty years, however, the development of digital map storage and colour display screens in the USA, Japan and Europe have made commercial systems possible. Car manufacturing companies, such as Honda, recognized sat-nav's marketing potential, and from the mid-1980s started to pioneer early sat-nav systems, alongside Mitsubishi, Pioneer and Magellan.

The devices are not only location finders, but also have security and safety benefits, assisting in tracking and tracing lost or stolen vehicles. Some research also indicates that using these devices increases road safety, although they are subject to error and they don't work in tunnels or other covered areas in which the signal cannot be received.

Integrated systems built into the vehicle are available, but low-cost, all-in-one portable devices have become hugely popular consumer items. TomTom NV is one of the leading brands within the sector, founded in 1991 in Amsterdam, and is now a global company integrating communication and smart navigation technology. Integrated systems have the advantage of greater reliability, but portable units like the TomTom 920 use an accelerometer to compensate.

DATE: 2008

MANUFACTURER: Tom Tom NV

PART 13

Futures

THINGS TO COME

The future is notoriously difficult to predict. Yet visualizing the future is a recurring obsession – a project that has fascinated film-makers, science-fiction writers, architects, designers and futurologists. Ironically, each decade seems to have predicted the future as a version of its present, and so many of the images shown in this section simply reinforce the cultural and design trends of their own time.

In some ways the use of future fantasy has become an industrial design aesthetic in its own right. One important source for futurist imagery is derived from science fiction, an essentially twentieth-century form of literature that has become an important genre. The most important figure in this context is the writer H.G. Wells, but later exponents whose work has influenced designers are Isaac Azimov, Arthur C. Clarke, and Philip K. Dick. Their written descriptions of fantasy scenarios have inspired countless illustrations, films and video games and helped to construct the visual landscape of the future. Also important are the countless comic books and popular published sources that include visual representations of the future. These should not be discounted as merely ephemeral: there is a real relationship between the imagery produced for young adults and children and the design ideas of many futuristic clothes and objects.

Artists, too, have explored the future. Max Ernst's Surrealist collages, for example, explore the territory of prophetic dreams. With Ernst, as with other Dadaist and Surrealist artists, a fascination with elaborate mechanical machines and robots shows in their drawings and paintings.

At the beginning of the twentieth century, a number of architects attempted to produce realizable plans for the new city of the future. Inspired by the potential of the century's new technology, architects such as the Italian, Sant'Elia, and, later, Le Corbusier, laid out plans for the city that included towering skyscrapers, linked by walkways; although they remained unbuilt, these visions became important

METROPOLIS

blueprints for city planners after 1945. Gradually in some of the world's largest cities, most notably New York or Brasilia, these visions began to take shape. Providing people with a glimpse of the future became part of every major exhibition and industrial show of the twentieth century and the best-known example of this remains the 1939 New York World's Fair. The whole concept of the exhibition was to provide the viewer with a glimpse of the way technology was going to reshape the future.

The period after World War Two was the time when societies truly embraced the future. The promise of technology underpinned the whole political and philosophical credo of the 1960s and the British Prime Minister Harold Wilson referred to it as "the white heat of technology". At

the same time important writers like Marshall McLuhan engaged in the theoretical implications such changes would have on the nature of society. These changes were seen in a positive light, but slowly a counter-movement gained a growing voice. Technology, the argument went, led to dangerous side effects. It produced ecological problems and was not the way forward. In response, future imagery demonstrated that it was not only about dark, overpowering visions of change, it also began to concern itself with low-tech self-sustaining technologies, projects that would involve recycling and the reuse of materials to build the future.

This division of feeling about the future has been thrown painfully into focus as we go further into the twenty-first century. The beginning of any century is an important moment, but the start of a new millennium is historically charged with significance and portent. The new millennium indicates the arrival of the future in which we look forward to building a better life while at the same time many fear that technology will overwhelm the individual. With this in mind designers and leading companies are asking themselves some basic questions. What will life be like in 2050? What will people want in terms of design in the future? What will interest them and make their lives more fulfilled?

Traditionally, new products have been introduced mainly through technological innovation, but the rapid development and merging of technologies is making it increasingly difficult to predict the future. In order to stay in business large companies, such as Sony, Philips and Ideo, as well as smaller concerns, like Tangerine, have to try to predict the future. Their prototype products – or "future gazing" concepts

– propose ways in which new developments in technology could improve the quality of people's lives. Companies have also been forced to recognize that technological innovation for its own sake is no longer acceptable. They recognize that products and services will have to come closer to meeting human needs and desires. Design will have to reflect the increasingly complex relationship between people and technology.

Until now our obsession with the future has focused on images of high tech and the power of the machine. The emergence of ethical and ecological concerns now challenges this vision. In the twenty-first century it will be interesting to see how the interplay between high-tech and sustainable low-tech shapes the next generation's predictions of the future.

Une Cité Industrielle

DATE: 1904

DESIGNER: Tony Garnier
(1869–1948)

Tony Garnier received a traditional French Beaux Arts education, where he was a star pupil, winning the coveted Prix de Rome prize. In spite of his conventional training, he completed an extraordinary series of drawings at the beginning of the century that established a blueprint for twentieth-century town planning.

Garnier was the first architect to produce a plan for the industrialized city with *Une Cité Industrielle*, which was first published in 1917. More than any other designer, he established the idea that architects should direct their attention to the city as a whole, rather than the private house or the individual grand building. Garnier introduced the single and most influential precept in town planning, a method of organizing and regulating the industrial city – the idea of zoning. He divided his imaginary city of 35,000 inhabitants into distinct areas – industrial, residential, transport, sport and health. It was this categorization of the activities of modern life that proved so influential on architects such as Le Corbusier in the 1920s.

Garnier also recognized that the new technology of industrial materials could be used to create the modern city of the twentieth century – significantly, he chose reinforced concrete for all types of buildings. His two-storey residential houses are simple cubic shapes with classical forms which predated the look of Modernism. Garnier's aesthetics of simple cube houses, dramatically cantilevered public buildings and his use of reinforced concrete set a standard for subsequent city planning. His revolutionary urban vision remains with us to this day.

La Ville Radieuse

La Ville Radieuse (The Radiant City) is arguably among the most influential intellectual concepts of the twentieth century. It saw Le Corbusier draw on the ideas of early visionaries such as Tony Garnier and Sant'Elia to produce a model of the modern city and how it should be organized for maximum benefit of its inhabitants. It was a culmination of a series of city plans Le Corbusier had worked on in the 1920s. La Ville Radieuse was based around the use of zones for the key functions of modern life and work, arranged in a sequence of bands that could expand horizontally into the landscape. Particularly influential was his idea of layering the city – for example, placing the pedestrian above the car in walkways – which had an enormous impact on postwar planning. The reunion of man with nature was one of Le Corbusier's most important town planning principles. Consequently, his buildings were all raised above ground level on pilotis, releasing the land for use as "green" space.

There was one fundamental drawback to Corbusier's grand visions: to work properly, such cities had to be rebuilt from scratch. In practical terms this meant the imposition of zones – whether the inhabitants wanted them or not – the demolition of existing buildings, the wiping clean of history and the control of people's lives. While Le Corbusier did move away from this authoritarian position, many suffered as a result of huge postwar rebuilding programmes based on his town-planning schemes that are now seen as inhumane and brutal.

DATE: 1930

DESIGNER: Le Corbusier (1887–1966)

Things To Come

DATE: 1936

DIRECTOR: William Cameron
Menzies (1896–1957)

More than any other writer, it was H. G. Wells who established the genre of science fiction writing in the twentieth century, and his visions of the future have exercised an extraordinary influence. In an early story, *The Sleeper Awakes*, Wells imagined the city of the future, a remarkable image of huge metal-framed buildings, and one which predicted the work of Modernist architects such as Le Corbusier. *Things To Come*, adapted from a later Wells novel, extended this theme and became one of the film sensations of the decade. The story covers a period of a hundred years of civilization. It begins in 1940, with a war that devastates the entire globe and exterminates most of mankind. The film ends with the

Futurist utopia of 2040, in which human hardships have been eliminated and the population is assured of all its material as well as spiritual needs.

Directed by William Cameron Menzies, the film is noted both for the remarkable visions of the future created in its sets and for the extraordinary special effects by Ned Man (1893–1967). Using models and buildings to give the impression of lifesize dimensions, Man also created fantasy machines, including vision telephones and the delta-winged aeroplanes that attacked London. The English public laughed at the idea of an air attack on their capital city in 1936. Within five years, however, this fiction had become reality.

Metropolis

DATE: 1926

DIRECTOR: Fritz Lang
1890–1976)

Produced in Germany in 1925, *Metropolis* was a hugely expensive film, with production costs reaching almost £2 million. Memorable for its futuristic sets and choreographed set-pieces which employed a cast of nearly forty thousand extras, it quickly established itself as the most significant science-fiction film of the silent era. *Metropolis* was both widely admired and highly influential – Hitler and Goebbels were both deeply impressed. Virtually every subsequent science fiction films owe a debt to its original vision of the future.

In the film's introductory sequences, Fritz Lang reveals a gigantic city of the future – a city of gleaming skyscrapers, connecting bridges and aeroplanes – where people live in comfort, devoted to intellectual and physical development. Although the film preaches a moral message about the threat technology represents to human spiritual life, the alternative to such progress is illustrated by the workers of the subterranean city who enjoy no individuality – a crowd from which personality rarely projects itself.

Using a refined cinematic language, *Metropolis* contained technical innovations which influenced Hollywood over the next two decades. The film made extensive use of uneven lines, the nameless crowd, contrasts of light and dark, half-shadows and silhouettes, much of which still serves to suggest mysterious and menacing actions or emotions. *Metropolis* established the potential for a film image to generate meaning – an example being the well-known scene in which the robot with its glittering female body, stylized breasts and inhuman mask makes its entry. Lang also shapes space with the help of human bodies and uses light so intensively that it takes the place of sound.

Perisphere and Trylon Structures

DATE: 1939–40
World of Tomorrow Exhibition,
New York City, USA

DESIGNER: Henry Dreyfuss
(1904–72)

By the 1920s, the USA had established itself as the world's most powerful industrial nation. The country led the way in new methods of industrial production. For the Americans the machine was not only a reality but a potent symbol of the future. In 1939 this vision was realized in the World of Tomorrow Exhibition, which was held in New York. Here was an attempt to create the future in microcosm – a man-made future where visitors could enter Henry Dreyfuss' Democracity – the 60-metre (200-foot) diameter Perisphere and the 200 metre (700-foot) tall Trylon. These soaring white geometric shapes gave visitors the promise of a streamlined lifestyle and universe of the future. People could marvel at the universe of televisions, robots, transcontinental highways, the promise of space travel and a range of the latest electrical domestic products. The impact of the New York exhibition was, however, severely restricted by the outbreak of the World War Two. This was not the moment for Utopian dreams of the future, and more pressing concerns became the priority. The spirit of 1939 was held in abeyance until the political and economic stability of the postwar years returned.

City of the Future

DATE: 1946

DESIGNER: Frank R. Paul
(1884–1963)

Throughout the twentieth century, comics and science fiction books published visual representations of imagined futures. Far from being ephemeral or trivial elements of popular culture, these illustrated stories became an important medium through which we acquired ideas of the future. Well-known science fiction illustrators, such as Frank R. Paul, visualized the future through the present – effectively recording the cultural aspirations of their own time. There is also a real and potent relationship between this kind of popular imagery and design culture – this creative visual language has been borrowed time and time again and appropriated for the visual landscape of mainstream design.

Plug-In City

DATE: 1964

DESIGNER: Archigram–Peter
Cook (born 1936)

During the 1960s, the Archigram group produced some of the most Utopian and futuristic designs of the twentieth century. Archigram served as an umbrella for a group of young British architects which included Ron Herron, Warren Chalk, Dennis Crompton, Peter Cook, David Green and Michael Webb. They came together with a shared enthusiasm for the work of the Italian Futurists and the new Pop culture of science fiction, space age, throwaway consumerism, and the inspiration of their guru, Buckminster Fuller. They believed that mainstream architecture was too bound up in history and tradition and wanted to replace this with an architecture more in tune with the period. They set up the magazine *Archigram* to show

their projects and revitalize architecture. The group rejected the idea that architecture needed to be permanent, arguing that if society and peoples changed, then so too should their buildings.

The projects in the pages of *Archigram* concentrated on an expendable architecture which drew its imagery from the new technology. Typical of this approach was Peter Cook's Plug-In City of 1964, which created a framework of basic utilities – such as water and power – onto which standardized living units could be attached. Although their work remained conceptual, it had an enormous impact on the major architects of the last twenty years, including Richard Rogers and Nicholas Grimshaw.

House of the Future

This husband-and-wife team was part of a young generation of postwar British architects inspired by the Modern Movement. Their interpretation of modernism, which used the new materials and construction methods developed in the 1930s, became known as New Brutalism because of its uncompromising forms using exposed steel beams and raw concrete. They were, however, interested in reworking the ideas of the Modern Movement to make it more relevant to their age and more in keeping with the consumer-orientated society of the 1950s. The Smithsons became some of the most important architectural thinkers in postwar Britain. The House of The Future represents their ideas of what the modern house should be in the new era. Built for the popular "Ideal Home" Exhibition, it expressed their ideas of the house as an appliance designed to facilitate everyday activities. It was moulded in plastic to form free-flowing internal walls that were easy to clean. The lighting and fittings were all moulded into this wall surface. Visionary concepts included the kitchen, streamlined and fitted to produce not traditional food but prepackaged meals, and compartmentalized washing facilities with a sunken plastic bath and a pod-like shower unit. The Smithsons' idea that architecture could be consumable and disposable proved extremely influential and their moulded plastic furniture and fittings had a profound impact on 1960s design.

DATE: 1956

DESIGNER: Alison Smithson (1928–93) and Peter Smithson (born 1923)

Barbarella

DATE: 1967

DIRECTOR: Roger Vadim (born 1927)

Barbarella provided a Pop-design vision of the future. It was not the stark streamlined vision found in such television programmes as *Star Trek*, but an image of the future as Pop culture. Interiors featured a satin bed, fur-lined walls, inflatable furniture and huge plastic membrane environments.

Barbarella appeared ahead of its time and inspired the architectural underground with its exploration of installation-type spaces – the curved, pliable and continuously adaptable areas echoed the experimental work of many designers of the 1960s, such as Verner Panton and Joe Columbo.

New materials, such as blown polyurethane foam and PVC, led to surprisingly sexual forms in furniture, with swelling shapes covered in tightly stretched, brightly coloured fabric. These witty Pop designs found a large audience through the styling of films such as *Dr No* and *Barbarella* and in this way cinema created some of the lasting future environments of the decade.

Future Fashion

In the 1960s Paris couturiers recognized the style revolution that was affecting fashion from the street upwards. With the new independent boutiques setting the pace, it was not long before the great French fashion houses looked for ways to define the new modern woman of the period. In this context images of the future were particularly important. Their look for the new woman now included streamlined all-in-one cat suits, visor sunglasses and space age helmets such as Pierre Cardin's futuristic 1967 designs shown below. In 1964 Courrèges was the first couturier to include the mini-skirt in his collection and his theme, "the moon girl", used white plastic boots and beautifully cut body suits in black and white, inspired by the new geometry of Pop Art.

Another key fashion theme was new materials. Plastic, of course, was important, but Paco Rabanne extended this to include chain-mail minis, made from squares of brightly coloured perspex, metal and acrylic. With its tradition of superb cut and innovative fabrics, Paris soon re-established the lead in 1960s fashion.

DATE: 1967

DESIGNER: Pierre Cardin (born 1922)

Blade Runner

DATE: 1982

DIRECTOR: Ridley Scott (born 1929)

More than any other film of the 1980s, *Blade Runner* established a visual landscape of the futuristic city which continues to dominate the popular imagination. Adapted from Philip K. Dick's novel *Do Androids Dream of Electric Sheep?*, the film stars Harrison Ford as a cynical hero whose job is to retire "replicants" – androids with a human instinct for survival – in an overcrowded Los Angeles of 2019. The famous opening sequences show a city of the future, dominated by advertisements projected onto skyscrapers, "cars" that can fly, and an oppressive, dark, chaotic urban vision.

Art-directed by Douglas Trumbull, who worked on the influential *2001: A Space Odyssey* (1969), *Blade Runner* continues to influence films, advertising and fashion design. The effects were created by a kind of add-on architecture constructed from buildings and sky-scrapers which extend onto existing structures. To create this darkly oppressive city, layers of texture were built up so that visual information is densely packed on to the screen. Details proliferate throughout, which leads to the view that, as a movie, *Blade Runner* was designed rather than filmed.

Eve Machina

In the 1980s the Eve Machina design was part of a widespread attempt to humanize the industrial aesthetics of the machine. The choice of name was no accident – the Eve in the title is the woman of forbidden fruit fame, and GK Dynamics described the bike as a "love toy". This startling prototype design, by the largest industrial design group in the world, suggests nothing less than a woman and machine joined in the sexual act and in doing so reinforces the strong connections between motorbikes and male sexual power. Strongly reminiscent of the sculptures created by Allen Jones in the 1960s, the concept has aroused strong criticism for its submissive portrayal of the female form.

DATE: 1980s

DESIGNER: GK Dynamics Incorporated, Tokyo, Japan

Urbanization

DATE: on-going

Another great challenge for the world of design in the twenty-first century is the growth and spread of cities. The United Nations predicts that by the end of 2008, half the world's population will live in cities. Mexico City (pictured below) is one of the largest cities in the world after Tokyo, Shanghai, Mumbai and New York. More than one-fifth of the entire population of Mexico lives in the Metropolitan Area of Mexico City, and it is estimated that the population will reach 30 million by 2020 compared to Greater London's estimated population of around 7.5 million. For architects and designers, urban sprawl presents serious problems. As cities grow, services and transport have to grow with them, but as they do, the boundaries push out again.

Finding solutions to the demands of city life is incredibly complex. The causes of traffic and pollution in the city are exponentially worse in dense urban centres; smaller living spaces mean that it is not easy to store rubbish for recycling; and higher wages mean more goods are consumed by city dwellers. The challenge for design is to seek innovative ways to alleviate the worst effects of city living: new materials enable cheap and sustainable housing to be built, solar street lights reduce reliance on electricity, reusable bags cut the amount of plastic waste. Improved insulation in new buildings reduces energy use, while car-sharing schemes and "swop shops" such as the Freecycle Network™ rely on a large pool of local users to work.

Industrialization

One of the major perceived threats to Western economies, and the planet's eco-system, comes in the shape of industrialization in Asia. The first country to switch from mass-produced goods production to heavy industry was South Korea. Others followed suit, notably China, assisted by low labour rates, stable economies and low import duties. Heavy industry such as ship-building, steel production and coal-mining, has almost died out in many parts of Western Europe, whereas China has whole areas (such as Shanghai, pictured) devoted to these endeavours. The "energy crisis" of recent years is said, at least in part, to be driven by high demand from these countries for fossil fuels. In addition, concerns about global warming often focus on the increased use of fuel – and the concomitant increase in pollution – by heavy industry which is conducted free of the Western world's heavy anti-pollution regulations. Despite the best endeavours of the Green movement, some in Western Europe use the booming manufacturing industries in Asia as an excuse for doing nothing, on a "what difference can I make compared to them" basis.

China's success, however, is not all bad news for the rest of the world: increased prosperity has meant that China is now an importer of cars from companies such as VW and General Motors, as more and more people can afford them. Other Asian economies have also benefitted from an increase in imports to China as her economy has boomed.

India has taken a slightly different tack, moving from heavy industry to manufacturing and, most notably, service industries, which can take advantage of the large well-educated and English-speaking sector of India's population. Twenty-first century designers and manufacturers in the west need to be able to counter cheapness and availability with durability, quality and sustainability.

DATE: 1980s–2000s

Global Warming

DATE: 2008

DESIGNERS: Shop (creative advertising agency); EbOY (illustration); PAM (direction and animation)

This artwork was commissioned for a TV advert for Christian Aid Week 2008, developed by the UK based charity whose work is focused on practical solutions as well as campaigning. Jeff Dale, Head of Marketing at Christian Aid, has been responsible for helping the charity refocus the perception of its work on practical solutions. Indeed the charity has made great strides to overcome its traditional, and for some negative religious image to connect with wider groups of people. Interested in setting agendas, the focus of the campaign was the threat of flooding brought on by global warming. The creative idea came from the advertising agency Shop. It was drawn by a group of German illustrators called EbOY, comprising Steffen Sauerteig, Svend Smital and Kai Vermehr, who use pixel objects and make highly original artwork, and directed and animated by PAM (Paul Plowman, Anthony Burrill and Malcolm Goldie) who met as students at the Royal College of Art.

Christian Aid's brief was to reflect their work in DRR (disaster risk reduction work) in Latin America, using the best of contemporary communication design to show the simple message that prevention is better than cure. Christian Aid are taking a proactive lead on how DRR can reduce human catastrophe and offering simple and practical solutions to save lives.

Recycling

DATE: 2006

DESIGNER: Arnout Visser, Arnhem, Netherlands

MANUFACTURER: Kitengela Glass, Kitengela, Kenya

Africa is a vast continent facing both great challenges in terms of its peoples and great opportunities in terms of its future potential. This project, a collaboration between a western designer and African makers, shows a potential way to move forward. With its diverse economies and governments, each African country has its own particular concerns, but as a region, the African continent also has common challenges in the face of a rising population and the need to reduce the number of people living in severe poverty. The skills and creativity of its diverse peoples are not in question, but the infrastructure of manufacturing and design are limited. Dutch designer Arnout Visser has been visiting the Kitengela Glass works in Kenya since 2000. In this picture, two of the workers are creating a carafe with a separate space inside it for ice, so that fluids can be kept cool without getting melted water in them – this is called a "kangaroo carafe". All the glass used is recycled; pieces of broken window glass are collected in Nairobi, cleaned and then loaded into a furnace. The burner of the furnace uses recycled oil. The melted window glass only stays flexible for a short time and is very irregular in structure, so it requires great skill. Visser and the glass blowers have also experimented with recycling used bottles. Each object they produce is unique. While countries like China and South Korea have expanded into heavy industry, others such as India and Africa have had to diversify. India in particular, with its mobile phone repair street stalls, seems to embrace both the love of brand new technology and the age-old skills of repair and reuse.

Index

Acknowledgements

The publishers would like to thank the following sources for their kind permission to reproduce the pictures in this book:

Architectural Association Picture Library/FR Yerbury 59/ Dennis Wheatley 60/W.Arets 93/Lewis Gasson 85; AEG 235; The Advertising Archive Ltd. 14, 233, 252, 259, 344, 388; Airbus Press Room 269; AKG London 86, /Erik Bohr 57; Alamy/© Bildarchiv Monheim Gmbh 75; Alamy/© Coaster 337; Alamy/© EKp 394; Alamy/© D.Hurst 395; Alamy/© Motoring Picture Library 268; Alessi spa 202, 204, 205; © Arnout Visser 421; © 1960 Allegra Fuller Snyder Courtesy, Buckminster Fuller Institute, Santa Barbara 414; Alvar Aalto-Museo 58, /M.Kapanen 189; Courstesy of Apple Computer Inc. 391; Ron Arad Associates Ltd 145; Aram Designs 125; Arcaid 100 /R Bryant 50, 51, 68, 70, 83, 98, 102, 103, 106, 117, 119 / Michael 54/Dennis Gilbert 69/ Ken Kirkwood 82/Dave G Houser 260/Museum of Flight 262/ Esto 63; Archigram Archives/© Peter Cook 1964, 410; Archivio Gio Ponti ©Salvatore Licitra 229, 240; Archivio Storico of Olivetti, Ivrea, Italy 349; Giorgio Armani 31; Artemide GB Ltd/ Aldo Ballo 165; Baron & Baron/© Steve Klein 303; BFI 279, 404, 405; Bang and Olufsen Holding A/S, Denmark 374; Jonathan Barnbook 299; Barneys, New York 101; Bauhaus-Archiv, Museum fur Gestaltung, Berlin/Gunter Lepkowski 158, 186; Tim Benton 56; Bibliotheque Nationale 407; Braun, Germany 232; British Architectural Library Photographs Collection, RIBA London 191, 400, 401, 403; Neville Brody 293; Bulthaup BmBH & Co 242; CDP, London 352; Canon 386, 387;

Cassina S.p.a/Andrea Zani 130/Aldo Ballo 139, 140; Catalytico 172, 173; Jean-Loup Charmet 84; Prunella Clough/Irongate Studios 55, 87; Branson Coates Architecture Ltd/Fred Rotkopf 104, Phil Sayer 417; Coop Himmelblau/Gerald Zugmann 72; Corbis /UPI 10, 25, 256; Corbis UK Ltd 45, 46, 47, 48, 49, 60, 64, 65, 66, 67, 71, 123 / Bettman 16, 52; Bettmann 406/ UPI 415; Christian Aid 420; Christopher Kane/ Relative PR 41; Corbis/© Yann Arthus-Bertrand 418; Corbis/© Bojan Brecelj; Corbis/epa/©Jason Szenes 40; © Dean Kaufman 79; Department of Health 357; Design Council Archive, University of Brighton 194, 234, 238; Design Museum, London 6-7, 34, 44, 90, 126, 127, 138, 148, 162, 168, 169, 170, 174, 180, 184, 187, 195, 196, 201, 207, 217, 220, 224, 231, 258, 274, 276, 285, 296, 340, 341, 347; Dissing & Weitling 94; Dyson Appliances Ltd 218; Establishes & Sons/© Jasper Morrison 153; E.T.Archive 230/Museum Fur Gestaltung, Zurich 342; ©FSI GmBH, Fuse 298; Fiat Auto SpA 91; Flos Ltd 165, 171; Fuseproject XO-1 245; Sir Norman Foster & Partners Limited 142; GCI Group 237; Abram Games 282; Ken Garland 281; Gebruder Thonet GmbH 116, 121; Geffrye Museum 129; Getty Images/ Time & Life Pictures 23; Getty Images/AFP 53; Getty Images/Image Source 73; Getty Images 392; Google Communications & Public Affairs 302; ©J Paul Getty Trust & Richard Meier & Partners/Tom Bonner 74; Peter Gidal 97; Ronald Grant Archive 261; The Graphic Unit 276; Kenneth Green Associates Ltd 329; Sally & Richard Greenhill 27; Haagen-Dazs/Bartle Bogle Hegarty/ Jean Loup-Sieff, Maconochie

Photography, London 355; Habitat UK Ltd 95; Habitat/© Tord Boontje 176; Habitat/© Naoto Fukasawa 212; Robert Harding Picture Library 61; Heal & Son 118; © Hella Jongerius 211; Hisao Suzuki 78; Hollington 367; © Hotwire PR 396; Hulton Getty 17, 18, 19, 21, 28, 408, 409; IBM UK Ltd. Photographic Services, Hursley 280, 390; Imperial War Museum, London 346; Imagination Ltd 99; Infoplan Limited, London 226; © Ilttala Glass, Finland 188; Jam, London 243; © Jasper Morrison 213; Karla Otto LTD/© Andrea Matiradonna 113; Ben Kelly 105; David King Collection 183; Photo : Nick Knight . Sarah Wingate for Yohji Yamamoto. Paris 1986, 30; Knoll, New York 147; The Kobal Collection 22; Levi Strauss/Bartle Bogle Hegarty (Artist: Nick Kamen/ Rick Cunningham)354; Leica 383; LGI 29; London Features International Ltd./Frank Griffin 32; London Transport Museum 253, 275, 343; McDonalds Restaurants Ltd 325; Manx National Heritage 181, 272; Enzo Mari/Aldo Ballo 198; Michael Marriott 149; © Maarten Baas 150; Mash & Air 109; David Mellor 203; Metadesign plus GmbH, Berlin 288; The Montreal Museum of Decorative Arts/ The Liliane & David M.Stewart Colelction 166, 167; Moto Cinelli 257; Photo: Musee des Arts Decoratifs, Paris, collection Albert Levy, tous droits reserve 88; ©1997 The Museum of ModernArt, New York 300/ petit model armchair (1928) Gift of Phyllis B.Lambert 124; © The National Gallery 360; The National Trust Photographic Library/Dennis Gilbert 89; Collection New York Central System Historical Society Inc, Ohio 251; Nikon UK Limited 384; Nokia 366; OMA/© REM Koolhaas 76; The Robert Opie

Collection 284, 307-313, 315-319, 321, 322, 324, 326, 328, 331, 332, 334, 345; Osterreichisches Museum Fur Angewandte Kunst 182; N. du Pasquien 206; © Paul Simmons 210; Pernette Perriand 122; Philips Corporate Design 175; Picture Desk/The Art Archive / Staffordshire University / School of Art, Staffordshire University 193; Pictorial Press Ltd/Rankin 38; Pira Ltd 209; Politecnico di Torino, Sistema Bibliotecariom Biblioteca centrale di Architettura, archivo "Carlo Mollino" 92; Popperfoto 250; Porsche design GMBH 219; Priestman Goode 239; Psion 393; Quadrant Picture Library 249/ Paul Sherwood 263; Retna Pictures Ltd: Frank Micelotta 33; Reuters 39; Rex Features Ltd 156, 412 /Barthelemy 36/ Rolf Neeser 236; Rex Features 37; Rex Features/Warner Br/ Everett 416; Rexite Photo Archive 227; Riverford/Julie de Pledge & Martin Ellis 336; © Ross Lovegrove 177; Rowenta 225; SCP Limited 146; Saatchi & Saatchi Advertising 353; Saba Personal Electronics 381; Sainsbury Centre for Visual Arts, UEA, Norwich 159; Studio Levien 241; Stefan Sagmeister/Bela Borsodi 361; Schopenhaur Gruppo Fontana Arte 143; Science & Society Picture Library 254, 389 /Science Museum 216/NASA 264, 265; ©Jon Sievert 287, 350; © Sebastian Bergne 208; Dave Carr Smith 110; Sony UK Ltd 376, 377, 378, 380; Sothebys 157, 185; Space Studio Ltd/ Mario Testino 144; Specialized 266; Stedelijk Museum Amsterdam 120; Studio Castiglioni 163; Superstock Ltd 248; Svenst Tenn AB Stockholm 200; TBWA Simons Palmer/Lewis Multatero 330 /Tim O'Sullivan 359; TKO Product Design/Ian McKinnell 371; Theatre Arts,

Harry Ransom Humanities Research Centre, The University of Texas at Austin/ Mrs Edith L. Bel Geddes 223; Thirst 294; Topham Picture Point 12, 13, 20, 24, 26; © TomTom International B.V; Courtesy of Toyota GB PLC 267; ©Tupperware Coporation 199; Ty Nant Spring Water Ltd 330; V&A Images/Victoria & Albert Museum 197; View/© Tim Street Porter 100; Vitra/© Ron Arad 151; Vitra/© Jasper Morrison 152; © Visual Arts Library/Stockholm, Modern. Tatlin, Monument a la 3e International 402; Vitra Design Museum Collection, Weil am Rhein, Germany 128, 131, 132, 133, 134, 135, 136, 141; Vitra Museum, Basle 161; Volkswagen 351; Jon Wealleans 96; The Trustees of The Wedgewood Museum Trust Limited 192; Wolfgang Weingart 286; Paul Straker Welds 373; Westminster City Archives 15/Liberty's 11; Whirlpool 244; Elizabeth Whitting & Associates 108; ©Wolford Tights, photo: Helmut Newton 358; Zaha Hadid Architects 77; Zanotta spa/Marino Ramazzotti 137; Zanussi Ltd 221.

Every effort has been made to acknowledge correctly and contact the source and/or copyright holder of each picture. Carlton Books Limited apologizes for any unintentional errors or omissions, which will be corrected in future editions of this book.